PRAISE FOR

EVERYTHING I'M CRACKED UP TO BE

"This Boston alt-rocker's novel reads like the best rock movie you've
never seen."
                                        —*Minneapolis Star Tribune*

"Trynin's breathless recollection of whirlwind corporate courtship pro-
vides a glimpse into a recording industry desperate for trends and
quick fixes . . . refreshing."   —*The New York Times Book Review*

"Trynin's *Everything I'm Cracked Up to Be* did for me what *Cockamamie* never did until I read her book—grabbed and held. Scanning a
page before filing it away, I kept going for 15, then went back to the
beginning and swallowed the thing lickety-split. . . . I've read enough
biz books to be certain this is one of the best. . . . Read it quick."
                                        —*The Village Voice*

"[Trynin] writes beautifully. . . . *Everything I'm Cracked Up to Be* is con-
versational and poetic at the same time and flashes past in an impres-
sionistic blur, as those years must have. Trynin perfectly captures the
wall-of-death feeling of celebrity in America."
                                        —*The Oregonian* (Portland)

"Trynin's memoir takes us on a Mr. Toad's Wild Ride of music business

executives, managers, 'head honchos' and underlings, all vying for her attention and her ink on their dotted line. . . . A real find for anyone who has written her first song and has a dream of 'making it.'"
—*The San Diego Union-Tribune*

"Although the current soundscape seems to favor pop confections, there's a long tradition of tough female rock artists whose amps go to 11, and whose comets usually end in cataclysm. Ask Joan Jett, or Marianne Faithfull, or Genya Ravan—or read this fiery book." —Reuters

"[Trynin] nails what it feels like to have her sense of self rattled to the core by an industry in which timing can hold more weight than talent. . . . Trynin is sarcastic and cynical. . . . She's also honest and self-mocking, however, and it's a kick to read about her efforts to embody 'cool,' since most rock-and-rollers are too 'cool' to admit to making such an effort."
—*The Boston Phoenix*

"Delightful . . . Alternately richly comic and heartbreakingly poignant, the book offers a detailed account of the label A&R reps' seductive sweet nothings, the heady thrill of a fat advance and the enervating, almost hallucinatory progress of a cross-country promotional tour . . . refreshingly free of any taint of bitterness." —*The Hollywood Reporter*

"In an extremely entertaining memoir, Trynin documents her experiences with an insider's eye, a musician's flawless timing and a born writer's way with character and story. Even without the fame she wanted as an entertainer, she still rocks. Grade: A." —*Tucson Citizen*

"One of the funniest, most poignant and thoughtful books ever on almost famous-ness . . . terrific."
—*Boston Herald*

"Jen's passions and insecurities are totally relatable." —*Jane*

"Outstanding . . . The book has elements of tragedy . . . but that just makes it all the more addictive. . . . It helps that Trynin is not just a good writer but an exceptional one. . . . Trynin's memoir is an essential document of the time, and a strong (and often hilarious) warning to anyone who shares her ambitions, regardless of the era." —*Long Island Press*

"Trynin's label chewed her up and spit her out, but she enacts stealthy, delayed revenge with this ingratiating, winningly candid book, emerging from her flirtation with pop stardom older, wiser, and blessed with one hell of a story." —*The Onion*

"[Trynin] expertly captures the vertigo induced by endless meet-and-greets, plastic A&R guys and conceited DJs with names like 'the Boneman.' Trynin is refreshingly human. . . . The book's coda is priceless." —*Magnet* magazine

"What happens when you get what you want? The question haunts this funny, ultimately poignant memoir of a rock-and-roll fairy tale becoming a rock-and-roll nightmare. . . . Terrific reading for anyone interested in rock and the music industry." —*Booklist*

"A brilliant, blast-ass chronicle of a dreamy rock nightmare. Jen Trynin gets right to the heart of the modern absurdist comedy called the music business. The wonderful thing is that Trynin survived 'rock stardom' with her own head and heart intact. To anyone with her own dreams of hitting it big in the scene: First read this book." —Brad Watson, author of *The Heaven of Mercury* and *Last Days of the Dog-Men*

"WARNING: Writing a batch of good songs in one's apartment may lead to having one's ass kissed by numerous multinational corporations for an indeterminate period of time. This may in turn cause one to lose one's sense of self, become unable to differentiate between fantasy and reality, develop eating disorders, chain smoke, enter into inadvisable relationships, suffer from depression, and ultimately even quit writing songs. See Jen Trynin's completely brilliant *Everything I'm Cracked Up To Be* for more information, or consult your entertainment physician." —Adam Schlesinger, of the band Fountains of Wayne

EVERYTHING I'M CRACKED UP TO BE

JEN TRYNIN

EVERYTHING I'M CRACKED UP TO BE

A ROCK & ROLL FAIRY TALE

A HARVEST BOOK
HARCOURT, INC.

ORLANDO   AUSTIN   NEW YORK
SAN DIEGO   TORONTO   LONDON

Requests for permission to make copies of any part of the work should be submitted
online at www.harcourt.com/contact or mailed to the following address: Permissions
Department, Harcourt, Inc., 6277 Sea Harbor Drive, Orlando, Florida 32887-6777.

www.HarcourtBooks.com

The Library of Congress has cataloged the hardcover edition as follows:
Trynin, Jennifer, 1963–
Everything I'm cracked up to be: a rock & roll fairy tale / Jen Trynin.— 1st ed.
p.   cm.
1. Trynin, Jennifer, 1963–   2. Rock musicians—Biography.   3. Women rock musicians—
Biography.   I. Title.
ML420.T833A3   2006
782.42166'092—dc22   2005015240
ISBN-13: 978-0-15-101148-3   ISBN-10: 0-15-101148-6
ISBN-13: 978-0-15-603296-4 (pbk.)   ISBN-10: 0-15-603296-1 (pbk.)

Text set in Bulmer MT
Designed by Linda Lockowitz

Printed in the United States of America

First Harvest edition 2007
K J I H G F E D C B A

*"A man's life is interesting primarily when he has failed,
for it's a sign that he tried to surpass himself."*
—GEORGES CLEMENCEAU

★

"What you think can't happen can."
—BAZOOKA JOE

EVERYTHING I'M CRACKED UP TO BE

ONE

1994. NOVEMBER 1. 4 P.M.

"91 South! There! On the left!" Buck is turned around in the front passenger seat. "You're clear! Go!"

Robby swerves left, to much horn-honking and raising of fists from other drivers. "Yikes," he says. "Touchy."

"Oh yeah?" says Buck, rolling his window down, sticking his hand out and giving someone the finger. "How about this?" he says, sticking out his other hand, giving the double finger.

The sun is low in the sky and flashing across the highway. We're on our first band trip to New York and I'm feeling slightly delirious and very pinch-me. We're playing at Brownie's, the kind of skanky rock dive I've been dying to play. In my previous life, the mere mention of Brownie's caused me deep pangs of inferiority and what-about-me.

"You know that guy," someone might say. "Freddy? From Brownie's?"

"Sure," I'd say, "the booking guy," hoping I wouldn't have to admit that I'd been calling Freddy from Brownie's for over two years to exactly zero avail.

Until a few weeks ago, when he'd finally called me back.

"Yeah, this is Freddy from Brownie's," he said when I answered. "I'm looking for Jennifer Trynin?"

"This is Jen," I said, my heart pounding up a storm.

"Oh, hey. Well, like, I got your 45 with the big boots on it and—that's yours, right? This is you, right?"

"Yeah," I said. *How in the world did Freddy from Brownie's get ahold of my 45?*

"Well, I think it's really good. Where you from?"

"Boston," I said.

"What're they puttin' in the water up there anyway? A lot of great bands comin' outta Boston. How come I never heard of you?"

Shit shit shit. I didn't want to admit that until very recently, few people cared about my music one way or the other. So I began coughing, fake choking-coughing—which unfortunately dislodged something in my lungs that really did catch in my throat, causing a real coughing fit.

"Hey, you okay?" asked Freddy. "Want me to hang on? Maybe get yourself some water?"

"No, no, I'm okay," I wheezed, pounding myself on the chest. "Just getting over a cold."

"Sounds like a bitch," he said. "Anyway, you want a gig?"

"You alive back there?" asks Buck.

"What?"

"I said do you like the Clash?"

"I guess," I say.

"You guess?" says Buck, turning around, leaning over the back of his seat and hitting me on the head with a magazine. He smiles. "Go back to sleep, rock star."

I smile, closing my eyes, the sunlight catching in my lashes, and for once I'm not dreaming. This is the way I'd always imagined it would be. Me and my bandmates goofing around in the van, roaming the highways. I have the feeling I used to get driving down to the Jersey shore with my family when I was maybe six. I'd pile blankets into the back-back of the station wagon and make a fort where I could be alone, but not really alone. I remember wanting never to get there, wanting always to stay just like we were in that car, together and forgiving, because there was nowhere else to go.

I'm walking toward Brownie's big black door, which is covered with band stickers and graffiti and chewing gum—when someone bursts through from the other side.

"Hallefuckinluiah!" yells this short guy with long black hair who's sucking on a lollipop. His fingers are dirty. "You're Jennifer, right?" He has a black leather jacket and a long nose with two silver studs.

"Are you Freddy?"

"Ready Freddy and willing," he says. He's clacking the lollipop around in his mouth a mile a minute. "Hey, you didn't tell me this was gonna be a fuckin' showcase. You got some pretty big dudes calling. You gonna be a rock star or something?" Freddy yanks the lollipop from his mouth with his dirty fingers and whips it toward the street, hitting the side of our van where it shatters and falls to the ground.

"Hey man, that's our van," I say, not giving in to my fear of people like Freddy. I don't know what kind of life they really lead but I always picture it damp and poorly lit, filled with knives and heroin.

"Oh," he says. "Sorry 'bout that, partner. Listen, I'll go get some crew guys to help with your gear," and he disappears inside again. This is the first time anyone from a club has ever offered to help me do anything. I feel like I've been let in on some kind of secret handshake. For a moment, I imagine never having to carry my equipment again, but after a while, when no help materializes, I start dragging my amp across the sidewalk and life rubberbands back to normal.

Inside, Brownie's is no frills, just a big rectangular room with a bar along one wall and a stage at the end. Freddy counts through a ream of brown paper tickets and hands me twenty-four. "Good for domestic beers or a buck off mixed drinks," he says. "I'm giving you guys extra cuz I'm stoked you're playing here tonight."

"You are?" I say.

"Yeah," he says. "You know, it's good for the club when this kinda shit goes down."

"What kinda shit?"

"You know, sharkfest," says Freddy. "Mark my fuckin' words."

"Awesome," says Robby.

"Words marked," says Buck, putting his arm around me, squeezing me tight, then pushing me away. "Stop *hugging* me all the time," he says.

I rip the tickets into eights and hand Buck and Robby theirs.

"Whoa," says Robby. "Can I sell some of these?"

"You trying to get us drunk, little lady?" says Buck. "Planning on taking advantage of us after the show?"

"Do I have to wait that long?" I say, smiling at my guys. They seem to be glowing, as if the highway sun is still shining on them, as if they're the best friends I've ever had and we'll be like this forever.

1968, age four: I begin taking piano from the old lady down the street. She calls me "Jenny my dear" and smells like an attic.

Eight: My cousin is married to the guitar player Robben Ford. He's on tour with Joni Mitchell, which is how I end up backstage in a brightly lit room with lots of tables and mirrors and people smoking.

"This is Joni Mitchell," says Robben.

"It's so nice to meet you," says Joni Mitchell. Her hand is pale and cool and her eyes shine right through me.

I listen to the cassette my mom buys me of Joni Mitchell's *Blue* on my brother's little black tape recorder, but the songs I love most make me so sad I don't listen to it very much.

Nine: My father leaves. I peek at my mom from behind a chair. She's lying on the chaise on the patio, gazing out across the lawn, smoking a cigarette, flicking the ashes on the ground at the end of her long, beautiful arm.

Eleven: My parents enroll me and my brother in a snooty private school located in the middle of a tough neighborhood, where black kids skid by on undersized bikes and whip rocks at us.

I quit piano, get a guitar, and start writing songs. I pretend I'm a real singer, like Joni Mitchell—beautiful, fearless, sauntering through strange cities, tossing love affairs over my shoulder like salt.

Thirteen: When I'm not wondering who in the world I'm going to tag along after once my brother Tim leaves for college, I'm writing songs. I'm allowed to play a song I write for Tim at his high school graduation and get a standing ovation, deepening my next-Joni-Mitchell conviction—until it begins dawning on me that I'm not the greatest singer in the world. So I focus on my songs, hoping that the beauty of the music will camouflage my subpar singing.

Fourteen: Tim leaves. I become a hippie. I stop eating meat or watching TV or going to movies or even listening to the radio. Not like I was listening to the radio much anyway, because the songs I love most still make me sad, and all the other songs just make me feel creepy. I can't help but picture the people I imagine playing the music, a bunch of scraggly guys in a dirty basement in some seedy town. So I read books, take pictures, write songs. Or I duck into the woods and drink beer. Kiss boys.

In college, I major in creative writing and smoke pot. I play my songs at coffeehouses or in the occasional dorm room if a guitar is being passed around and I want some guy to notice me. In the summers, I sing in restaurants by the seashore when I'm not waiting tables. I throw in a few originals, but mostly I play covers. Janis Joplin's a cappella "Mercedes Benz (Oh Lord, Won't You Buy Me A . . .)" always brings down the house.

Junior year, Tim visits me and we stumble into a party where a band with the skinniest guys in the world is playing loud and angry and fast—the epitome of the kind of music that has always creeped me out. Everyone's thrashing around, slamming into each other, or they're just standing, staring, especially girls with skinny arms and dirty hair and long thin hands jammed into their back pockets. The singer's guitar is hung to his knees, a cigarette dangling from the corner of his lips with the ashes fluttering down like snow and sticking to the back of his hand. Later, at some bar, I ask Tim what he thought of the band. He tells me they look like a bunch of greasy-ass losers who can't get laid.

Senior year, I'm in my first real rock band. Just before we graduate, we play a party where the cops shut us down. I've never had so much fun in my whole life.

After graduation, I land in Boston, where I begin freelancing at a monthly parenting publication and waitressing at Doyle's, a beer and burger joint down the street.

On November 1, in a post-Halloween sugar daze, I decide to make a record.

I have no idea how to do this.

I end up slipping a homemade cassette of some of my songs into the pocket of a cousin-of-a-cousin at a family funeral. I think this guy owns a recording studio and I'm just looking for a break on price, but it turns out he has his own little jazz label in New York called Pathfinder Records. My cousin's cousin tells me that, while my music isn't jazz, it does have "a certain something, reminds me a little of Joni Mitchell."

I record a five-song EP for Pathfinder called *Trespassing* down in New York with a bunch of coolcat musicians. At Pathfinder's urging, I assemble a "touring band" that includes a born-again Christian bass player I get from an ad.

Trespassing receives a smattering of good reviews and I even hear one of my songs on a college station's "New Coffeehouse Hour." But just as my band begins practicing in each other's apartments at low volume, Pathfinder folds, bankrupted by an ill-advised attempt to re-launch an early-80s star who was single-handedly responsible for that period's *OOH ooh OOH!* phase.

I curl up on my futon couch, eating pizza and watching reruns, with the wind whistling through the cracks in my windows.

I manage to book a few shows here and there, mostly in suburban clubs on Sunday through Wednesday nights as the first of three or four bands featuring chick singers with acoustic guitars. The cops never come close to shutting us down.

I keep writing new songs.

Every now and then I see *Trespassing* in a music store somewhere.

I meet Guy, a keyboard player turned wunderkind producer who has his own recording studio. He's very tall and skinny with long blond hair pulled into a ponytail. Recently he produced a demo for a band that got signed to Atlantic, after which he immediately got fired, "because that's just the way things go," he says. He tells me he's seen me play a few times, that I have a lot of potential, but that I should ditch my band and he'll hook me up with "more appropriate players."

A few weeks later, we begin recording.

One morning at 6 A.M., after we've been up all night in the studio, Guy and I are drinking a beer in the lounge, where the sun is blasting in. Guy is tilting back in a chair with his feet up on the windowsill, leaning into the shadow I'm making. He tells me he's always wanted to be in music, even though deep down he's always known he's far better at things like math and science. He says he wrote songs for his college band until he finally faced the truth: He was a terrible songwriter. Then he says, So how'd you end up here? and I'm like, Here where? and he says, Doing music. You don't seem like the type.

A bunch of us pick Guy up to go out drinking and I'm the only one who knows he's just been mugged. Guy gets into the backseat next to me and I squeeze his thigh once, then quickly pull my hand away because no one knows we've kissed yet either. Nobody ever seems to know anything about Guy except for the obvious. He's smart, stubborn, and funny. He uses words like *superfluous* and *fuckhead* in the same sentence and it works. He loves three things: music, pro sports, politics.

Then the studio gets booked by someone else for a week. So night after night after night, Guy and I stay up together, talking, drinking. When Guy makes a chicken, I eat some even though I haven't eaten meat in years. When I go on for too long about my Theory of Everything—how wave forms are like architecture are like song structures—Guy never looks at me like *What?*

At 3 A.M. on the last night before we go back into the studio, Guy and I are at the Store 24, buying can after can of tomato juice, because my cat, Ranger, has just crawled through my window reeking of skunk. Back in my bathroom, Guy and I kneel side by side, leaning over Ranger, whom I've stuck in the tub. I ask Guy to hold Ranger down— even if Ranger goes berserk, even if I scream to let him go—and Guy says he will. The second a drop of tomato juice hits Ranger's back, Ranger begins to wail and I start to scream, but Guy hangs on. When it's finally over, there's tomato juice everywhere—all over the bathroom and Guy and me. Guy's laughing as he pats Ranger dry with about a million paper towels, saying how he looks like a piece of ziti.

Later, as the sun's coming up, I tell Guy about the time I thought I was going to die, how the plane was suddenly dropping and the alarms were going off and everyone was freaking out like this was it. I tell him how ever since, I've been plagued by these nightmares—I'm falling over and over, out of the sky, off cliffs, from the tips of buildings. This is when I start to cry and Guy pulls me close. Just before I fall asleep, he whispers that he loves me. When I wake up, I'm scared to death because I know I'm going to marry him.

I form a new quasi-band with a revolving combination of Guy's "more appropriate players," whom I'm able to corral about once a month for gigs in pubs or small clubs with crappy sound systems. Guy usually tags along and ends up fiddling with the PA to make it sound better. I beg Guy to commit to being my live soundman, but he won't do it. He says that he's done his time in bands, that he's a studio guy now and that's it, but I figure it's only a matter of time until I break him down.

When I'm not doing band stuff, I go to open mics, solo.

My first open mic ever is at Ye Ol' Vienna Coffee Haus, where there's no alcohol and an endless procession of what Guy refers to as "talentless no-necks playing James Taylor covers."

When my name is finally called—I'm thirty-fifth on the list—my heart begins to beat so fast and loud that I rush through both my songs, missing the high notes, forgetting lyrics and dropping my pick. When I'm finally done, there's an even sparser smattering of applause than there'd been for the buck-toothed harpist who'd played a rigorous version of "Mr. Tambourine Man."

On the way home, Guy and I stop at a bar, where I drink two martinis and break a glass. I tell him I'm quitting music. He says, If you can't stand the heat. I say, It's not the heat, it's the stupidity. He asks if I've ever considered comedy.

I become a rising star on the open-mic scene, thanks to a clever little number I call "Undercover," whose refrain focuses on "getting up and doing it" but is really about "staying in bed and screwing it." It's the first and last song I ever write that borders on funky. I play most of "Undercover" by popping the bottom two strings of my guitar with my thumb, creating a tone not unlike the bass line from the *Barney Miller* theme song.

People are always very impressed with this maneuver.

I submit a cassette of *Trespassing* to Ron, the owner of Passim, Boston's premier acoustic venue, known for launching the careers of people like Suzanne Vega and Tracy Chapman. I'm convinced I'll be a shoo-in.

A week later, Ron still hasn't listened to my tape, so I go back down to the club. I'm standing in front of the little desk in the little office where Ron is wearing the same shit-brown sweater he'd been wearing the week before, only today there's a stain on the chest. He's not looking at me.

I ask Ron if he's listened to my tape.

"No," he says.

"Oh," I say.

"Wait. Trynin, Trynin," he mutters, shuffling through all the crap on his desk. "It's here somewhere. I did listen to it. Hang on."

He pulls my tape from a huge pile of cassettes. "Here it is," he says, holding it out to me. "Not for us."

"What?"

"It's not Passim material," he says.

I take the tape. "But," I manage to say, and then nothing.

"Didn't like the voice," he says. "Sorry. I'm sure you're very disappointed."

I'm back on my couch, eating more pizza, watching more reruns, my brain circling like a bat.

I return to the doldrums of the open-mic scene, getting the occasional solo gigs and playing with my revolving quasi-band in what I'm quickly coming to know as the Sunday-through-Wednesday-night-folk/acoustic-chick-band wasteland. Nobody even remotely cool ever shows up, and these gigs aren't leading to anything besides more crappy gigs at these same crappy clubs where the audiences drink tea and stare at their shoes. Meanwhile, I'm getting drunk and cursing during my set. Suffice it to say there's not a lot of love being lost between me and the folk/acoustic scene.

At Guy's recording studio, I'm out in the big room on the other side of the glass, adjusting my headphones, when some lanky blond chick appears at the control-room door wearing a tight black jacket, shin-length pants, and black Doc Martens army boots. All the boys lounging in the control room are suddenly standing, smiling, pushing their hair out of their faces. When she turns to leave, all eyes follow her out the door.

When I ask who that was, they all say, "Aimee Mann," like they're saying "Elvis Presley" or "Marilyn Monroe." Come to find out, Aimee was the lead singer and songwriter in the Boston-band-made-good 'Til Tuesday, which had a hit back in the early 80s called "Voices Carry." Guy's been working with her for a few years.

A few weeks later, Aimee stops by with this beautiful orange Gretsch guitar, a semi-hollowbody electric with a Bigsby whammy bar. She lets me borrow it. Suddenly, Guy is scrambling all over the studio, plugging me into Fender combos, Marshalls, HiWatts, lining up pedals in this order, that order:

Tubescreamer into a T-wah into a Big Muff.

Play.

How about a Big Muff into a Tubescreamer, forget the T-wah.

Play.

Phase Shifter into a Real Tube into a Tape Echo.

Play.

Three chords in, Guy's waving his arms at me, telling me to stop strumming like I'm playing acoustic.

By the end of the week, I'm in love with electric guitar.

But the week after that, I'm crushed when Guy starts bringing in "real" guitar players to do all the tricky-dick guitar noodles that begin working their way into all the corners of what will become my earnestly wrought twelve-song cassette.

I get some cash from my family for my birthday and search everywhere for a guitar just like Aimee's.

I never find one.

But I do find a totally swank Gibson ES335 circa-1967 semi-hollowbody with a Bigsby whammy bar, which is close enough. Then I get a 70s Fender Super Reverb amp (blackface, with a red grill cloth), a wah-wah pedal, and a Real Tube.

My excitement knows no bounds.

I go down to Aimee's rehearsal space, plug everything in, turn it up, and let 'er rip.

It sounds awful.

And fanTASTIC.

I begin playing electric guitar in my revolving quasi-band, but we're still being sequestered into the Sunday-through-Wednesday-night-folk/acoustic-chick-band wasteland. We're playing shows labeled "Spotlight on Women" or "Songwriters' Showcase."

I begin turning up.

People begin sticking their fingers in their ears.

I tell Guy that he *has* to be my live soundman because I'm afraid we're always sounding like shit.

Guy won't do it.

I start flirting with the house soundmen, trying to get any of them to give a damn.

We open for some acoustic chick I've never heard of who screams a lot and the place is packed with chicks who look like guys.

"You could always go the lesbian-folk-rock route," says Guy. "Built-in audience."

"But I'm not a lesbian."

"They don't know that."

When the screaming chick gets signed to Elektra, I revisit the idea of using homosexuality as a marketing tool.

I go out to a rock club to be with people who're loud and drunk and sick of it all. There's some band onstage that's noisy and fucked up and they kind of suck but they're also kind of great. Everyone in the place has weird clothes and dirty hair, and people are fighting and flirting and kissing in the corners. Now *this* is what I'm talking about. *This* is where I want to be. Why oh why am I still stuck playing the *fucking* Tam O'Shanter at *fucking* eight o'clock on a *fucking* Monday night for *fucking* "Songwriters' Serenade"?

"For starters, because you're not a rock band," says Guy.

"But what does that *mean*?" I say.

"I don't know. Lots of things."

"Enlighten me."

"You don't have a steady band, you go by your own name, your lyrics are, umm, lyrical, and just the way your songs, you know, move."

"Move like how?"

"They can be a little complicated."

"Complicated?"

"Rock music is usually a little more straightforward than your stuff. The old one-four-five. Verse, prechorus, chorus, repeat. No frills. Do you know what I'm saying?"

"My music has choruses."

"Well, sure. And they're good, you know, interesting. They're just not rock choruses."

"And that's bad?"

"Not bad. Just not rock."

"Oh, so I should dumb down my music, is that it?"

"You think writing a great chorus is 'dumbing down'?"

"Listen. My music's just as rock as all those stupid-ass bands put together and if those assholes can't see that, then fuck 'em. Fuck the whole thing."

"Fine," says Guy. "Then stop complaining."

"I will."

"Fine."

"FINE!"

Guy makes me a tape labeled "Great Pop Rock Songs" and leaves it on my desk. I shove it in a drawer.

We finally finish recording my earnestly wrought twelve-song cassette, which I'm listening to through headphones at three in the morning, drinking vodka and smoking. Fuck the stupid rock bands with their straightforward choruses. At least my lyrics *mean* something.

I do the artwork with a friend. A four-panel multi-fold with all the lyrics. The colors are blue and black with a picture of me in silhouette on the cover. It's an eponymous release.

Guy plays my tape for a trusts and estates lawyer who's trying to break into the music business. The lawyer offers to shop it, claiming he knows a few people and explaining how "music biz folks" are infinitely more impressed receiving a tape from a lawyer rather than directly from an artist. Guy figures it couldn't hurt, since the few people he'd gotten to know at Atlantic have already been fired, and that a trusts and estates lawyer is better than no lawyer at all. So I give the trusts and estates lawyer a bunch of my earnestly wrought twelve-song cassettes, which he sends out to anyone he can think of. Then he and Guy set up a showcase for me down in New York, where it doesn't matter that my revolving quasi-band doesn't get onstage until 2 A.M., because no label people ever show up.

Back on couch. Pizza. Reruns.

Is it possible I'm such a genius that people are simply having trouble getting their minds around the enormity of my talent?

———

One evening, I'm at the office of the parenting publication, where for the past few years I've done everything from proofreading to ghost-writing to paste-up, but mostly I compile and format their monthly "What's Happening?" section. Sarah, the graphics chick who always wears black, is listening to a college station that usually plays stuff I think sucks. But at that moment, a song comes on that's the most beautiful, ferocious, heartbreaking thing I've ever heard.

"Who is that?" I ask Sarah.

"Nirvana," she says, monotone, not looking up.

"Are they popular?"

Sarah looks at me. "Do you, like, *live* under a rock?"

I can't understand a word of it, but something about the music suddenly feels like everything I've ever tried to do. The colors. The intensity. The simplicity. The inevitability. It's as if it's been here all along. And the chorus—both straightforward and unique.

That night I lie awake, staring at the water marks on my bedroom ceiling.

So.

Someone else has already done it.

Someone else is the Voice of My Generation.

Despite the enormity of my talent, the fact is I'm not a genius.

Nirvana.

They're geniuses.

Me?

I'm just another chick with a guitar.

So now I know, so now it's done.

(CouchPizzaReruns.)

On my twenty-ninth birthday, American Airlines loses my luggage. Something explodes in me and it's like I pop out of a manhole.

So I'm not the VoMG! And maybe nobody's having any trouble whatsoever getting their minds around the enormity of my talent. But there's no way in hell that I suck any worse than all those other motherfuckers getting record deals. If I can just get out of the Sunday-through-Wednesday-night folk/acoustic-chick-band wasteland and into the rock scene, I *know* I'll do better.

I'm going to try one more time, *just one more time,* and if something really *wow* isn't happening by the time I'm thirty, I'm done.

Gonzo, baby.

Outta here.

I stay up all night listening to Guy's "Great Pop Rock Songs" tape, which includes Joe Jackson's "Is She Really Going Out with Him?," The Police's "Every Breath You Take," Squeeze's "Tempted," and The Cars' "Just What I Needed." Something's dawning on me, but I can't tell what it is.

I begin studying the local rock bands whose music is anything at all like mine. Come to find out, getting rock gigs is a tricky business having to do with where you work and what you drink and where you rehearse and who you're sleeping with or used to sleep with or who you might be sleeping with really soon. It's what kind of guitar you play, rig you have, pedals you use, jeans you wear. It's how you say hello: "Yo," "Dude," or "'Sup?"

I stop cutting my hair with nail scissors and go to a salon for the first time since high school. I get my hair cut straight across at my shoulders, leaving long bangs covering the left half of my face. I chuck my black jeans, ankle cowboy boots, and brown suede jackets and go to the cool thrift stores, where I find myself an old blue corduroy jeans jacket, a pair of big black-laced shoes, and three ugly print polyester shirts. As I'm trying on pair after pair of super-slim corduroys, I admit that I could lose a few pounds.

I spend two days rolling years of change into paper tubes, which I exchange at the bank for $368.70. I scour the city for the coolest gear I can get for my money: an old purple Telecaster made from a kit, a used Tubescreamer pedal, and a black leather strap.

I take four songs from my earnestly wrought twelve-song cassette and make a new tape with a bright pink cover. I call it *Flank* and send it out to a short list of local rock journalists and DJs with the specific intent of getting gigs in cooler clubs on better nights in later slots.

Bing.

Bang.

Boom.

Flank receives good reviews in a few cool local 'zines and one of the songs even gets played (once) on a rock station's "local show."

I get offered a semi-decent gig (so-so club, Thursday night, 10 P.M. slot), but none of the tricky-dick guitar players in my revolving quasi-band can make it.

Fuck.

FUCK!

I take the gig anyway because When In Rock, you can't be such a wiener.

On the night of the gig, when we get to the first tricky-dick-guitar-noodleless expanse, I don't know what the hell to do, so I just bang on my guitar—WHAM!—and slam on my wah-wah pedal—WAH!—and just let the fucker ring out with the most ear-splitting feedback—WAAHHEEEEOOOOHHAAAHHHEEEE—and the whole place goes nuts.

NUTS!

Okay, not the whole place. My table of friends and Guy and Aimee and a few other people. But this is the night I discover My Sound and swear off tricky-dick guitar players forever.

Meanwhile, Guy's been recording two of the most popular pop rock bands in Boston, Skivvy and Shineaway, both of whom have been signed to one-offs with indies and are beginning to attract major label attention.

I start watching them like a hawk and quickly realize that putting out cassettes is for chumps. Cool bands put out singles—45s, those old-school 7-inch records with the big holes (except if you're cool, you make them with *little* holes)—with an all-important indie-label logo on the back cover. So I make a few calls to this or that local indie on the pretense of asking their advice on 45 manufacturing, hoping that someone will jump at the chance to release a single for me.

No one jumps.
(CouchPizzaReruns.)
No.
Fuck that.
In 292 days (not that I'm counting), I'll be thirty.
Zero is how much time I have to waste.

I make up a label called Squint Records and sign myself. I get a second phone line and an answering machine with an outgoing message that begins, "Hey. You've reached Squint Records. . . ." I create a logo, and with the $1,250 I get from American Airlines for my lost bag, I buy a fax machine and a printer and print up stationery. I pick another song from my earnestly wrought twelve-song cassette and shorten the title from "Don't Make Me Beg" to "Beg" (because cool bands use one-word song titles). I choose "Undercover" as the B-side (because old insecurities die hard). For the cover art, I use a picture of a weird cat I saw in the newspaper (because cool bands usually have weird nonsensical artwork). Then I slap a Squint Records logo on the back cover and take everything to one of the 45 manufacturers I'd heard about through all the indie-label people who didn't want anything to do with me.

I send out "Beg" to an expanded list of local press and radio. Then I drive around to record stores begging all the greasy-haired counter guys to take a few of my singles on consignment.

The response is fanTABULOUS. "Beg" gets highlighted in lots of cool 'zines and repeated airtime on four local radio shows. ("Undercover" is, thankfully, ignored.)

A live review describes me as "the *lovely* Jennifer Trynin," which tickles me completely pink. The first line of a new song ends up being "She is lovely," because I can't get the word out of my head.

I get asked to be in a "Women in Rock" fashion spread in the *Boston Globe*'s Sunday magazine. All the other rock chicks at the shoot are much cooler than I am, with their tattoos and multiple earrings and dyed hair. I wear a hideous paisley polyester shirt and blue cords. The magazine people pick the shot where I'm screwing around with these horns on my head and laughing with my mouth open. I look like the Devil. It's fanTASTIC!

I finish writing the "She is lovely" song and call it "Everything's Different Now," after the chorus, which is straightforward and decidedly uncomplicated. We're recording it one day when Aimee happens to stop by with Dave Gregory from XTC, and Dave ends up playing a ridiculously cool guitar solo on the track.

In January 1994 I'm picked as a "Face to Watch" by a rock writer at the *Globe* and a photographer wants to take a picture of me in my kitchen. On the morning of the shoot, I wake Guy and tell him to skedaddle. Guy doesn't officially live with me, but he's been more or less staying at my place for the past three years. I try to keep our relationship on the down low because I don't want people getting the wrong idea. Like he's my Svengali or something. Like I can't do my thing without him. I can do my thing without him. I *choose* to have him produce my records. This is what I tell myself.

The picture comes out great and it's the first time I get compared to Chrissie Hynde of the Pretenders in print. I tape the article to my refrigerator.

I start making plans to release "Everything's Different Now" as my second single, enlisting the help of a real graphic designer and a photographer who are willing to help for next to nothing. For the cover, we use a picture of a friend's sculpture, which is just two huge black work boots nailed together, with a handle glued to the side of one boot. But before we're ready to roll, I'm solicited by a local indie label for a song to include on a compilation of local chick-lead rock bands. I'm not crazy about the "chick" part but I'm delirious about the "rock" part, so I give them "Everything's Different Now."

The press eats up the compilation, and "Everything's Different Now" is singled out like crazy.

We're back in the studio recording my newest song, "Snow," which doesn't even have a chorus but works anyway. Aimee says she wants to sing on it. It sounds so beautiful that for a little while I forget all about polyester shirts and 45s and folk vs. rock and just play music again.

I release the "Everything's Different Now" single backed with "Snow." My picture is in all the 'zines and the local radio shows play both songs for weeks. I'm finally getting gigs in cooler clubs on better nights in later slots. I'm also beginning to be accepted by all the cool rock-band people and hang with them backstage, where all they ever seem to want to talk about are their favorite bands: Cheap Trick, Big Star, Gang of Four, the Meat Puppets, Hüsker Dü , the Replacements, Elvis Costello, the Pixies, Mission of Burma, Sonic Youth. While I guess I've heard of most of these bands, I couldn't pick out a single one of their songs in a lineup. So I just smile and nod like *Oh yeah, sure, Cheap Trick, they're great,* because the last thing I want to do is admit that I've never even owned a turntable. I have exactly one album: *Trespassing.*

A bona fide entertainment lawyer calls me up. We meet in his office downtown on swanky Beacon Street. He tells me how he and some manager friend of his are "starting up" a publishing company, how they want to "sign me," and that they will shop my songs and give me "free advice" in exchange for half my publishing. Since I don't know what "publishing" really is, I think the whole arrangement sounds pretty neato.

Until Guy—who's been learning a lot by watching Skivvy and Shineaway—explains that any publishing deal should come with an advance, and that without it, it sounds to him that this guy is going to be acting more like a lawyer/manager than any kind of publisher. And in that case, customarily, in exchange for securing and brokering record deals and giving career advice, lawyers and managers get 10 to 15 percent of your advances—"not fifty percent of the worth of your publishing for the rest of your life." He advises me to tell Mr. Beacon Street to piss off.

"But what if he really *does* know people and really *can* get me a deal and then something really *does* happen—I mean, isn't keeping fifty percent of some money better than keeping a hundred percent of no money?"

Guy tells me I'm going to end up in the poorhouse with that kind of attitude.

"But I'm in the poorhouse now," I say.

"Now isn't later," says Guy.

Kurt Cobain, the lead singer and songwriter of Nirvana, kills himself.

I sit at my kitchen table, guitar in my lap, but I can't breathe.

I'm playing guitar with the TV on and the sound off. Suddenly I sing, "Maybe we could talk in the shower," which ends up being the first line of a song I stay up all night working on, trying more than anything else in the world to keep the fucking thing *simple*.

A few days later, I play the song for Guy and Aimee.

When I'm done, Aimee smiles at me for maybe the first time ever.

"Now that's a fucking chorus!" says Guy.

"What're you gonna call it?" says Aimee.

"'Better Than Nothing,'" I say.

"Why don't you call it 'I'm Feeling Good,'" says Guy, "like the words in the chorus?"

"Because the song isn't about feeling good," I say.

I get asked to be in local rock station WBCN's annual Rock 'n' Roll Rumble and it's like I've died and gone to heaven—until I don't even make it out of the first round.

Evidently, I'm still not getting my point across.

I start wearing tighter pants, bigger shoes, and a white leather jacket.

I buy a black 70s Les Paul Custom guitar and a Big Muff distortion pedal.

I put my revolving quasi-band on notice and begin looking for a couple of rock guys to play bass and drums—the kind of guys who never tune and don't have cases and always need rides.

In July, a real live New York City entertainment lawyer calls me up, telling me he represents Skivvy and has been "hearing about me" and is "curious." Mr. Skivvy explains how he's way too busy to make it up to Boston, so he's wondering if I'll be playing "down in the city" anytime soon. I tell him I'll let him know. After we hang up, I jump in the air and clap my hands.

Two days later I'm standing in a packed Cambridge club, shredded with envy. I'm watching Tracy Bonham, a classically trained violinist (of all things) with a top-40, jingle-pretty voice who just started playing guitar and writing songs like yesterday. The second she gets offstage, she's swarmed. My friend points out an A&R geek, a record company asshole, and over there, the guy with the creased jeans and the Lacoste shirt—Mr. Skivvy.

The tail I don't have is between my legs as I slip out the door.

I'm on a local radio show talking about how I'm almost done recording a full-length record and am looking for a committed band to go out on tour with me (like there's a tour for me to go out on). I give my number over the air.

The next day, there's a message on my machine from a guy named Robby who used to play in some hardcore band but is currently in some art band that's breaking up. He says he wants to be my drummer.

We meet at my rehearsal space. Robby's cute, with shaggy black hair, long shorts, and an orange-and-black striped T-shirt. He's lived around Boston all his life and went to the Berklee School of Music. He works freelance for a furniture maker and is "kinda engaged" to his girlfriend who lives "out of state." His drums are dirty and his cymbals are cracked. He hits hard and doesn't ask me about time signatures. He has an old yellow van that smells like a wet dog. He holds a door open for me.

He's perfect.

Robby and I begin playing shows with my old revolving bass players while we audition new bass players, but no one's fitting just right,
just yet.

In August, I send out two hundred "Everything's Different Now" 45s
to radio stations across the country from a list I get from a friend of
Guy's. Stuck inside each 45 is a self-addressed, pre-stamped postcard
with the following boxes to check:

☐ We're playing your 45!
☐ We'd like to get your CD!
☐ We'd like you to play in our town!

I tell Guy that I think it'll help my overall marketing strategy to go by a
band name.

"Like what?" says Guy.

"That's the problem," I say. "I can't think of anything I really like.
I mean, I could do like an inverse feminism thing that might be kinda
cool for a while, like Hooker or something, or Get Some, or Pussy,
but I'm afraid that it might get misinterpreted."

Guy looks at me. "Ya think?"

By September, we finally finish recording. Then Guy and I mix, sequence, second-guess, re-sequence, and master my new record. I
bring it to a manufacturer to be made into Squint Records' first (and
only) CD. The artwork is spare and colorful and features a red toy
chair I found in a junk shop. The song titles are short and sweet (or
purposefully long and cheeky). I call the CD *Cockamamie*. I call myself Jennifer Trynin.

After a gig one night, a guy in a baseball cap and ripped jeans approaches me, smiling, drunk, flirty. He has nice eyes.

"I'm Buck," he says. "I like your music."

"Thanks," I say.

"I hear you're looking for a bass player," he says.

"I am," I say.

"Then you're in luck," he says, "because I just happen to play the bass."

"Well, lucky me," I say.

"Yeah," he says. "Lucky you."

A few days later, Robby and I meet Buck at the rehearsal space. He has one old bass (a P-bass—the cool kind), a very old SVT head missing the handle, and no car. He tells us how he's been playing in bands for years, mostly punk or alt-country, and how he writes songs too and is always happy to oblige. He says he grew up with his mom and his brother in the bad section of some Boston suburb, but these days, he's living at his girlfriend's house. He's back in college full-time, majoring in English. He pulls a paperback out of his jacket pocket and smacks it against his hand.

"*London Fields,*" he says, holding up the book, tapping the cover with his finger. "You should check it out."

We play through a bunch of my songs, and Buck sings well and has good feel. He rocks back and forth while he plays, just like all the cool rock bass players.

When we take a break and go out for iced coffees, Buck offers to treat until he realizes he's forgotten his wallet. Then he slips my wallet out of my back pocket and waves it over my head, asking me if I'm missing something. After we get our coffees, we all grab straws and Buck blows the paper off his at my head. So I blow the paper off mine at his butt.

When we're done playing, Buck asks me for a ride back to his girlfriend's. I drop him off at a dilapidated three-story in a dicey neighborhood, where he runs up the walk and hugs a pretty girl in overalls wearing gardening gloves. She has a small shovel in one hand and a nice smile. Buck points at her and yells to me, "Laura!" Then he points to me and says something to her.

Laura waves.

I wave back.

We rehearse a few more times and after a couple of "audition gigs," Buck's in.

———

My mailbox is stuffed with postcards, and every box is checked. "Everything's Different Now" is getting played all over the country, on college stations, commercial stations, the coolest station in Philadelphia, the biggest station in Michigan.

"This is unfuckinbelievable," says Guy.

And it is. Shit! Had I known it was going to be this easy, I'd have put out my own music eons ago.

"Don't get cocky," says Guy.

But I'm getting cocky. Fuck major labels! I'm going to put out *Cockamamie* myself (whatever that means).

"That's nice," says Guy, "but we're still shopping it, just like we planned."

"But I don't need a major label. I just need some help with stuff like publicity and distribution at, you know, Squint Records."

"You're losing it," says Guy.

"All I gotta do is follow up on the postcards, see where my song's really happening, then reservice—"

"Getting tricky with the lingo, aren't we, my little record mogul?"

"—then *reservice* those stations with *Cockamamie,* follow up on that, and then set up a tour in the towns where they're playing my songs. Bing bang boom."

Guy kisses me on the forehead. "Go crazy," he says. "We're still shopping it."

I decide to hire an independent radio promotion company to help me with all this follow-up. Record labels (both indie and major) hire radio promo guys to help promote their bands by including songs on tastemaking samplers and by hounding stations to play their bands' music. Indie promo companies will also track your songs so you know what's getting played where. Some of these guys will work for anyone if the money is right, but I want the guys at Gimmee, who're known for pushing only cool music. I send them an "Everything's Different Now" 45 and an advance cassette of *Cockamamie* and feel cooler than cool when they agree to take me on. This guy Billy explains how when they're helping out *real* artists, artists who're making it work on their own, artists like me, they charge "like nothing, like two-fifty a week"—as opposed to what they charge the majors, "cuz those corporate motherfuckers can afford it, right?" The plan is for Gimmee to track my "Everything's Different Now" 45 for a few weeks, put one of my songs on their midwinter "Gimmee More" sampler, and then help me release *Cockamamie* to college radio, indie-style, just after New Year's.

I need a band picture for the *Cockamamie* press kit, so I have a friend follow me and Buck and Robby around Cambridge with a camera. It's warm and sunny and I feel tremendous in my tight blue cords, strawberry T-shirt, big black shoes, and white leather jacket—just me and a bunch of boys wandering the city. I'm so into being the person I'm trying to be that I don't even mind Buck's hand on my knee as we're sitting on the church steps. Or his arm around my waist as we're walking along Mass. Ave. Or his fingers against the back of my neck as we're leaning against the fire escape.

We choose the picture in the parking lot behind Cambridge Music where Buck and Robby are standing by this big black car while I'm lying on its hood with my arms propped against the windshield behind me. I'm peering up over my Peter Fonda/*Easy Rider* sunglasses and grinning at the camera with my hair falling across my face just right. Everyone tells me what a great picture it is, how it really looks like me, but I know that's not true. It's just one of those pictures of you at your best, a best that doesn't really exist. I dream that night of people with heads like cameras—of an entire world I can wield to see me always in that perfectly impossible light.

The *Cockamamie* CDs are finally back from the manufacturer. Guy and I are drinking coffee and making lists of whom to send them to. We decide that I'll take care of the usual suspects while Guy will send them to the industry people he's beginning to know through working with Skivvy, Shineaway, and Aimee. Guy reminds me that no matter who expresses interest at the beginning, the first step is to secure a lawyer. When I tell Guy that Mr. Beacon Street has been back in touch from New York, where he's working now for some big entertainment law firm, Guy says, "Once a scumbag, always a scumbag." But I send Mr. Beacon Street a *Cockamamie* CD anyway.

This time, it's different from the get-go.

We're still asleep when the phone rings.

Guy reaches over me and picks up the phone. After a groggy hello, he bolts up, clears his throat, rubs his face. "Oh, right, hi," he says. "No, it's okay. I had to get up anyway." Then:

"Really?"

"Well, I mean, that's what we were hoping."

"That's fuckin' great!"

"Yeah, Tuesday. Brownie's. She's on around ten."

"Yeah, no, I can't. I'm gonna be in L.A."

"Yeah, I know, rough life."

"Fantastic. I'll let her know."

"Thanks. You too."

Guy reaches back over me and hangs up.

"Uh, Jen?" he says. "You gotta wake up."

I roll over. "I'm awake."

"That was Neil Krakow. He got the record and he's flipping out."

I sit up. "Neil Krakow? The Shineaway lawyer?"

"Yeah."

"He's flipping out?"

"Flipping *way* out."

"What?"

"He's already given dupes to like ten people and he says everybody's flipping out." Guy climbs out of bed, puts on his jeans.

"Are you fucking with me?"

"I'm not fucking with you," he says. "I'm making coffee. He's coming down to your show Tuesday and he's bringing people."

"People like who?"

"People like people. I don't know."

"This is good, right? I can be excited, right?"

Guy bounces back onto the bed, takes my face in his hands, kisses me on the lips. "Oh, this is good," he says. "This is very good."

Ring-ring!

★

At 9:30, Brownie's is dark and hot and just beginning to rev. Every time Freddy walks by, he winks at me. I've never heard of the other bands on the bill—Paisley Pants, Fudrucker, Girly—but for once I'm not looking to glean cool status from anyone else. For the first time what matters is that *we're* playing, that the sharks are here to see us, and thinking about this too directly feels a little like looking into the sun.

Paisley Pants are wearing (eye roll) paisley pants as they play through their Beach Boys–inflected love songs. The club is still pretty empty. Here and there people cluster, chatting, looking like birds. Birds on wires or clumped in trees. One bird up and goes and others follow. Or they circle one another, never touching, like spinning magnets with opposite poles.

Buck and Robby are next door getting pizza. I can't eat. I can barely swallow. Except for liquor. I'm trying not to think about how much is hinging on this gig. I've heard stories about bands doing showcases and getting so drunk they can't sing, blowing the only chance they may ever get.

I get another beer from the bar and stand against the wall, hair in my face, head down, eyes up.

I'm trying to figure out who in the crowd might be any of the music biz people who've been calling me over the past week.

A small clump of industry types are conferring in the corner. They're dressed very New York in that black, deep-blue, super-sleek sort of way, and each of them is wearing big black trendazoid eyewear. One of them is staring at me. I look over at the bar where two chicks are talking, one pretty with red hair, the other short and dumpy and laughing loud with her mouth open like a claw. They're staring at me too. I look at the floor.

"Hey," someone mumbles.

I turn. *Yes? Yes?*

"Got a light?" says some chick with a big hoop hanging from the center of her nose.

Oh.

I give her a light off the tip of my cigarette.

"Ever get a butt caught in that thing?" I say.

"Once," she says, and walks away.

I hear a familiar voice and peek out from behind my hair. Mr. Beacon Street is coming through the door in worn-out jeans and a brown wide-waled corduroy jacket, accompanied by a wavy-haired guy dressed in black. He holds up two fingers to the bartender, then leans against the bar and runs his hand through his hair. He shakes his head like he just can't believe something while the wavy-haired guy talks and smacks the back of one of his hands into the palm of the other.

Against the opposite wall, a small group is gathered around a tall guy in a suit with a heavy black beard. He's pointing at his ear and talking fast. Then he makes like he's shooting himself in the head. Everyone laughs, shaking their heads or grabbing their noses, like this is the funniest fucking story they've ever heard. Hovering on the outskirts of the group is Mr. Skivvy, laughing along, until he turns away and his smile disappears. He rubs his temples with the tips of his fingers, then pulls a handkerchief from his pocket and wipes it across his mouth. He looks up and catches me staring at him, then waves and smiles. He walks over and introduces himself.

"Thanks for coming down," I say.

"No problem," he says. "Sorry I haven't been able to make it up to Boston, but thanks for sending me your record. Really. I'm impressed. I mean, like I told you, I really liked your single, but I think this record is a major step in the right direction."

"Oh, well, good," I say.

Mr. Skivvy looks around the club, then back at me. "So I see you've already got your hands full," he says, looking down at his own hands, rubbing them together. "You still have time to come by tomorrow?"

"Sure," I say. "Sure I do."

I got all the time in the fucking world.

"Hey," says a woman, right into my ear. I turn to see the two chicks who were sitting at the bar before. The pretty one with the red hair smiles.

"We're not really talking to you," says the dumpy one, putting a finger over her lips like she's keeping a secret.

"You're not?" I say.

"Too dangerous with all these lawyer types around," she says.

"Oh stop," says the pretty one. "I'm Lizzy Johns," she says to me. "We spoke the other day? I manage the Liquorwhips, from Boston?"

"Oh right. Sure," I say.

"This is Becka Stein," she says, pointing to the other woman.

"We love your record," says Becka. "Okay. I said it. So shoot me."

"Why would I shoot you?"

"We're supposed to be playing it cool," she says.

"We just don't want to bother you tonight," says Lizzy, rolling her eyes around the room. "You've got enough on your plate."

"That's right," says Becka. "There'll be plenty of time to talk tomorrow, right? Four o'clock, right?"

"Right," I say.

"Looking forward," says Lizzy.

"Me too."

"Break a leg!"

"I'll try!"

Fudrucker is blaringly loud—not that there's anything wrong with that, but they also suck. Someone is yelling something at me and when I turn, it's the tall guy in the suit with the heavy black beard who was making everyone laugh. I edge toward him, staring at his mouth instead of his eyes because I'm trying to read his lips.

"What was that?" I yell, so close to him it's like we're going to kiss.

He cups my elbow, pressing my finger farther into my ear. "Hi," he yells.

"Hi," I yell back.

"I'm real whacked now and stop her over my damn shorts. Drinks are at eight."

I look at him. "What?"

"I'm Neil Krakow from Klopner Rosenzweig and Schwartz. I think you're great!"

Fudrucker launches into their next song, which, while still sucking, isn't nearly as loud.

"You're Neil?" I say.

He smiles. "I'm Neil."

"You're that lawyer."

"Well, I'm *a* lawyer."

I've been hearing about Neil Krakow for years. He represents *real* bands who get *real* record deals with *real* record companies.

"It's so great to meet you," I say.

"Same here," he says.

Neil seems both older and younger than I thought he'd be. He's forty-something, with a nice build and a big smile and shining eyes. His shirt is open at the collar and I bet his tie is in his pocket. He's wearing a gold Rolex and a wedding band.

"So you had a good ride from Boston?" he says.

"Yeah, it was fine."

"I love Boston, you know? How can you not love Boston? Especially this time of year. The foliage?" Neil puts his hand on his watch and twists it around his wrist. "So," he says. "Your record. Can I tell you something? I get records like every day, all day, all the time, these records, those records, but *your* record—I love it, like LOVE," he says, framing LOVE with his hands in the air as if it's in Hollywood lights. "You're like a real songwriter, you know? Melodic. Good lyrics. But the thing rocks. And something about it. I don't know. It's like, timeless. Do you know what I mean?"

"I think so," I say.

"So I'm really looking forward to your show," he says. "How's your band? Are you guys good? Great? Whaddaya think?"

What am I supposed to say? That we've only been playing together for a few weeks and I'm ecstatic when we make it through the set without breaking anything?

"I guess we're pretty great," I say.

"That's what I was hoping you'd say," says Neil.

Fudrucker rips into another blazing ball of noise over which Neil yells something like *Can I let you appear,* but I figure is really *Can I get you a beer,* so I nod and he smiles, giving me a thumbs-up, mouthing, *Be right back.*

The tail I don't have is wagging like mad.

I know I shouldn't but I'm getting drunk anyway. More people are filing into the club and I don't know if they're all really looking at me or if I just think they're looking at me.

Someone waves.

I wave back.

Buck appears with two small plastic cups filled with what looks like urine.

"For you," he says, holding one out to me.

"Where's Robby?"

"I think he's still next door on the phone. You know, talking to *her.*"

"Great," I say. "Nothing like keeping your eye on the ball. Hey. Neil Krakow's here. He said he *loves* the CD and then he went like this with his hands like he was putting it in lights."

"You just tell me where to sign. Take this already," says Buck, putting the shot in my hand.

"This is *so* not the time to be doing shots," I say.

"Au contraire," he says. "This is *exactly* the time to be doing shots." Buck smiles, holding up his plastic urine drink for me to clink with.

We clink.

Buck downs his. I take a sip of whatever it is and wince.

"Aw, come on," he says. "One shot's not gonna kill you. And if you get all crazy and out of control, I'll take care of you," he says, putting his arm around me.

It feels good. I don't know why and I don't want it to, but it does.

I can see Neil telling stories again, fast and laughing. He's holding a beer and I'm wondering if it's the one he got for me. I push Buck's arm away and down the rest of the drink. The room takes one swerving dip, then rights itself with a slight wobble.

"I don't think I should've done that," I say.

Buck grabs me by the arms, looks me up and down. "You seem okay," he says, pulling me into him, whispering in my ear, "Don't think so much."

Fudrucker finally stops and a few people clap.

The house lights come on, shooting my adrenaline up like a flare. We're next.

The lead singer of Fudrucker is taking his sweetass time getting off the stage, pushing his long, greasy hair behind his ears again and again as the chick with the nose ring chats him up.

I wish I had a horn I could honk.

I HAVE TO SET UP MY GEAR!

CAN'T YOU SEE I'M IN A FUCKING HURRY?

MY WHOLE GODDAMN LIFE'S ON THE LINE HERE, MR. FUDRUCKER!

"Break a leg," says someone, and when I turn, it's Mr. Beacon Street.

"Oh, hey," I say. "Thanks for coming down. I didn't really see you—"

"Yeah yeah yeah. So," he says, waving his hand over the room. "You wanted buzz? You got buzz."

"I do?"

Mr. Beacon Street looks at me. "Come on," he says. "Listen, I gotta take off right after your set, so I'll see you tomorrow, right?"

"Absolutely."

"Got a lot of meetings tomorrow?"

"Kinda."

"I don't wanna know," he says, taking a deep breath, letting it out. "Okay then," he says. "See ya." As he turns, he almost bumps into

Neil, who's bouncing up with a beer in his hand. Mr. Beacon Street gives Neil a quick glare, but Neil doesn't even seem to see him.

"Jen," says Neil, holding out the beer, lightly pounding his chest, pretending to be out of breath. "I got waylaid, talking about *you*!"

We finally get our gear onstage with beers on the amps and everything tuned. My guitar is slung around my back as I adjust the mic stand. "Yo," I say into the mic, nodding at the soundman. The house music goes down and I give a quick peek up through my hair. I can see them: Mr. Skivvy, Mr. Beacon Street, Neil.

Neil waves at me.

The lights go down and the room goes quiet. Someone lets out a *"Woohoo!"* My throat's tight and my mouth's dry. I look at Buck. *Ready?* He smiles and nods. I turn to Robby, who winks and salutes me with a drumstick. I look down at the set list next to my pedalboard with my heart pounding in my eyes like a fist. I stomp on each of my pedals to see the little red lights, just to double-check, triple-check, quadruple-check that they're working. Very fast in my head: *What could make me happier than sitting right here? Bars on the windows and the boys down in the street there . . .* The first words of the first song are the head of a snake. As long as I can remember them, I can remember everything.

Usually.

I can do this.

House music goes on. Lights come up.

Clapping!

Sweating.

Hair sticking to my face.

Hate that.

You guys fuckin' ROCK!

You got stuff for sale?

Where's your mailing list?

Spilling what's left of my beer while dragging out my swag

suitcase from behind my amp. It's filled with CDs, 45s, the mailing list, T-shirts.

How much are those?

You got change?

Reaching into my pocket. Fuck. Used my ones tipping the bartender.

"Jen!" (Neil, pointing down, eyes open wide, mouthing, *Tomorrow?* with both index fingers in the air like an eleven) "You guys were GREAT!"

At 2 A.M. I'm out on the sidewalk standing watch over the gear while Buck and Robby get the van. Across the street, two girls are touching hands and laughing. A car rolls by, booming with bass. The wind is warm and the moon is full and glowing from every window in the city.

We pull up to the curb in front of my father's building on the Upper East Side, and there's actually a spot. Buck opens his door and something shatters.

"Shit!" he says.

"Shhh," I say, hopping out and going around to open the back of the van.

The street is dark and rustling with leaves. I look up at my dad's windows on the fifth floor, making sure he isn't still awake, imagining for a moment that he might be worried. But his windows are dark. One floor below, a light's been left on for us in my stepmother's apartment. My father and stepmother met because they were neighbors and I've always thought it strange that my father would leave, only to end up with, literally, the girl next door. These days, they spend most of their time in their house out on the tip of Long Island, spitting distance from the Hamptons. They keep these apartments for a place to stay when they come into the city to see friends or go to the theater. They're here this week because my father says he has some business to take care of, but I think he's just spying on me.

As we're unloading the gear onto the sidewalk, an old man is wheeling his way toward us behind a shopping cart filled with junk.

I consider feeling through my pockets for change but I'm drunk and it's three in the morning. All I really care about is whether we can get all our equipment into the teeny-tiny elevator and up to my step-mother's in one trip.

I'm leaning deep into the back of the van when Buck says, "Jen, you got any money?"

"It's too late," I say, grabbing my guitar case.

"Too late?" says Buck. "Too late for what? To be poor? Is it after closing time for you?"

"What are you, a fundraiser?"

Buck slams his door shut. "Wow," he says.

"What?" I say.

He looks up at my father's beautiful brownstone, then back at me. "Just can't spare a dollar, huh?"

"First of all—"

"Oh, here we go," says Robby. "Jen's counting."

"First of all, I don't live here, my father does. And second of all, why don't *you* give the guy a dollar. I mean, who are you, the fucking Curator of Charity?"

Robby laughs.

"Ooooh, Curator of Charity," says Buck, swiveling his hips, doing a little dance, looking, I have to admit, completely adorable.

"You wanna know something?" I say, leaning into Buck and whispering in his ear. "You're kinda cute when you're being a dick."

In the teeny-tiny elevator, crammed with all our equipment and the three of us, Buck shifts position and one of his hands ends up under my butt. He gives a small squeeze.

"Cut the shit," I say.

"What shit?" says Robby.

"Not you," I say. "Buck."

"What?" says Buck. "I'm not doing anything." He gives my butt another squeeze.

We finally get to the fourth floor and slog all the gear and the bags down the hall and into my stepmother's apartment, which is just two rooms and a kitchenette, with a big empty terrace off the living room.

Everything is white—the walls, doors, radiators—painted over, year after year, in big gloppy strokes that have turned everything soft, as if covered in snow. I toss my bag into the bedroom and head to the little kitchen. Inside the half-fridge is a six-pack with a Post-it stuck to the side. "WELCOME!" it reads in dull pencil. "Hope show was FUN! DNR tomorrow? xo BB."

I bring three beers into the little living room, where Buck and Robby are already stretched out on the couches amid all our gear. I sit on my amp and say, "So."

Robby laughs. "So," he says. "Is that all you have to say?"

"What do you want me to say?"

"How about how awesome this is? I mean, we're getting a lawyer, right?"

"Well," I say, smiling, but not as big as I'd really like to. "I'd say it's looking pretty darn likely."

Buck is staring at the ceiling. "We're a good band," he says. "I like us."

"To kicking ass," says Robby, toasting me with his beer.

"To kicking some *serious* ass," says Buck, swinging his legs to the floor, sitting up. "I just want you guys to know," he says, raising one eyebrow, smiling at us, "that this is all affecting Buck very very well," and he raises his beer. "To the big bad music business. May they give us a record deal and then go fuck themselves!"

TWO

The lobby of Neil Krakow's building shines with marble and buffed wood and reverberates with echoes like a canyon. I'm walking toward the big elevator doors when someone says, "Hey you!"

I turn around and see an old guy with a badge sitting high up behind a round reception desk and pointing his finger at me. "Yeah. Over here."

I skitter over.

"Who you seein'?"

"Neil Krakow?" I say.

"Your name?"

"Jennifer Trynin?"

The old guy begins shuffling through papers, tapping his pen, exhaling like I'm the biggest pain in his ass all day.

"He expectin' you?"

"Yeah."

"Could ya spell it?"

"Sure," I say. "K R A—"

The old guy looks at me and says he needs to see some I.D.

After checking my name off his list, he tells me middle elevator, fifty-sixth floor.

I get into the elevator with two men wearing dark suits and carrying coffee in white Styrofoam cups. One of them pushes button 55 and turns to me. "You're going up to Klopner, right?"

"That's right," I say. "Floor fifty-six. How'd you know?"

"Wild guess," he says, and pushes the button. I'm wearing the same clothes I had on last night—orange cords, big black shoes, white leather jacket, just with a different ugly shirt. This is what I think rock stars are expected to do. Wear the same clothes. Smell like a bar. Not give a fuck.

The elevator doors slide shut and the thing begins to climb, my ears popping like crazy.

"So, are you guys, like, lawyers?" I say.

"No. We're the Rolling Stones," says the button-pusher, scrunching his nose at me. "And you're, like, what. A brain surgeon?"

"Yeah," I say, smiling. "Need a lobotomy?"

The other guy laughs.

The doors ting open on the fifty-fifth floor and they get out.

On floor fifty-six, the doors open into a high-ceilinged reception area with one large desk facing the elevators and two striped linen couches to the right and left. A beautiful blond is lounging behind a desk with nothing on it but a phone, a pink pad, and a pen. She looks like a model in that way that makes you bet she really is a model.

"I'm Jennifer Trynin, here for Neil Krakow?"

She picks up the phone with her impossibly long arm, softly saying something, then pointing to her left. "Enda da hall on ya right," she says with about the thickest New York accent I've ever heard.

When I reach the end of the hall, someone screams, "WHAT THE HELL ARE YOU *TALKING* ABOUT?"

An older woman with hair in a bun is sitting behind a small desk cluttered with stacks of paper and unopened mail and manila envelopes with bumps in them, which I figure are cassettes people are sending to Neil.

"Jennifer?" she says, standing up, sticking out her hand. "I'm Debbie. I lo-ove your record."

"Wow," I say. "Thanks. I can't believe you listened to it."

"YEAH? WELL THAT GUY'S A FUCKIN' *DOUCHEBAG!*"

Debbie rolls her eyes. "Don't mind him," she says. "I can't believe you're on time! Rock stars are never on time."

"I guess that's cuz I'm not a rock star."

"Maybe not yet," she says, as the screaming resumes, moving on to dicks in hands and taking things up the butt.

Debbie does a quick mini-massage of her temples. "Just go on in," she says.

Neil's talking into a headset and squeezing a tennis ball. He gives me a quick smile and motions for me to sit. On his desk are a picture of a woman and two kids, a baseball signed in red ink, and a bowl of apples. One wall of the office is glass, floor to ceiling, with a view of Central Park like a postcard.

Neil's still looking at me, smiling. Then, "DO I *LOOK* LIKE AN ASSHOLE?" he yells. "THAT'S CRAP AND YOU FUCKIN' KNOW IT!" He holds out the bowl of apples to me. "SO TELL HIM TO GO FUCK HIMSELF!" I shake my head. "WHAT? *WHAT?*" Neil shrugs, and puts the bowl of apples back on his desk. Then he starts tapping his finger on his mouthpiece. "HE*LLO?* THIS THING *MUST* BE FUCKIN' BROKEN CUZ THERE'S NO *WAY* YOU JUST SAID WHAT YOU SAID!"

On the walls are a Woodstock poster (signed by a bunch of the Woodstock artists), a framed platinum record by Bruce Springsteen, and a sepia-tone antique map of Central Park. "YOU'RE *KILLIN'* ME OVER HERE!" On the floor, leaning against all the walls at least ten deep, are more rock-star posters and more platinum records, some of them still with cardboard around the edges as if they'd just been unpacked, but I have the feeling that they've been there for years. "TRAGEDY?" yells Neil. "TRAGEDY IS TWINS BORN WITH FUCKIN' *BRAIN* TUMORS!" He rips off the headset and slams it on his desk. "*Jesus* Christ." He picks up the headset and looks at it. "I keep breaking these things," he says. He puts it back down, hits a button on his phone, and tells Debbie to hold his calls.

"Anyway," he says. "How you doing today, you okay?"

"Yeah," I say. "I'm pretty good."

"Good, good. Me, too. That," says Neil, pointing to his phone, "that was bullshit." He stretches his arms over his head, then claps his hands and leans toward me. "So," he says. "Where're the boys from Boston?"

"They had to get back," I say. "Work, school, you know, stuff."

"Well, all I gotta say is last night. *Jesus!* You guys were fuckin' great! *Great!* And you never know, you know? Sometimes you hear these great records and then you see the band and it's like, *ehhh*—but you were fuckin' great, okay? And, you know, I just want you to know that it's been a long time since I loved a record the way I love your record. You got songs. You got something to say, you know? So I just want you to know I'm on board, like *on board.* So here's the deal: You play the music, I take care of the rest. You got no manager, no label, no booking agent. And I'm telling you, people are gonna be lining up and it's a lotta mouths to feed. Are you excited? Of course you're excited. Are you nervous? Sure you are. But it's all good. I've been here before and I know how these things move. And I can't emphasize this enough: timing timing timing. Massaging. These things can be like eggs, you know? Delicate. Cuz these people? These people are temperamental fucks and it'd *kill* me if you ended up in the wrong hands. All I'm saying is I hope you're gonna be careful. You take your time. You think. But just know that I'm all in." Neil leans back in his chair, puts his hands behind his head. "I have a good feeling about this one, like goose-pimple good." Then he leans back across his desk at me. "You got any questions?"

"I'm not sure," I say.

"That's okay. You don't have to be sure. That's where I come in. We can do it together. Let me bring it in, you know? I gotta land this sucker."

Back on the street, I watch myself walk by in a store window, wondering if my entire life has been leading to this moment.

I'm trying not to think about the money, but I know I'll be getting at least some, enough to pay my brother back the $5,000 he lent me, enough to get a new clutch for my old car, enough to make the past seven years amount to more than my own stubbornness.

Mr. Beacon Street is next. He tells me what scumbags the Klopner lawyers are, what weasels, how with him, I can rest assured that everything will always be on the up-and-up.

Mr. Skivvy speaks in bullet points—his firm, his experience, his education. His precisely cut blond hair seems matted and dull. Maybe he already knows he can't hold a candle to Neil. Maybe he's as distracted as I am by the sun just beyond his windows, streaking through the clouds like heaven.

When I get outside, the sun has gone behind the clouds. I take the subway down to the East Village and walk maybe ten blocks before I realize I'm shivering. I duck into some aren't-we-cool clothing store, and suddenly realize that I've been here before. It was years ago with Tim, and I'd been too intimidated by his nice clothes and Wall Street job to buy some secondhand coat I wanted.

I zero in on a rack of sweaters. New sweaters, expensive, like forty bucks. I let my fingers touch them as I circle the rack. I take one off its hanger—a green one with a zipper. I remove my white leather jacket and put it on, and it feels good. I rip the tag off the pocket of the sweater, put my jacket back on, and head for the counter.

Two more meetings but I'm wilting. I haven't eaten since yesterday. I can't. Or I won't. It's easier this way, my eyes a blur, my head full of fuzz. It's almost like I'm not really here at all.

The doorbell's loud: BING! BONG!

"Yikes," I say when the door opens. "Nice bell."

"I just had it installed. It's craaaazy, right?" says Hooper, wiggling his fingers in front of his eyes and making a silly bing-bong kind of face.

I don't know if Hooper's his first name or his last, and I don't care. I also don't care that he manages some cool band from Australia whose name I keep forgetting. All that really matters is that Hooper is that "manager friend" of Mr. Beacon Street's, the one in cahoots with him about taking half my publishing—i.e., Hooper's a slimebag. I'd agreed to meet with him anyway because, frankly, I'm so excited that anyone wants to meet with me at all. But now that I'm standing here in his super-mod studio apartment/office ("Because this way," as Hooper tells me about fifty thousand times, "I'm here for my bands twenty-four seven . . ."), even if this guy wasn't a slimebag, I'd never work with him anyway because, among other things, he has black dinner plates.

Lizzy Johns is sitting at a white Lucite desk with neatly stacked piles of folders on the floor all around her.

"Excuse the mess," she says. "I just moved my office." Then she tells me the "sad story" of the Liquorwhips who got signed, moved to New York, got dropped, and were back in Boston all within a year. It was rough, she tells me, but she sticks with her bands. Through thick and thin.

"Don't tell me you started without me," says Becka, hands on her hips in the doorway, silver hoops dangling from her ears. Then, "YOU," she yells, waving her finger at me like I'm in big trouble. "All I gotta say is were you born with a guitar in your hands or *what*?" She launches into an awkward sequence of air guitar moves, arms everywhere, head thrashing. She stops short with one of her earrings straddling her nose. She shakes her head and it falls off. "So, has Lizzy told you?"

"Told me what?" I say.

"We're teaming up," says Becka, putting her arm around Lizzy and squeezing her. Lizzy grins. "Frick and Frack, right? Isn't that what you're thinking?"

"I guess," I say, but Mutt and Jeff is more like it.

"We're joining forces. New letterhead, new office space, new everything, and now—new you! We want you to be our first artist together. Maiden voyage."

Lizzy nods.

"It'll be like a chick thing, right?" says Becka, smiling, staring at me, waiting, evidently, for an answer.

"Totally," I say.

By now it's dark. I walk a few blocks, then take the 6 back uptown.

When I get to my stepmother's, I leave the lights off. I lie on the couch and close my eyes. Listen to the traffic. The wind picks up, spinning leaves in the air. Birds begin circling the building, pecking at the gutters, scratching on the terrace. A man stands by the window, his back to me, looking out, so when the wind roars and the door blows open, I'm not afraid.

We're at Gino's, which is where we always go—a one-room restaurant that's been here since the dawn of time, along with the orange walls painted with zebras. The place is filled mostly with old people who've been coming here since their own personal heyday. The waiters—old men in white shirts and red vests who all speak with the same unplaceable accent—all know my father.

"I love this place," says my dad, which is what he always says after his first martini. "The décor. The clientele. Look at that poor old codger." He motions toward an old man hunched alone at a small table against the wall. "Nice ascot, though, huh?" he says, leaning into me like he's telling me a secret.

My father's been pointing things out to me my whole life. When I was little, it was usually pretty basic, like the snow or the moon. But gradually he began drawing my attention to the tilt of a man's hat or the way a woman walked into a room. I don't even think he knew he was doing it. I think he was just talking, trying to fill the space between us.

My father puts his hands against his ears. "What's all that racket?" he says.

There's a commotion at the entryway. A big group arriving, talking loudly, laughing, yelling out drink orders. The maître d' is all smiles and handshakes, snapping his fingers at the waiters, who begin scraping tables together, billowing a large tablecloth, clinking down silverware.

"Mr. Sorvino," says the maître d', extending his arm toward the big new table, and the group begins moving past us like a single spindly organism, arranging itself into seats.

BB, my stepmom, returns from the bar, where she's been smoking. "Ooh la la," she says, sitting down, one leg folded under her. "Movie stahs."

Tim grabs my arm under the table. "Holy shit," he says. "Isn't that Quentin Tarantino?"

My father leans back, takes a quick peek, pulls his chair back to the table. "Asshole," he says.

Tim rolls his eyes.

"Oh, sweetie, now, come on," says BB.

"Who's an asshole?" I say.

"That foolish Tara-whatever-his-name-is," says my father.

"We heard him on a talk show," says BB, "and every other word was a bleep."

"I don't know what it is about you kids today, your whole generation," says my father. "There's no romance. No class. This Tarantino fellow, acting as foolish as some, I don't know—*rock* star, with his sunglasses, smoking a cigarette." He shakes his head. "Idiocy."

"Shut up, sweetie," says BB, smiling, squeezing his shoulder, as the big table roars with laughter.

"So how was your show last night?" says Tim.

"Good," I say. "I think it went really well."

"Where did you play?" asks BB.

"Brownie's," I say.

"Brownie's?" says my father.

"And people came to see you, right?" says Tim. "Like, the lawyers?"

"Yeah, they did," I say.

"What lawyers?" says my father. My father's a lawyer.

"You know," I say. "Entertainment lawyers."

"Bunch of crooks," says my father.

"Anyone from a record company?" asks Tim. "Like those A&R people?"

"I'm not sure," I say, "but I think so. I mean, the place was pretty packed."

"Shit," says Tim. "I can't believe I couldn't go."

"We got another gig tomorrow night, downtown somewhere, at this place called Ludlow."

"Awesome," says Tim. "I'm there."

"We've got," says my father.

"What?" I say.

"We've got. We have got. We've got another gig."

"Actually, no," I say. "What I said is that we got—"

"Oh, sweetie, let's go," says BB. "A rock club! Rock and roll! I'll wear my white boots!"

"*If I were a rich man, bahda bahda bahda bahda bahda bahda bahda bah . . .*"

Everyone looks over at the big table.

My father's face lights up.

"*All day long I'd piddy piddy pum, if I were a wealthy man!*" Paul Sorvino and Quentin Tarantino stand, arms around each other, glasses of wine in the air. "*Wouldn't have to work hard, bahda bahda bahda bahda bahda bahda bahda bah . . .*"

"Now that's music," says my father, tapping his fingers on the table.

"*All day long I'd piddy piddy pum, if I were a wealthy man!*"

My father, singing along quietly.

After dinner, Tim and I head to a bar for another drink.

When we sit down, he asks what I'd like and then orders for us both, saying just one more and then he's got to hit the hay.

"What, no date for you tonight?" I say, like I'm teasing him, but really I'm just wondering how long until he ditches me.

"Naah," says Tim. "I'm beat. And I gotta get up early." He looks at his watch, then back at me. "You have the life, right?" he says, smiling, reaching out and digging his fingers into my knee. "Party all night and sleep all day?"

I hit his hand away and laugh. "Fuck you," I say.

"Hey, I'm not knockin' it, I'm fuckin' *jealous*," he says, slurring his words to make them sound dramatically New Yorky, like he's a truck driver. "*I'm* the one who works his *balls* off at Yale, and his *balls* off at Wharton, and now *you're* gonna be the fuckin' rock star? And rich? And famous? My little sister?" He smiles at me, not winking, but it feels like he's winking. "Gotta hit the bathroom," he says, and he gets up.

Even in his suit and tie and tasseled loafers, Tim has the same sauntering swagger as ever, as if he's still making his way off the soccer field to another party, where all the girls will love him.

When I get back to BB's, I call Guy at the studio in L.A. where he's working with Aimee. I tell him about all the meetings, Neil's impressive building, Mr. Beacon Street's bad-mouthing Neil, pushy Becka Stein.

"Neil's already called me three times today," says Guy.

"What? What for?"

"Jen, I'm telling you. He's going nuts over the record. And he says everyone's going nuts. He's bringing like everybody and their brother to the Ludlow show."

"But I haven't even hired him yet."

"He says he can't help it."

The next afternoon, Buck and Robby and I are out in front of my father's, loading gear into the van.

"You missed us like hell, right?" says Buck. "Be honest."

"I was just about to kill myself," I say.

"So how'd the meetings go?" says Robby.

"Everybody loves us, right?" says Buck.

"I guess it's kinda looking that way," I say.

"Who do you like," says Robby, "like for a lawyer."

"I'm pretty sure we should go with Neil," I say.

HONK!

I fall against Buck, a taxi missing me by a hair.

"Are you okay?" says Robby.

"Fuck that was close," I say.

Buck begins touching me all over, saying, "One piece. One piece. This may be broken," he says, wiggling my pinky. I laugh, slapping his hand away.

"You better be careful, O'Trynihan," says Robby. "We need you alive."

"Yeah," says Buck. "That'd be great. 'Oh, gee, sorry, Mr. A&R guy. Jen's dead. But we'll play!'"

"That'd go over big," says Robby.

"How about you guys shut the fuck up," I say.

Ludlow is half club, half pizza joint, with booths around the edges and a stage in the front window. We got this show last-minute, opening for Flint Raft, a young rock band who recently relocated to Boston from Connecticut and are making a record with Guy. We're also playing with them tomorrow night at some club in Worcester.

It's already crowded when we load in our gear and begin arranging it on the stage. There's no official soundcheck, just a line check to make sure everything's working. Then it's "set it and forget it."

"So who all is coming down tonight?" says Robby, setting up his kit.

"I'm not really sure," I say. "You know, Neil, and the other lawyers and those managers I met with and a bunch of people are coming with Neil and then some other people Guy told me about but I forgot the list at home and I don't really remember. Exactly."

"Our fearless leader," smiles Buck.

"Is Guy still in L.A.?" says Robby.

"Yeah," I say. "He's working."

"Work, work, work," says Buck.

Part of me wishes Guy were here. To help with the sound. To keep track of what's going on. To just be here. But another part of me is excited to be alone.

"Jennifer?"

A guy is standing in front of the low stage dressed in a trench coat, sticking out his hand and smiling.

"I'm Merv Csisick," he says. His hair is dark and messy.

"Merv Sick-it?" I say, shaking his hand.

"Siz-ik," he says, pumping my hand like he's blowing me up.

"Sorry," I say.

"I know it's a bitch," he says, giving my hand a squeeze, then finally letting go. "So, I got your record," he says, patting the pocket of his trench coat, then scratching his head. "And I just got one question."

"Shoot," I say.

"Where you been all my life?" says Merv. He smiles.

"Thanks," I say.

"Just wanted to tell you that. Go back to what you were doing. Don't mind me." Merv looks over at Buck and Robby. "Hi guys," he says, smiling, giving a short wave, and he walks away.

"Who was that?" says Buck.

"I don't know," I say. "Merv Sick-it or something."

"Here he comes again," says Buck.

"I almost forgot," says Merv, holding out a business card. "Just in case we don't get a chance to chat after the show. I'm with Mercury Records. Oh, and here," he says, pulling a pen from his pocket and writing something on the card. "That's my direct line, you know, just in case."

"Thanks," I say.

Merv turns, waves, and goes back to his table.

"In case of what?" says Buck. "You remember who the murderer is? Just one more question," says Buck, pretending to write on his palm. "Were you sleeping with the defendant?"

I laugh.

"Hey, but Columbo works for Mercury," says Buck. "That doesn't suck."

Over at the bar I see my father and BB, and my heart jumps.

"Hey, Kiki Dee," says Tim, who's suddenly right in front of the stage.

"You're here," I say.

"I told you I was gonna come."

We hug with my guitar between us.

"I didn't think *they* were coming," I say, pointing toward the bar.

"They said they were curious."

"I don't want anybody feeling Dad's whole 'You're all a bunch of crooks' thing."

"Oh, come on. He'll behave himself. I'll watch him."

"Don't let him talk to anybody," I say.

"Settle down, Kiki," says Tim. "I just wanted to let you know we're here, but c'mere."

I bend down toward him.

"There are all these people talking about you over at the bar," says Tim.

"Really?"

"Yeah. You know. Like how *Cockamamie* is so great and how you're gonna be like a tough one to get and stuff like that."

"You're kidding."

"No."

"Wow."

"I know." Tim smiles at me and gives my arm a squeeze. "Don't worry about it. Just do your thing," he says.

I stand back up.

"You want a drink?" he says. "Hey," he says to Buck and Robby, "you guys need drinks?"

I'm hooking up my pedalboard when I feel someone staring at me. A small woman with light hair, her arms crossed at the chest, a small smile on her face. She's older, maybe sixty, with a tan sweater down to her thighs, tan slacks, tan shoes, and a big black bag.

"Can I help you?" I say.

"I'm just watching," she says.

"Oh," I say. "Watching what?"

"You," she says and smiles. "You see," she says, "I've learned over the years that sometimes, with guitar players in particular, there's so much to witness in the before, in the setting up of things. Some of the greats—Verlaine, Lloyd—when I worked with television, there was always something to learn. Sometimes I can tell how someone's going to play by the way he—or she in this case—how you sling your guitar strap over your head."

"Do you play guitar?" I say.

"Me?" She laughs. "Good god, no. I wish. I just do A&R. I'm just a facilitator. I like to think I help people. People like you. Most of the time, I try to help by staying out of the way."

"I'm Jennifer," I say, sticking out my hand.

"I'm Lola," she says, and we shake. Her hand is warm and small and she lets go at just the right moment. "*Cockamamie* is amazing," she says. "Truly. Beautiful. Powerful. I'd love to work with you, but the truth is my company's going through a strange time, and I just wouldn't feel right approaching you, officially, until we've gotten back on our feet." Lola smiles. "I'm looking forward to your show and I'll be in touch again when things settle down at The Company. Who should I contact? You or Neil? Neil's your lawyer, right?"

"Well, not exactly. But probably. I mean, it's not official."

"He's a good man," says Lola. She raises her small fist into the air. "Go get 'em," she says, and turns, walking back into the crowd.

"Where is *she* from?" says Robby.

"She didn't say," I say.

"This does *not suck*," says Buck.

"Your money or your wife."

I turn.

It's Neil.

I smile.

He smiles.

"I don't have a wife," I say.

"So take my wife, *please*," he says.

I like this guy.

"So introduce me already," says Neil.

I introduce Neil to Buck and Robby.

"The boys from Boston," says Neil. "Fantastic. You guys were great the other night. I loved it! I can't wait for tonight. Jen. Can I talk to you?" Neil motions me down to the floor. "So I've been giving people copies of the CD, okay? I hope that's all right—you know, you haven't really hired me yet or anything—but, I'm telling you, people are fucking freaking out, okay? So I brought some folks down tonight, just to check it out, but don't let that throw you or anything, you know, don't be nervous about it. But Jen, you gotta listen to me. You're really gonna need some help soon, like fast. That woman who was just talking to you? Lola? She's the real deal. You should take her very very seriously. Just her being interested in you takes you onto a whole 'nother level."

"She didn't say where she works."

"Warner Brothers," says Neil. "A&R. She's been with Warners forever and is highly *highly* respected. It's like Lola don't have to report to *no*body."

"Really?" I say.

"Yeah," he says. "She goes after one, maybe two people a year."

"She said things were fucked up there or something."

"Well, yeah. See, this is what I'm talking about. You're gonna need help seeing your way through this kinda crap. And these things can happen fast, so time is definitely of the essence. Do you know what I'm saying?"

"Yeah," I say, trying to be cool, but my excitement meter is pinning to the RIGHT RIGHT RIGHT.

"Okay," says Neil. He waves to Buck and Robby. "All right, boys. Rock on, okay?"

Neil hasn't taken two steps before he's shaking some woman's hand and laughing. She has dark curly hair and is wearing an oversized black leather jacket with an MTV logo on the chest and the sleeves rolled up. She keeps looking over at me, and then she's walking my way, chewing gum and smoking.

"Hi," she says, flicking a little white card in her hand with her thumb. "We said hi the other night at Brownie's? When I was on line for the bathroom?"

"Sure," I say. "I remember you." And I almost do.

"You know, Neil can*not* stop talking about you. I'm Cinda Weinstein. I work at Sony Publishing. And, so, well, here," she says, giving me her card. "I mean, I hate being so formal and like icky business-y, but I'm afraid I'm not gonna get a chance to really, you know, *talk* to you tonight, and I just wanna make sure I'm in there, you know? But here I am and we're talking so I guess I might as well just tell you that your record, it's like my favorite record in like, *forever*, and I know it's a little early to be getting all over you because you're just gonna be like *de*luged with people and the last thing I wanna do is like con*fuse* you even more, but I want you to know that I really get what you're doing. I mean, I really see *into* it. I mean, cuz you know, everyone's like the Women in Rock thing and yadda yadda yadda," she says, moving her fingers like a little mouth. "But you don't need that. You're like—you play guitar like a *guy*, for Christ's sake," she says, ruffling some feather deep within me. I've always hated my tomboyishness, my pottymouth, my Jerseyhood. But lately, everything feels topsy-turvy, like my weaknesses are suddenly my strengths.

"I throw a ball like a guy too," I say.

"But there's such contrast on your record. I mean, all this rock but then there's this other side, the softer side, almost like singer-songwriter-y," she says, sending my I'm-Not-Folk flag right up the pole.

I look at her.

She looks at me.

"I'm coming on too strong, aren't I," she says, chewing her gum a mile a minute. She takes a drag off her nubby cigarette and then throws it on the floor, stamping it out with the tip of her pointy black boot. "I don't wanna be this way. Everyone's gonna be this way," she says, looking around the room. "Ever notice how few chicks there are in the business?"

I don't tell her that I'm so used to dealing with guys in my own little rock world that, no, I hadn't noticed at all. But now that she's pointed it out, the fact is I like dealing with guys.

"Guys guys guys," says Cinda, pulling a pack of Marlboro Ultra Lights from her purse. "Cigarette?"

"Thanks," I say.

"Light?"

"Sure," I say, as she takes out one of those lighters that has a girl with a bikini on it, which disappears when you turn it upside down.

A cute guy with dark hair walks up, looks at me, looks at the ground, looks at Cinda, looks over Cinda's shoulder.

"Oh," says Cinda. "Hi Randy."

"Hi Cinda," he says.

"This is Jennifer Trynin," says Cinda. "And this is Randy Sway. Manager to the stars."

"Well, I don't know about that," says Randy.

"C'mon," says Cinda. "John Hiatt? Liz Phair?"

"Hi," I say.

"Hi," says Randy. He's wearing a black leather jacket, the nice kind you might get in a men's department store, not the rocker/biker kind. "I got your record from Neil because, you know, he thought I might like what you're doing, and I really do. It's hard to define, you know, pin down, and that's a good thing. I think that's a good thing." He's speaking from somewhere so deep in his larynx that it's a little hard to tell if he's saying something or just clearing his throat.

Cinda's nodding her head, blowing smoke out of a corner of her mouth, away from Randy. "Ditto," she says.

"Thanks," I say.

"I used to manage a band from your neck of the woods," says Randy. "Treat Her Right, Mark Sandman. You know those guys?"

"Sure," I say. Treat Her Right was one of the most successful bands in Boston when I moved there. They'd been signed and dropped years ago, but the lead singer, Mark Sandman, was and still is the coolest guy in the world. Scary cool, not chill cool. "I loved those guys."

Cinda looks at her watch. "Oh, shit," she says. "I gotta go meet someone. But I'll be back." She reaches into her purse and pulls out a box of Altoids. "Mint?" she says, holding them out to me, then to Randy.

We both take one.

"Back in a flash," she says, and gives me a wink. "Break a string!"

Randy and I suck on our mints. He looks like Jerry Seinfeld but handsomer. And more nervous. And not funny.

"So, I'll let you get back to, you know, whatever you're doing," he says, "but it'd be great if you could come by our office at Vibetone and take a look around, get to know us, you know, when you're ready." He gives me his card.

"Great," I say.

"Okay then," says Randy.

Buck and Robby come over.

"Did that chick say she was from Sony Publishing?" says Robby.

"Yeah," I say.

"Ah, yes," says Buck. "They're a nice little company."

"And that guy manages Liz Phair or something," I say. "He used to manage Treat Her Right."

"Not bad, not bad," says Buck.

Robby's eyes go all puppy-dog. "You know, Jen," he says, and he touches my arm. "I just want you to know that, well, this is really cool. And I'm really happy to be playing with you."

"Me, too," says Buck. "In fact, all told, I'd say I'm even happier than Robby."

Robby laughs. "You are not," he says, putting up his dukes.

"Am too," says Buck, smacking Robby on the arm.

"Are not," says Robby, smacking him back, which leads into a full-scale rock-em-sock-em fake fight complete with karate chops and scissor kicks.

Three beers later, it's like I'm walking through a car wash with random hands turning me in circles. Mr. Skivvy (*Do you like tennis?*). Hooper and Mr. Beacon Street (*We should've gotten in when the gettin' was good, right?*). Lizzy and Becka and an entourage (Becka: *This is Jennifer, our new guitar goddess!*). And more managers, A&R people, publishing people, booking guys—offering drinks, cards, advice, everyone wanting to throw their hat in the ring—*Love your record. Can't wait for the show. Just wanted to say hi, throw my hat in the ring.*

"Hey, O'Trynihan," says Teddy Z. "What's shakin'?" Teddy Z. is the bass player for Flint Raft.

"C'mere," I say, and grab his arm. "Take a break with me."

Teddy Z. knows everyone and everything, and people are always trying to steal him from Flint Raft—including me, before I found Buck. He's like my brother's rock-guy doppelgänger, with his you-can-talk-to-me eyes and I'll-make-pancakes-in-the-morning demeanor. All the chicks dig Teddy Z.

"What the hell's going on here?" he says. "It's like a dweebfest."

"I guess a few people came to check us out," I say.

"A few people? Jesus. Everyone's like talking about you all over the place. *Fuck*," he says, holding out a pack of Camel Lights. I shake my head. He takes a cigarette and puts it in his mouth, letting it bop in his lips as he talks. "This chick over there was saying how she went to high school with you or something and I'm like, Where'd you grow up? And she goes, San Diego. And I'm like, Sorry, Jen's from New Jersey."

"That's weird," I say.

"*Fuckin'* weird." He lights his cigarette.

Theo comes over. Theo is Flint Raft's singer, a stocky guy with a big head and a great voice. He plays the farfisa and reads Thoreau. "Greetings," he says, standing stiff, looking up over my head.

"Thanks for these gigs," I say.

"Thank Ted," says Theo.

This is about as far as my conversations ever go with Theo. I take a deep breath and let it out. "All right," I say. "Thanks, Ted."

Teddy Z. blows smoke at Theo and then salutes me with his cigarette.

"I better go freshen up," says Theo. "Gotta look pretty for all the weasels. Because they really give a shit." He walks away.

Teddy Z. laughs. Blows smoke at the ceiling. "Give 'em hell," he says, and kisses me on the cheek.

"I'm gonna try," I say.

"Just send us your sloppy seconds, okay?" he says, and goes back to the bar.

———

"Jennifer?" says a man with his hand on my elbow. He's completely bald and wearing a black suede jacket that smells like a horse. "I'm Philippe," he says, "friend of Neil's. Welcome to the Big Apple."

"Thanks," I say.

"Got a minute?"

"Sure."

"Great," says Philippe. "I'm with Columbia."

"Columbia?"

"You familiar with Columbia?"

I laugh and say yes.

"Good," says Philippe. "Listen. It's no secret what's going on here. But let's pretend none of this is happening. Like I'm just me and you're just you and we're just two people here in this bar having a drink. Okay? No pressures." Philippe's earlobes are very long, with gold studs in each. He has bushy eyebrows and seems around forty. "Cuz all we're really doing is talking about tunes, right? I mean, that's all it comes down to for me cuz I love music, and I gotta tell ya, your songs are something else. Artists like you make jerks like me look good, you know? I mean, take that 'Feelin' Good' track—"

"'Better Than Nothing,'" I say.

"'Better Than Nothing.' I mean, come on. Did anyone order a hit song?" Philippe snaps his fingers in the air. "The thing is, I don't know what's up with some of these labels these days not just coming out strong. I've seen more bands go down the fuckin' tubes cuz of id- iots pulling their punches, waiting on the hit song, saving it for later. Later when? Later why? When's later? If you got a hit, you go for it. Bam. You don't start screwing around, trying to be all *indie*," he says, rabbit-earing his fingers around the word *indie*, "releasing the *cool* song first,"—air-quoting *cool*—"making a *low-budge hip video*"—air- quoting *low-budge, hip,* and *video,* continuing his diatribe in an air- quoting frenzy, bouncing his fingers around words like *precious, passionate, arty, money,* until it seems like the only words Philippe ac- tually means are ones like *the* or *and* or *yeah*—"but what's the point?" he says. "This ain't rocket science. Just go for the gold, right?"

"Right," I say, as if I'm as tired of all this hanky-panky marketing mumbo jumbo as he is.

"I mean, let's get real," he says. "You know, grass roots and slow build and blah blah blah. Fact is, your average moron isn't gonna get anything he's not smacked over the head with, right? It's like what that circus guy said. You never lose money overestimating people's intelligence."

"Underestimating," I hear myself say.

"What?" says Philippe.

"*Underestimating* people's intelligence," I say, a little quieter, feeling like my father, crossing other people's T's uninvited.

"Right," says Philippe. "See, with you, the beauty is once we hook 'em with the hit, then we can start digging, cuz your record is that kinda record. It's so deep, I'm friggin' drowning over here, and far as I'm concerned, that's numero uno importante. Cuz let's say hell freezes over and your 'Feelin' Good' song isn't a hit. So what? We got 'One Year Town' to—"

"'One Year Down,'" I say.

"That song's killer. And then to back up those kinds of tunes, we got other stuff. That bluesy one and that song at the end?"

"'Do It Alone'?"

"Right. Wow." Philippe puts his hand over his heart and shakes his head. "Whaddaya want me to say? I played that track for my girl-friend," he says, putting his finger to one eye and slowly dragging it down his cheek. "Tears," he says. "Brought tears to her eyes. It's fuckin' beautiful."

I can't tell if this guy's for real or if he's just blowing smoke up my ass.

"Thanks," I say.

"No, I'm the one thanking *you*," says Philippe, taking a pack of Doublemint from his pocket and holding it out to me. "Gum?" he says.

"No thanks," I say.

Philippe unwraps a piece, bends it in half, and puts it into his mouth. He picks a bit of lint from his sleeve. "See, I know where you're coming from because I used to be one of you. I was in the

Hamfisters," he says, pausing, staring at me, as if he's waiting for me to say, *Oh yeah, I remember you guys.* But if I lie and say I do, I'm afraid this will devolve into a discussion of the intricacies of the Hamfisters' discography and I just don't think any good will come of that. So I stare back at him like I'm entranced by his fascinating tale and hope he'll just keep talking.

"Ever hear of us?" he says.

Shit. I purse my lips. Look up at the ceiling. Mumble, "Uhhh," and then stare down at the floor.

"The Hamfisters," he says again. "Back in the early eighties? We were Punk—I mean *real* Punk, not like the fake crap."

"The Haaaaamfisters," I say slowly, beginning to nod my head as if it's all coming back to me now, but I can tell Philippe isn't buying it. He looks over my shoulder, his tongue in his teeth, his expression vacillating between insulted, betrayed, sad, and bedraggled. It's like I can see his whole life flashing by right between us. He closes his eyes and puts his hand over his mouth, pulling down along the sides of his lips as if smoothing a long mustache. He takes a deep breath.

"Anyway," he says. "That's not important. What's important is you, and I just want you to know that I get it. You need to be with people who have vision, for you as an individual, but also for your career. I'm talking about good old-fashioned artist development. Longevity, and that's what we're about at Columbia—the long haul." Philippe gives a quick look around the club and then leans back into me. "Most of these jokers, all they think about is money. Money money money. But at the end of the day, you and I know that's not what it's about, right?"

"Right," I say.

"All I want is for you to go with who-fuckin-ever makes you feel comfortable." He winks at me. "I know where you're coming from, for you," he says, pointing both index fingers at me like guns. "Not for them," raising his hands above his head in a flurry, "but for you," gun-pointing me again.

I look down at my wrist, checking the watch I don't have. "Oh, man. I gotta go do something," I say.

"Sure," says Philippe. "I'm sure you got a million things to do. So I should be in touch with Neil?"

"We haven't really finalized anything, but, yeah. Probably."

"Great. All right. Well, I can't wait to hear your set, and I'm really glad I got this chance to chat and tell you how great your record is and, you know, throw my hat in the ring."

I'm almost to the bar when someone says "Almo," right into my ear, warm, moist, monotone. "I'm Johnny. I can't say your stuff is terribly original but I think I could sell it," says the voice, jack-in-the-boxing the horrid articulation of my biggest fear.

I whirl around to see who it is and knock into Buck, spilling his beer on his shirt.

"Thanks," says Buck.

"Oh, Jesus. Stop fucking with me," I say.

"Fucking with you?"

"*Fucking* with me."

"Believe me," he says. "I'd know if I was fucking with you." He smiles.

"Ha ha," I say.

"Buck!" yells Robby, pointing with both hands toward some skinhead-looking dude standing next to him.

"Scuzzy!" yells Buck. "Holy shit," and he heads over there.

I order a beer at the bar and pull out a cigarette.

"Light?" asks a guy wearing a black SubPop T-shirt and holding out a black Zippo lighter.

"What? Oh, yeah, thanks," I say.

"Didn't mean to scare you," he says, flicking the lighter at the end of his skinny arm, which is completely covered in a swirling tattoo that ends abruptly at his wrist, as if his hand had been sewn on separately. He's tall and lean with tangled sandy hair, black jeans, and a nice smile. Part of me is hoping he's just a regular person who thinks I'm cute, but then he pulls a business card from his pocket. "I'm Drake," he says, "record company asshole."

I laugh. "I'm Jennifer Trynin," I say.

Drake smiles. "I know who you are," he says.

I look down at his card, which has nothing but the name "Drake," a phone number, and a cool logo that's half record, half moon. "I like your logo," I say.

"I like *your* logo," he says.

"I don't have a logo," I say.

"Sure you do," says Drake. "You're your logo."

I can't tell if he's flirting with me or if in the real bigtime music business, it's common knowledge that a person can be his or her own logo.

Drake looks around the room. "Jesus," he says. "I hate these things."

"What things?"

"These things," he says, dismissing the entire club with a wave of his hand. "I hate being called up and told how *great* somebody is and how I *have* to hear their record and go to their show. I don't like to play that game. But the thing is, I just got *Cockamamie* FedEx from this bud of mine in Boston who's been going on and on about you, but I mean, he's like that about a lot of bands. But then I listened to your record," says Drake, shoving both hands in his pockets, looking very aw-shucks. "I listened to it like five times, I *swear,* and I mean I *never* do that. But Jesus Christ, the thing fucking *rocks,* but it doesn't *just* rock, it rocks without being, you know, obvious. And you play some kick-ass guitar."

"Thanks," I say.

"And you got Dave fucking Gregory to play on a track, and Aimee Mann?"

"I'm lucky."

"She's a fucking goddess and XTC is the balls," says Drake. "Well, they used to be the balls. But, I guess they're still the balls, in a way. But, anyway, you fuckin' rock."

"Thanks," I say.

"And I'm sure everyone's jumping all over that shower song cuz, like, obviously that's a great song. But you wanna know my favorite?"

"Absolutely."

"That song about the snow. *That* one fuckin' kills me," he says, looking at the floor, running his fingers through his hair. "Some of your stuff, it's like, like Patti Smith meets Alex Chilton, you know?"

"Who?"

"What?"

"Alex Chilton?"

"You're joking, right?" says Drake. "Big Star."

"Oh, Alex *Chilton*," I say. "Big Star. Yeah."

"I bet you listened to a lot of them," says Drake.

"Totally," I say.

"I don't know," says Drake. "I just really love your record and I totally respect your whole DIY thing and no doubt you're like wary as hell about the whole major-label game and you should be, you know, cuz you know how those people are. They're all about throwing bands against the wall just to see who sticks. They're about as loyal as a cat."

"I love cats," I say.

"Oh, no, I love cats too. I'm just saying I don't think a regular old major is the place for you. Atlas is different. We're like the best of both worlds. We're like indie meets major. East meets west. Yin and yang. Because we're like our own little universe where you can get all the attention you need while also getting all the trimmings of a bigger label, cuz we're under the *umbrella* of A&M—" says Drake, drawing a big circle with his hands, "—giving us *access* to A&M as if we *were* A&M. Like for distribution and stuff."

"But you're not A&M."

"Well, no," says Drake. "Listen. I know you're going to get a million offers from labels way bigger than Atlas, but I think it'd be a huge mistake. People like me don't work at the big labels and I mean, you need to be working with people who get it. Who *really* get it. Not some asshole who's like, Oh, I *get it*," he says, air-quoting *get it,* which makes me instantly clammy. "I mean *get it* get it," he says, no quotes, "for real. And I know it's really tempting to give in to the bigger companies with all their *money* and *influence,*" he says, sneering over the words *money* and *influence* as if these aren't bona fide advantages of going with a big label—"but at the end of the day, you need people who're really gonna be there for you long-term, not just for this song or that song. I know you know what I mean, we're on the same page, right?"

I nod, wondering exactly what page it is that we're both evidently on.

"So blah blah blah," says Drake. He smiles. "You're from Boston, right? I used to live in Allston. Near that diner? Next to Bunratty's? You know that diner?"

"The Deli King?"

"The Deli King, that's right. I love that place."

"Yeah, me too. It kinda sucks that it's gone now."

"The Deli King's gone? That place totally ruled!"

"Yeah. But it's like a Boston Chicken now."

"Boston Chicken? What do they serve, like, chicken?"

"Oh no," I say. "They serve a lot more than just chicken. They should call it Boston Chicken And We Don't Just Serve Chicken If You Know What I Mean." I smile.

"Hmm," says Drake, as if he's carefully considering this new information. "You know that band Wonderlush?" he says. "They're from Boston."

"Wanderlust?" I say.

"No, Wonderlush. W-o-n-d—"

"Sorry to intrude," says Philippe. "Hey Drake."

"How's it hanging, Phil?" says Drake.

"Can't complain," says Philippe. "Saw you at the Jets game."

"You were there?"

"Freezing my ass off."

"Great game," says Drake.

"Unreal," says Philippe.

"I see you've met Jennifer," says Philippe.

"I think she likes to be called Jen," says Drake. "I heard you prefer Jen, right?"

"It doesn't really matter," I say, finding it hard to believe that anyone's had an actual conversation about what I prefer to be called.

"I was just wondering if you're staying in the city tonight," says Philippe. "Maybe I could take you to lunch tomorrow?"

Drake laughs, then puts a hand over his mouth and pretends to clear his throat.

"Wow, that's really nice of you," I say, "but we're taking off pretty early. We have a gig tomorrow night back in Boston."

"That's okay," says Philippe. "Maybe next time."

"Sure," I say. "Definitely."

"Mr. Rosenberg," says Neil, putting his arm around me, squeezing, taking it away, shaking Philippe's hand.

"Mr. Krakow," says Philippe.

"Always a thrill," says Neil.

"Likewise," says Philippe.

"How you doing?" Neil says to Drake. "Neil Krakow."

"Drake from Atlas," says Drake.

"Fantastic," says Neil, putting his arm back over my shoulder. "You'll have to excuse us for a minute," he says, and he pulls me away.

"I see you were talking with Randy Sway," says Neil. "He's top shelf, okay? You should take him very very seriously. So listen. We really need to talk soon, like yesterday. This room is buzzing with a capital-B buzz. You need a lawyer. Now. Bad. Call me, okay? Like soon."

I'm dizzily making my way to the bathroom when I feel someone looking at me again. Some guy leaning against the wall in a worn leather jacket and blue jeans. Brown messy hair. Kind of tall and cute. He smiles. Actually, he grins. I look away, but as I'm hurrying past him, he leans toward me.

"Having fun?" he says, warm, moist, monotone. I'm almost at the bathroom when it hits me. That was the Voice. Johnny.

There's a line for the bathroom, but everyone seems to know who I am and they let me go right in. I close the door behind me, slide the lock, and I'm alone. The walls are black cinderblocks. One bare bulb hangs from a cord just above the toilet, and the place reeks of disinfectant. There's no toilet paper or paper towels, and the toilet seat is dull with dried piss.

I pee standing up, then stare at myself in the mirror, which is cracked and fingerprinted and has KISS ME YOU BADASS scrawled in red lipstick. My face is pale and my hair is hanging stringy across my eyes. My stomach twinges and I feel out of breath.

This is it. This is real. People are here because I'm good. Because they understand what I'm doing and they want to help me be my best. There's no other explanation, right? Fuck that Johnny guy. It's *good* that they think I might have a hit song or two. Isn't that what I wanted?

I run water over my hands. Let myself cry just a little.

Fuck it. Just go out there and play your songs. Everyone's on your side.

But I know everyone's not on my side.

I turn to the door and put my fingers around the knob, which is cold and wet. I slide the lock open. "Kiss me you badass," I say, and head back out into the club.

It's around 2 A.M. when we get back to BB's, everyone drunk and laughing, crammed into the little living room.

"You guys were great," says Tim. "Really. It was a great show. And all those people? Like, it was just fuckin' great." Tim looks at me and smiles his goofy smile, the one I live for, the one he smiles when he's filled with real feeling and doesn't know quite what else to do.

"So what's going on?" says my father. "I mean, Jen," he says, looking at me in that way that I know he's really looking at me. "Is this for real? Who were all those people? How do they even know who you are?"

"I don't know. It's kinda confusing," I say. "They're, like, industry people. Everyone seems to be duping the CD and passing it around."

"Far cry from that gig a couple of years ago," says Tim. "You guys didn't go on till like two in the morning and nobody was there."

"Yeah," I say. "Thanks. I remember."

"That's cuz she wasn't playing with us," says Buck.

"Who's this Neil Krakow fellow?" says my father. "He seems awfully fond of you."

"You *talked* to him?" I say, shooting Tim a look. He smiles and shrugs.

"Don't get excited," says my father. "I just want him to know who he's dealing with. I don't want him thinking you're some country bumpkin coming from nothing. I don't want any of these cats thinking they can take advantage of you," he says, causing that familiar swivel in the center of my chest—*help me, I don't need your help.*

"So what's the plan?" says Tim.

"The first thing is to pick a lawyer. Then I guess he shops the record around."

"You guess?" says my dad. "Kiddie, I hope you know what you're doing."

"Is anyone talking money yet?" says BB. BB used to work on Wall Street. She's the first one to admit she doesn't know anything about art, but money she understands.

"No one's mentioned money yet," I say.

"Richard's son Dicky is in some band on Sony," says BB, "and he says Dicky still has to wait tables."

"Yeah, well I bet Dicky didn't have a million labels after him when he got signed," I say.

"Meaning," says my dad.

"Meaning I don't think I'm gonna have to be waiting tables after my deal comes down." I don't really think this. I just don't want my dad and BB knowing that I don't know what I'm talking about.

Tim is smiling at me again. "This is fucking cool," he says.

"Well, I hope you pick a good lawyer," says BB, picking up her shoes from the floor and walking toward the door. "Nighty-night," she says.

My father stands. "Very exciting, kiddies," he says. He looks out the window. "What a beautiful night." He takes a deep breath. Lets it out. "Life's a grand adventure, isn't it?" he says, and points up in the sky. "Did you see that moon?"

At 4 A.M. I'm lying in bed, listening to the heat bang through the building. I'm happy and shaking and tired. And scared. And suddenly lonely. And wishing more than anything in the world that someone was in bed with me. Preferably someone I don't know, who doesn't know me, who wouldn't ask questions, who would just let me sleep.

★

We're heading back toward Boston, north on 91.

"Life on the road," says Buck. "It's a bitch."

"But someone's gotta do it," says Robby.

"In the middle of our first tour," says Buck.

"God, we've been out forever," I say.

"Two whole nights in a row," says Robby.

"Hey, rock star," says Buck, turning to me in the back. "When do we get a bus?"

"When we get a million dollars," I say.

"So when's that? Like tomorrow?"

"Yeah. Sure. Tomorrow."

"Hey," says Buck, turning back to the front. "How do you get a million dollars, tax free?"

"How," says Robby.

"First, get a million dollars. Then, don't pay your taxes. When the IRS comes, just say, 'I forgot.'"

Robby honks the horn. "Bad one!"

"Very funny," I say.

"What's the matter," says Buck, turning around again. "My humor too plebeian for you?"

"Plebeian?" I laugh.

"Plebeian?" says Robby.

Plebeian?

PLEbeian?

PleBEian?

We pull into the parking lot behind Bowler's, where we're opening for Flint Raft again. Buck and Robby go into the club to find out what's what while I watch the gear.

The night is warm and sprinkling with rain. I'm leaning against the van with my mouth open, the cool rain on my tongue, when I hear footsteps.

"Yo, dudette." It's Kramer, Flint Raft's manager. He's from Boston and also manages Shineaway, whom he got signed last year. Kramer's big stuff in Boston. He rubs his hands together, sticks them in his pockets. "So how's it going?" he says.

I look behind me to see if anyone else is there. I know Kramer through Guy, though "know" is a little strong. Every time I've recorded anything, Guy's gotten a copy to Kramer, and every time I've heard exactly nothing from him, including when Kramer got an advance of *Cockamamie* about a month ago.

"It's going okay," I say.

"Krakow says it's going nuts already. Are you freakin' or what? He's a trip, right?" says Kramer.

"Yeah," I say. "He's pretty crazy."

"So are you talking to any managers yet?" says Kramer.

I look at him. Smile.

He smiles back.

"I guess I've been talking to a few," I say.

"Well, I just want you to know that I'm up for it. Let's have a sit-down, just you and me, okay? You free tomorrow?"

"Hmm, tomorrow," I say, pulling out my cigarettes. I take one from the pack, reach for my lighter, light it, take a drag, put the lighter back in my pocket. "Tomorrow's no good," I say.

"Okay, that's cool. So maybe next week? Maybe Monday?"

"How about if I call you," I say.

"Cool. That's cool," says Kramer. He looks at his watch, then down at the ground, then back at me. "You think this is kinda fishy, right," he says.

"What?" I say.

"You know. I never really help you out before and now I'm kinda comin' at you."

"Yeah," I say. "It's a little fishy."

"Hey, it doesn't mean I don't love your record. It fuckin' rocks. It's fuckin' great."

"Thanks," I say.

"Yeah, well, whatever. Just consider me, okay? That's all I'm asking."

"Okay," I say.

"Okay," he says.

A van roars into the parking lot and comes at us, its headlights bearing down on us until Kramer yells, "What the fuck!" We scramble to get out of the way, knocking into one another, our feet sliding on the gravel, as the van skids to a stop inches from where Kramer and I have ended up basically in each other's arms. The horn honks and we let go of one another. The driver side door opens and Teddy Z. jumps out.

"Caught in the act," he says.

"You're a fuckin' asshole," laughs Kramer.

The rest of the band gets out and there's much laughing and shit-giving and cigarette smoking, until it's decided that as long as I'm watching my gear I should watch their gear too and they all go inside and it's quiet again.

The rain has stopped and the moon's come out. I lean back against Robby's van and light another cigarette, trying to blow smoke rings. The only light in the parking lot is shining down on me and I feel like I'm in a movie. But I can't tell if this is how it begins, or if this is just before the screen fades to black.

★

It's 5 A.M. when Guy climbs into bed.

"Hi," I mumble.

"You smell like a bar," he says. He kisses the back of my neck, puts his arms around me. Stops. Lifts the covers. "You're still dressed," he says.

"Can't move," I say.

"Okay," he says. Lets the covers fall. Puts his arms back around me.

———

When I wake up, Guy is sitting in bed next to me, reading the paper and drinking coffee.

I roll over. "Hey," I say.

"Welcome back," he says.

"I smell like a bar," I say.

"Told ya," he says.

Through three cups of coffee, I tell Guy everything, right down to Cinda Weinstein's bikini lighter.

"So who's the lucky lawyer?" says Guy, as if he's being nonchalant, opinion-free.

"I think I'm leaning toward Mr. Beacon Street."

"What?"

"Just kidding."

"You better be fucking kidding."

"I really don't think there's any choice."

"None."

I nod my head. "Neil," I say.

"The one and only," says Guy.

I call Neil, who yells, "WOOHOO!" and starts right in on how I have to send him this many CDs and that many press kits and how I need to write personal notes on my Squint stationery to this guy and that gal and those guys over there.

When we hang up, I write notes to Mr. Beacon Street and Mr. Skivvy, thanking them and telling them my decision. I drop the notes in the mail, and it's done.

I have a lawyer.

By the time I get back to my apartment, Neil's already faxed me a list of people coming to our show tomorrow night.

THREE

It's 6:12 P.M. on the second Thursday in November, and the parenting publication staffers are flitting around as if they're closing *Newsweek*. I've just finished paginating the "What's Happening" section and I'm sitting at a desk tapping my thighs, waiting for the pages to print out. All I have to do is paste them on the boards and I can get the hell out of here.

Across from me is Alicia, another freelancer who writes for the paper and comes in to help out on production night. She's around my age, which scares the shit out of me. She's wearing a mauve velour sweat suit with the jacket unzipped because she's too fat. Underneath is her "No. 1 Mommy" T-shirt. Alicia's just staring into space, chewing another sugar cookie from the Tupperware container on her desk from which she keeps encouraging everyone to help themselves.

"Alicia," I say.

Alicia stops chewing and looks around.

"Over here," I say. I know that I'm the last person in the office Alicia wants to deal with.

"Oh," she says, looking at me like I'm going to steal her soul with my rock and roll. She puts her cookie down. "God, where was I? Why am I such a space cadet?"

"See those?" I say, pointing to the pages slowly churning out of the printer. "If you could just slice them up and lay them out on boards forty-three through fifty-six, I could kinda get outta here."

This is a totally uncool thing to do and I wouldn't even be considering it if my boss were here, but I'm supposed to meet Buck and Robby to load our gear in forty-five minutes.

"I don't know," says Alicia. "I've never really done that before."

"It's easy. Just cut straight and the glue's on the table," I say. "It'd really help me out."

"Are you performing tonight?" she asks.

"Yeah," I say.

"Have I ever told you that I used to sing?" she says.

I take a deep breath. "I don't think so."

"Well, I did. Show tunes. You know, like musical theater? In college."

I look at her.

"Oh sure," she says, waving her hand in front of her face. "And then I was going to move to New York because what I really wanted was to be on Broadway, but then, you know," she says, pointing to her stomach. "Kids."

Tonight we're playing at an Irish pub called the Plough & Stars. It's a small bar with a few tables and charcoal drawings of local musicians all over the walls. It's one of those places that hires one band for the whole night. There's no stage or soundman, just an old mixing board and a couple of PA speakers in the far corner. The "stage" is the floor space under the speakers, between the bathroom and the steps that lead down to the basement. Whenever somebody has to take a leak or get another keg, you have to move to let them get by. I've been playing here once a week for about a year.

The first time hardly anybody came, but I didn't let it get to me because I was new.

The second time, about thirty people came and I was psyched.

The third time, there were maybe ten people, but it was snowing out.

The next few times, more and more people showed up until one week the place was almost empty again. I got drunk, turned up my amp, and didn't sing into the mic.

"That's great," said Guy. "You give a shitty show for the people who *did* come because you're throwing a hissy fit at the people who *didn't* come. Good move."

But lately the crowd's been growing again, especially since *Cockamamie*. Last week the line was out the door.

Tonight, the bar phone keeps ringing while we're setting up our gear. I can hear the bartender giving directions to the pub over and over again.

"If that's for Jen, tell 'em she's dead," says Buck.

"Yeah," says Robby, "but we're still playing."

A guy who looks like a bike messenger comes in and sits on the bench against the wall, smacking a *Cockamamie* CD against his thigh.

"Hey," I say to him.

"Hey," he says. He holds my CD up in the air. "I love your record. I've been listening to it all day. 'All This Could Be Yours' is like so X."

"Ex what?" I say.

"X," says the guy again.

I look at him.

"X," he says. "You know, John Doe? Exene? The band. X."

"Oh, right, sure," I say.

"You guys rocked Ludlow the other night. You guys were really great," he says, a little louder, so Buck and Robby can hear him.

"Thanks," says Robby.

"Just doing our job," says Buck.

"Far-fucking-out," he says, smacking the CD on his thigh again. "So, I'm with RCA and I just kinda wanted to talk to you." He hands me a card that says Erik Estrada, RCA.

"Your name's Erik Estrada?" I say. "Isn't he a famous singer or something?"

"That's Julio Iglesias," says Buck. "Erik Estrada is Charlie Sheen's brother."

"That's Emilio Estevez," says Robby.

"It's the guy from *CHiPS*," says Erik Estrada, rubbing his eyes.

"*Chips*?" I say.

"You know," he says, "that old cop show. The motorcycle cops?" He begins moving his hands like he's revving a motorcycle.

Oh right, right, we all say, nodding.

By the time we're halfway through our first set, the place is so packed that people are practically stepping on my pedals. My set list gets stuck under someone's shoe and walks off with her into the crowd.

"I guess the show's over," I say, laughing into the mic.

Oh no, moans the crowd.

"Well then would someone get the asswipe who just walked off with my set list?"

"I got it!" someone yells, waving my set list like a flag and making his way to me.

"Drake!" I say. "Fancy meeting you here."

Drake hands me the set list and a few people clap. "At your service," he says.

"Major points," I say, nodding my head, like I'm someone worth making major points with.

It's our break time and I'm at the bar reaching for a handful of napkins to wipe the sweat off my face.

"You're hot," says a woman to my right. She's sporting ultrashort dark hair and a green army jacket.

"You think so?" I say, smiling at her.

"I'm Beth," she says. "You don't know me, but I wanna change that."

I wipe my forehead and down the back of my neck. "Well, I hope you're in the music business, Beth," I say, "because otherwise, you're in for a big disappointment."

"What?" she says. "*Oh, no no no.* I meant you're hot like you sweat a lot. I'm not *gay*—" She reaches into her pocket and pulls out a card.

"Not that there's anything wrong with that," I say.

"I'm with Maverick Records, down in New York," she says, holding up the card like *See?* "Sorry I missed your Ludlow show. Your record is really great. And your show is really good, but I got the feeling with some time on the road—you ever been on the road?"

"No, not really, but—"

"Well it shows. I mean, you're obviously getting there, but road time would do you wonders. But here's the thing. We just signed this other rock chick whose record is slated for the summer and with radio climate being what it is, I'm not sure coming out with two of you is the best idea for anybody. I mean, not to be lumping things together. I'm just being realistic. I'm just being honest with you."

"Okay," I say.

"I gotta take off, but I'll be in touch," she says.

I'm looking for somewhere to throw the sweaty napkins when Cinda Weinstein appears. "Jesus," she says, looking around the room. "It's like white on rice around here. No other publishing vultures, though." She turns to me. "God, you're drenched."

"Yeah," I say. "Thanks for coming all the way up here."

"Oh, pshaw," says Cinda. "I gotta keep my finger on my property, right?" She smiles. "Not that you're my property. I don't know why I just said that. I can't believe you guys sound so good in this place. You were really funny, too. It's so great that you're so funny. I've always wanted to be funny. Have you always been funny?"

"Funny-looking," I say.

Cinda laughs. Pulls out a cigarette. Lights it with her bikini lighter.

"What's Maverick?" I say.

"Yeah," says Cinda, "I saw you talking to Beth. It's one of the little labels under Warners. It's Madonna's label. You know, like a vanity thing. You got way bigger fish to fry than them. Listen, I gotta go pee before you play again. There's no way in the friggin' world I'm walking through you guys to go to the bathroom. No way," she says and waves at me as a clump of her cigarette ash falls to the floor.

———

An arm goes around my shoulder and it's Guy, kissing me on the cheek.

"I thought you were working tonight," I say.

"I am," he says. "We're taking a break so I thought I'd shoot over here. How's it going?"

"Pretty good, I think," I say. "A guy from RCA is here, and some chick from Maverick and some of the people from the Ludlow show. You wanna, like, meet any of them? I could introduce you like my producer."

"*Like* your producer?" says Guy. "Anyway, I don't have time, I gotta get back. But turn down your guitar. You can't hear the vocals in the back."

"Nobody else has told me that."

"That's cuz nobody else really cares."

"If *you* really cared you'd stay and tweak the system for me," I say.

"Can't," says Guy. Then he cups my chin in his hand. Kisses me on the lips. "Knock 'em dead," he says.

I watch Guy as he makes his way back through the crowded club to the door, waiting to see if he's going to turn around to wave good-bye or good luck, or maybe just to see if I'm still looking at him, but then another arm goes around my shoulder.

"Nice set," says Drake.

"Drake, my man," I say, "you saved the day." I give him a hug.

"Wow," he says. "I should fetch you stuff more often." He smiles. "But you didn't play 'Snow,'" he says.

"Next set," I say.

"Cool," says Drake. "So I went by where I used to live, and you're right. The Deli King's a fucking Boston Chicken."

"Told ya," I say.

"So you went with Neil Krakow," he says.

"Yeah," I say.

"He seems a little like a tough guy."

"He does?" I say.

"I had to try him like three times before he finally took my call and then he was kind of a dick."

"No way," I say.

"Way," says Drake. "You better be careful. You better make sure he wants what you want, you know?"

"Yeah, I guess," I say.

"I mean he's big-time. Like all day, he's dealing with big artists and big money and he may not know what's best for somebody like you. I'm just getting the feeling he's gonna like whip this thing right into the stratosphere."

"Hey! Drake!" A group of skinny guys with long hair is waving.

"I gotta go," he says. "But, like, my boss is coming. His flight was late, but he'll be here."

"He flew in for *this*?"

"Drake!" yell the skinny guys.

Drake turns toward his friends. "You know the guys from Breakdown?"

"They rock," I say, even though I think they suck.

Drake nods. "They're old friends," he says. "Roommates actually."

"Well thanks a lot for coming," I say.

"Don't forget to play 'Snow,'" he says. "For me."

"Just for you," I say.

"Cool," says Drake, and he walks away, revealing an older guy right behind him who has no hair, big bulging eyes, and a very small silver stud in his right nostril. He's looking at me.

"That's a weird-looking Tele you got," he says.

"It's from a kit," I say.

"I'm checking you out," he says.

"Oh," I say. "How am I doing?"

"Not really my thing, but, you know, pretty good," he says, draining the end of his beer and turning back to the woman beside him.

Lizzy and Becka are sitting in a booth against the wall. They wave me over.

"Eeeeeeeeeh," says Becka, grabbing my arm and pulling me down next to her. "You. Guys. Are. Awesome."

"Hi," says Lizzy.

"Thanks for coming all the way up here," I say. "You really shouldn't have."

"Shouldn't have?" says Becka. "We can't stay away!"

"I love this bar," says Lizzy. "It's so *Boston.*"

"So what did Brimmer say to you?" says Becka.

"Who's Brimmer?" I say.

"That loser from Island," she says, pointing toward the guy with the bulging eyes at the bar.

"He's not a loser," says Lizzy. "We just don't trust him."

"He didn't really say much," I say.

"He's just fucking with you," says Becka. "That's what I'm talking about."

"They've already got Tracy Bonham anyway," says Lizzy.

Erik Estrada sits down. "Hey," he says.

"Motorcycle Boy," says Becka.

"Great set, Jennifer," says Erik Estrada.

"Thanks for the directions, Erik," says Lizzy.

"We have an artist with Erik," says Becka, "and it's going great. Erik's great."

"No, *you* guys are great," says Erik Estrada.

"No, *you,*" says Becka, reaching across the table toward his cheek, her fingers prepared to pinch, her elbow knocking into his bottle, spilling beer across the table and over the edge, into my lap.

I push my chair back, letting the rest of the beer drip to the floor.

"Oh God, I'm sorry," says Becka. "I'll get some napkins."

"Don't worry about it," I say. "People've been spilling beer on me all night."

"I love it," says Becka. "You're so *rock.*"

★

"Well, it was a long time ago, but we had some bloody good times all right," says Drake's boss in his pointy British accent, taking a drag on his Dunhill.

It's 2 A.M. and a bunch of people have come back to my apartment—

Buck and Robby and random friends, Drake and his boss and his boss's friend who's wearing a hat with a feather in it.

"So, what band were you in exactly?" asks Robby.

"Dexy's Midnight Runners," says Drake's boss, as Buck and a couple of other guys stand, drunk, and begin singing the chorus to "Come on Eileen" (*too-rah too-rah aye*).

"You guys gotta keep it down," I say.

"Oh, c'mon now," says Drake's boss. "You're a rock star! Be loud! Be crazy! Go nuts!"

I'm psyched as hell that Drake's boss is so dead set on signing us that he's dragged his and his friend's British asses not only all the way to Boston but all the way across town to my crappy kitchen in the middle of the night. But it's getting late and I'm tired and drunk and Drake's boss's friend is giving me the creeps. He's tilting back on one of my creaky folding chairs, legs spread wide, staring at me, with one arm wrapped around his skinny stomach, smoking his cigarette hard, like he's eating it. Like he's going to eat me.

Drake's boss is laughing and telling stories about this and that, but I'm having trouble focusing on what he's saying, because I can't take my eyes off his creepy friend's balls. There they are, right under his European designer jeans, which are riding so high up into his groin that I'm amazed he can swallow.

"You okay?" asks Drake's boss, suddenly snapping my eyes over to him.

"Yeah," I say. "Fine," but all I can think is, *Balls balls balls!*

Then a sudden rumbling is coming from my bathroom, which is just off the kitchen. It's followed by a clunk and then a bump and a boom and a *bam* and finally by Drake, who stumbles out of the bathroom accompanied by about a million Tampax, which roll out across the kitchen floor like a little white army. Behind him, two shelves are on the ground.

No one speaks. Drake's boss hangs his head in his hands.

"I'm so fucking sorry," says Drake, stepping carefully as if avoiding small dead bodies.

Robby picks up a Tampax and sticks it in his mouth like a cigar. Everyone laughs.

"I mean," says Drake, "I guess I knocked into that shelf with all those, like, you know, a shitload of those . . . those . . ." He points at the floor.

"Tampax?" I say.

"Yeah," says Drake.

Everyone's cracking up, kicking Tampax across the floor, and between each other's legs. Buck keeps yelling "It's GOOD!" and "GOOOOOOOAAAAAAAL!" and throwing his arms in the air.

Okay. So get this.

We're playing on top of a platform that's been wheeled into a cafeteria somewhere on the Sarah Lawrence campus. We're in the middle of our set and I keep almost falling over because the platform isn't remotely steady. The fluorescent lights are a real vibe-kill and some guy with one of those puffy chef's hats keeps peeking out from behind the door to the kitchen.

There are eight or nine kids sitting cross-legged on the floor in front of us. Behind them, with their arms folded or their hands in their pockets, are about twenty grownups representing many factions of the music industry. Some of them—Cinda Weinstein, Drake, Lizzy and Becka, Erik Estrada, Philippe—I've seen so much of lately, they're beginning to seem like friends. Some of them I don't know from Adam. As I watch them watching us, I'm wondering what it must feel like to have made the hike all the way up from Manhattan to suburban Bronxville, just to stand around in a room that smells like ham and Lysol, drinking Hi-C from plastic cups. Specifically, I'm entranced by Cinda's delicate yet sturdy jaws chomp-chomp-chomping on her gum.

We're playing a soft part when a huge clatter comes from the kitchen, snapping my mind back to the space-time continuum. I look down at my left hand and I'm lost. *There's my hand,* I'm thinking, *on the fifth fret in some configuration.* I still seem to be singing, but with each passing beat, a harrowing cliff is coming one step closer. My throat gets tight and sweat breaks out. *WHERE AM I?* I keep strumming as my left hand comes up off the fret board, en route to the next chord. *Is it up here? Down there? I CAN'T REMEMBER.* Music is stored in some underbelly of my brain, somewhere akin to the dark side of the moon. As soon as I try to see it, touch it, it disappears quick as a snowflake in the palm of my hand—the very hand which is presently dive-bombing toward the fretboard with no clear destination. My heart skips a beat. *Did I just finish singing the first chorus or the second chorus?* As in, *are we heading into the second verse or the bridge?*

At the last minute I leap, eyes closed. I land high up on the fret-board, letting my guitar scream out the first chord to the bridge at the same instant that I realize Buck and Robby are still padding along the trails leading into the second verse.

These kinds of moments are called "train wrecks," both because of their sonic similarity and because of the handy analogy of things being "off track." Train wrecks are about the last thing you want to happen during any gig, but especially when there are people in the audience who are (for lack of a better term) "evaluating" your performance. Train wrecks make you look like you don't know what the fuck you're doing, which at this particular moment, I guess I don't. But I can hear Guy's voice echoing in my head: If you're gonna fuck it up, fuck it up with confidence. So I just keep going, shooting one quick, sharp look toward Buck, then Robby: *I'm the singer here, goddamnit, and I wrote this song and I'm playing the fucking bridge SO GET WITH THE PROGRAM!* But what I'm really thinking is *Please God, let Buck and Robby figure out where the hell I am because I honestly don't know how to get back to where I used to be going.*

The second I get offstage, I duck outside to have a cigarette. It's cold, so I stand near the back door as if being closer to the building will somehow make me warmer. Up and down the driveway, black town cars idle with their parking lights on.

The cafeteria door swings open and out walks a guy wearing a dark coat. If he wasn't so cute, I'd be irked about having my privacy invaded.

"You shouldn't be smoking," he says, "being a famous singer and everything."

"I'm not a famous singer," I say, blowing smoke at him.

"Maybe not yet," he says. "Got one for me?"

"I don't know," I say, wondering why something about this guy feels familiar. "Are you a famous singer?"

"Used to be," he says. "Well, almost. Kinda. Like you."

I hand him a cigarette and light it, praying to avoid another Hamfisters moment.

"Nice train wreck," he says.

"Thanks for noticing," I say.

"We met the other night, but I guess our little princess was too busy flitting around to notice li'l ol' me." He smiles and takes a drag from his cigarette, then blows the smoke up into the sky.

"You're Johnny," I say.

"Very good, Princess," he says.

"Alamo, right?" I say.

"*Almo,*" says Johnny. "We don't rent cars."

"You're the guy who thinks I suck."

Johnny laughs. "I never said that."

"But you think you can sell my songs anyway. That's what you said."

"Listen," says Johnny. "If I thought you sucked, why the hell would I be sitting around in Bumfuck with a bunch of kids?"

"Because you want to torture me," I say.

"Wow," says Johnny. "Torture. I like the way that sounds."

"I don't even know what Almo is," I say.

"Just the perfect record company for you," says Johnny.

"Oh yeah? Why's that?"

"Because I work there," he says.

"So why didn't you come talk to me again at Ludlow?" I say.

"I don't know," says Johnny. "I guess I just wanted to watch. I don't need to rush. I already know you're gonna go with me."

"Really," I say.

"Really," he says, flicking his cigarette to the ground, stamping it out. "I got another show to catch back in the city."

"I guess you're a pretty big cheese, huh?"

"No need to get huffy," he says. "Afraid you'll never see me again?"

"Terrified," I say.

He turns and begins walking down the driveway. "See ya later, Princess," he says, as the parking lights shine red and soft against him.

"Oh yeah," says Buck. "Really glad we're playing in some summer town in the middle of winter. Good booking policy."

We're an hour south of Boston, playing at the Sea-Note by the water. There's nothing much else around. A Dairy Queen ("Closed For The Sea-son"). A few stores along a strip, some of them boarded up.

"Sorry," I say. "I booked it back when, you know—"

"It doesn't matter," says Robby. "I just wanna play."

Inside, the walls of the club are aquamarine, and there's a round bar in the center of the room.

"You the Jennifer Trying band?" asks a big, bald, fat guy wearing a Hooters apron.

After soundcheck I sit at the bar, smoking and reading a first-person account of what it's like to live with lung disease in *The New Yorker*.

I stamp out my cigarette.

The place is empty. Not empty like there's hardly anybody here. Empty as in there's no one else in the whole place except the Hooters guy and some skinny old lady reading the paper and sucking on her teeth.

Robby's still onstage fooling with his foot pedal, which keeps breaking.

Buck's playing pinball.

I go over and whack him on the arm.

"Cut it out," he says.

"Aw, come on," I say. "Come talk to me." I drape myself across the glass.

Buck's ball sails between the flippers and sinks into the hole. A siren sounds and he punches the sides of the machine.

"Why the *fuck* did you just do that?" he says.

I stand up. "Jesus. Sorry. Forget it."

Buck looks at me and smiles. He reaches out and mock-pinches my cheek. "Lucky you're so cute, or I might have to kill you," he says.

"I thought I was already dead," I say.

He puts his hands around my throat and pushes me against the pinball machine. "Not yet," he says, letting me go, touching his finger to the tip of my nose.

By the time we play, seven people have shown up. Three of them are at the bar; the other four are in front of us, standing about twenty feet from the stage. When I squint, they melt together in the swirling blue light spinning above the dance floor.

"Feels like things are picking up steam," says Robby.

"I've never understood that saying," says Buck. "I mean, how do you *pick up* steam?"

"With your fingers, dumbass," I say, kicking his seat.

Buck and Robby and I are heading back to New York for another Brownie's gig and tons of meetings.

The show at Brownie's is a lot like the Ludlow show but times ten. The lights are low, everything swirling with drinks and hands and teeth, and the talk is fast: *priority, roll out, capitalize, maximize, merchandise, marketing, BDS, BMI, SRLP*—Hello, JENNIFER TRYNIN. I heard about you through SOMEONE and I'm ME from WHEREVER and you should go with US because we're *small* or we're *big* or we have other successful acts *just like you* or we don't have *any* other acts *anything at all* like you or I'm from Jersey *too* or I used to play a black Les Paul *too*—so clearly, as anyone can see, WE'RE the *best best best* and I know you must be hearing this all the time, but I'm *sincere,* I'm *genuine,* I *get it*: your record/voice/songs/real deal/special/substance. Where did you? What are you? How did you? Who are you?

"Freaking," says Neil. "I'm freaking out. This is great. Great! I mean, I've seen things whip into a frenzy before, but this is fuckin' ridiculous. Here," he says, handing me a sheet with a long list of meetings and the relevant names and addresses and phone numbers. "And Danny Goldberg just checked in today and he *loves* the record."

"Who's Danny Goldberg?" I say.

"Well, he's about to be heading up The Bunny. He's kinda easing his way out of Atlantic right now. He used to head up Gold Mountain, who managed Nirvana."

"He loves my record?"

"*Loves.*"

"And he used to manage Nirvana?"

"Yeah," says Neil. "Is that bad?"

"Are you kidding?"

It's 4 A.M. Still awake. Alone in bed at BB's. Blankets. Ceiling. The heat ticking in the pipes.

The following afternoon, Philippe meets us in the lobby of the gargantuan building in which Columbia Records is way high up. He asks us if we're ready for "the dog and pony." Then we're hustled through I.D.-showing and security-pass-getting, then into this elevator, down that hall, into more elevators and through more doors, each new area leading sleekly into the next like the opening-credit sequence of *Get Smart.*

When we finally reach the inner sanctum, I realize that I've been imagining the offices of a major label to be a whole lot more like a rock show and a whole lot less like regular offices. There's not even any music playing. Philippe leads us down a plain old hallway into a plain old room where a couple of guys are sitting pushed back from a conference table and talking. One of them is wearing a purple silk shirt with a red silk tie and black slacks. The other one has on a stretched-out brown sweater and stonewashed jeans that have a hole just above the right knee—a small hole, very manageable and unfraying, a hole definitely made by a hole-making machine. They're both wearing sneakers.

"Sixty-three fuckin' yards!" the guy in the purple shirt is saying, motioning above his head as if to throw a pass, using a *Cockamamie* CD as his football.

"Unfuckinbelievable," says the guy in the ripped jeans.

Phillipe makes the introductions and we sit down. The guy in the purple shirt turns out to be Philippe's boss, Captain Talent. The ripped jeans belong to Marketing Maven.

"Okay then," says Captain Talent, putting his elbows on the table, holding my CD flat between his hands. "What I want to know is where have you guys been hiding. We get tapes and tapes and tapes and then this," he says, waving the CD in the air and then smacking it down on the table. "Perfection." The Captain continues in the usual way—*your record/voice/songs/real deal/special/substance* . . . He says he sees big things for us. Really big. Then he sits back and Marketing Maven leans forward.

"It's obvious you know what you're doing, or we wouldn't all be taking time out of our day to meet with you like this," he says, looking at his watch. "All we want to do is help you get to the next level. Our goal is to take the initial excitement you've created with Squint—that's your own label, right?"

"Right," I say.

"See, that's great. That's a great angle." Marketing Maven nods his head, wagging a finger at me. "So the first thing we do is develop a well-thought-out, fully integrated, *long-term—*" he says, finger in the air "—marketing campaign that includes all facets at our disposal, every arm of the company. Next, we pick the singles. Then we gear up for the major rollout. Radio, press, videos, TV. We get you out on the road, starting in the U.S., then branching out. Europe. Australia. Maybe Japan, depending on reaction at radio. And the radio promo guys are already chomping at the bit for these songs, but I want you guys to know that we'd also be keeping focused on the more subordinate goal of building your career because we're not just about racking up hit singles. Although we like hit singles. Who doesn't?"

Buck and Robby and I shrug our shoulders.

Next, Philippe leads us down the hallway to meet with the biggest wig here at Columbia Records. He keeps leaning into doorways, around corners, waving to people, pointing at us and saying, "This is them," and everyone's smiling and saying *You guys gotta come with us!* and *You guys rock!*

We approach a reception desk where a woman with bright red lips tells us to go on into BigWig's office. But Philippe knocks anyway and opens the door slowly. He peers in, then looks back at us with his finger across his lips, making a shushing sound.

BigWig's office is like another world. It has huge windows and wood-paneled walls and all the furniture is too big or too low or too high—very PeeWee's Playhouse, but with a lot less color and zip frivolity. BigWig is pacing around the room, smoking and yelling into a headset strapped to his skull: "WHADDAYA WANT FROM ME? BUT WHADDAYA *WANT* FROM ME?" He glances in our direction, sticking his large index finger into the air and winking. *One sec.* "BUT YOU'RE NOT EVEN FUCKIN' CLOSE! I MEAN WHAT THE *FUCK*?" He motions for us to sit.

Everyone takes a seat and when I plunk down into one of the gigantic brown leather chairs, it makes a small exhaling sound. The tips of my toes barely touch the floor. In the middle of where we're all sitting is a low coffee table the size of a pool table that appears to be made from a solid block of iron. On the table are flowers and bowls of oranges and apples and lots of neatly arranged magazines. The big black desk behind which BigWig is now pacing is enormous and gives the entire room a tilted, wrong-side-of-the-telescope feeling. "THEY CAME BACK WITH WHAT?" yells BigWig, slamming his fist against his desk, which makes me jump. He takes a drag off his cigarette and I wish I had a cigarette. Do I have any cigarettes? Could I smoke a cigarette, or would that be disrespectful? Or is that what people do? Is that what rock stars do? My mind is racing, even though number one on my list of Things Not To Do is to let my mind race.

Suddenly my neck feels prickly and now my knees are itchy. So is my hair. My throat is going dry and I'm staving off visions of coughing fits and back-pounding and vomiting on other people's shoes. That's when I realize I really have to pee, and my pits go damp. *Don't raise your arms* is number two on my list of Things Not To Do.

Number three on my list of Things Not To Do is *Do not climb atop BigWig's desk and take a whiz.* Ever since I heard a story about Courtney Love doing just that, the image of me peeing on someone's desk keeps popping into my mind like a Tourette's thought. I think it's less that I actually want to do it than that I want to be someone who *could* do it—or better yet, someone who'd already done it. But not only can't I imagine myself really doing it, I can't imagine how it's done. How do you get up on the desk in the first place? What do you wear? A skirt? Do you just reach up underneath and slide your underwear to the side, or do you somehow swingle your underwear off beforehand? Or do you plan ahead and just not wear any underwear at all?

"Of COURSE I WANT THIS TO HAPPEN," yells BigWig, stomping over to his fully stocked bar and stubbing out his cigarette in a glass ashtray the size of a pizza. "YOU WANT FUCKIN' BLOOD? IS THAT WHAT YOU WANT? CUZ THAT'S ALL THAT'S LEFT!" BigWig looks at me and mouths, *Sorry,* holding his finger up in the air again. *Just one more sec.*

The fact that BigWig is giving two shits that he's keeping me waiting is blowing my mind. It's only been two years since I sent out my earnestly wrought twelve-song cassette, which didn't register even a 1 on the Who's-Going-To-Get-Signed Richter scale. I still have my carefully compiled list of each and every person to whom we'd sent padded envelope after padded envelope, and at this very moment, I'm staring one of them right in the eyes.

Next on my list of Things Not To Do is *Do not make any reference to this bygone, we-don't-like-you period.*

BigWig finally removes his headset, apologizing for taking so long, but he's sure that we all understand that sometimes people are just real fucking idiots.

"No problem," says Philippe. "This is Jennifer Trynin," he says, pointing at me. "And this is Buck," he says, pointing at Robby, "and Robby," pointing at Buck.

"Actually," says Buck. "I'm Buck. He's Robby."

Robby waves.

"Great," says BigWig, coming out from behind his desk, walking over to the coffee table, and grabbing an orange. "Anybody hungry?" BigWig throws the orange in the air and catches it. "This fruit is the best in the fuckin' city. Catch," he says, tossing the orange to Buck. "You like oranges, Bob?"

"Buck," says Buck.

"All right then." BigWig goes back behind his desk. "Listen. I acknowledge that I'm in no way the first person telling you this, but your record, you know, it's really something, nice piece of work. And that song—" and here he begins snapping his fingers and bouncing, swinging his head from side to side, "*I'm feeling goo-ood, I'm feeling goo-ood* . . . well, *fuggedaboudit!*" He looks straight at me, raising his big hands over his head and waving them around. "HIT HIT HIT! Do I have to spell it? H-I-T! HIT!" BigWig talks like he just walked off the set of *NYPD Blue*. "And, I mean, sure," he says. "Hits. We love hits. We live for hits, let's face it. But you *got* the hits, and when you got the hits, we're talking about a career here." BigWig lights another cigarette and takes a drag, making the tip glow red as a stoplight. "You?" he says, blowing smoke. "You're a career artist. And we're a career label. I mean, take Toad the Wet Sprocket. Now those are some talented guys. Just like we're gonna do with you guys, we picked up their first record and released it *as is*. But then what happens? A lot of nothing. Second record, still nothing, but we make a third record with 'em anyway, right boys?"

The Captain, Marketing Maven, and Philippe all nod their heads.

"Did we drop 'em just cuz things weren't going as big-time as we'd anticipated?"

No way, no way.

"Fuckin-A no way. And why? Cuz that's not who we are. We're just not made that way here at Columbia. So then what happens? Third record, *bam!* Hit! Gold! Fourth record, bam boom! Hit hit! Platinum! And now we're making our fifth record with 'em and we couldn't be more excited. See, cuz we got patience. We're artist-friendly. We believe in careers." BigWig stands, takes another drag from his cigarette, and rests it in an ashtray on top of some shelves behind his desk. He walks over to his stereo and hits a button, then returns to his desk and falls into his black leather chair. He twirls it around once and stops, facing us. He says, "Listen to this."

Some music comes on, sounding very slick and Top 40 in a trip-hoppy sort of way. Then a woman begins singing about "knowin' watcha doin'" and there's tons of *baby baby* and *yeah yeah yeah yeah yeah*. It's not that I don't like the song, but it's making me nervous that BigWig is playing it for us. I'm afraid it means that he's seeing me like he sees this chick, as a solo act instead of as a band. And while the truth is that I *am* a solo act, I'm a solo act *doing* a band thing. It's essential to me that I'm marketed as a rock singer, a rock band, not as a solo, singer-songwriter act, because as I already know from my days in the Sunday-through-Wednesday-night-folk/acoustic-chick-band wasteland, that doesn't work for me. That's the main reason I want to bring Buck and Robby to all the meetings, so that it's clear that "we're" a band (even though we're not).

BigWig's elbows are resting on the top of his desk as he snaps his fingers to the song. His hands are the kind I like—square, big-knuckled, wide, not fleshy but sturdy—and I can't help but feel what I always feel staring at those kinds of hands: I feel them on me. A shiver goes up my spine. I've heard stories about this label, like how Big-Wig's boss married Mariah Carey and that's when her career really took off. I wonder if that's what it takes. Screw BigWig's Toad-the-Wet-Sprocket story. These powerhouse labels are known for a lot of things, but sticking with their artists isn't one of them. I'm afraid that if I want to be a star I'm going to have to leave Guy and start wearing tight dresses and lip gloss so I can get some big scary dude like Big-Wig to marry me.

Something small falls to the carpet behind BigWig. Now there's smoke curling up under his chair.

It's his cigarette.

BigWig's eyes are closed as he nods his head to the beat. The Captain's and Marketing Maven's eyes are closed too, and their heads are nodding. Philippe is checking his watch and glancing out the window.

Great.

I guess I'm the only one who knows this place is about to go up in flames.

At a sushi place, we're all sitting in a booth, staring at the menu, with the A&R guy from Geffen who signed Lisa Loeb. He's not much older than we are and his vibe is disheveled preppy: half-tucked button-down shirt, jeans with a black belt, hair parted on the side. Preppy Boy is cute and bashful, in a my-dog-ate-my-homework sort of way. He shuts his menu and looks at me.

"I love your r-record," he says.

"Thanks," I say.

"I r-really mean it."

Preppy Boy also has a bit of a stammer, which makes him even cuter.

He tells us some story about how Ethan Hawke directed Lisa Loeb's video "in one shot, one camera," and how he has all these video ideas for my songs. While I'm not wild about being allied with Lisa Loeb (solo act, singer-songwriter), I'm in love with the fact that Nirvana was on Geffen and that now maybe I'll be on Geffen too.

It's dark and brisk as we head downtown for the Hole show. Buck keeps flicking my ears with his fingers or tripping me every few steps, then pretending like he's not doing it.

"W-whoa there," says Preppy Boy as I stumble against him for the second time.

"Sorry," I say.

"Are you drunk again?" says Buck.

When we get to Irving Plaza, Preppy Boy takes us backstage and then leaves us there, saying he's going to find EdR, the president of Geffen, with whom we're going to, evidently, "h-hang."

So Buck and Robby and I just stand there, plastered against a wall, as famous person after famous person goes by, everyone much smaller than you'd expect. For instance, Drew Barrymore—it's not like she's an actual midget or anything, but she sure is teeny. I picture putting a drink down on the top of her head.

Some guy with a big red Afro and clownlike pants goes bopping by.

"Is that Carrot Top?" says Robby.

A tall guy with a clipboard and a headset taps me on the shoulder. "You Jennifer Trynin?"

We follow him down a long hallway, through a door and down another hallway, into a brightly lit room with a pool table covered in pizza boxes and beer bottles, up a set of stairs and down another through a labyrinth of road cases, down and up another set of stairs and ending, very Chutes and Ladders, at a black velvet curtain that Clipboard Boy draws apart with his hand.

"Hello, Cleveland!" says Buck as we find ourselves thrust into the center of the coveted VIP section situated to the right and well above the crowd, with a ripping view of the stage. Hole is already in full tilt, screaming about dolls and cheerleaders and phrases relating to what I guess life is like if you do a lot of heroin. Up here there are chairs and tables with little candles, and Preppy Boy is waving at me from one of them.

"Over h-here," he says.

We sit down at Preppy Boy's table, where a bunch of men begin nodding their hellos to us, with their faces glistening in the candle-light. When I'm introduced to Cliff and Peter, my stomach clamps. They run Q Prime, a powerhouse that manages bands like Metallica and Smashing Pumpkins. Neil's told me that these guys are "the real deal," that they're known for "tearing people new assholes" at record companies—and that they're interested in me.

I smile. Or I think I'm smiling. I mean, there's no telling what kind of crazy-ass shit these guys have seen, managing crazy-ass bands like

Metallica, and I can't help but wonder if they'll expect the same kind of crazy-ass shit from me.

Next to me is EdR, president of Geffen.

"Glad you could make it," he says.

"Thanks for getting us back here," I say.

Courtney Love is in her usual stance, one leg up on the monitor and her dress falling off.

"She's something, isn't she," says EdR.

"Yeah, she's pretty kick-ass," I say, which feels odd, saying "kick-ass" to someone who's almost as old as my dad, but I don't know what else to say. You can see Courtney Love's tits pretty much clear as day. "Nice tits," I say, because someone has to say it. I can feel EdR laugh beside me and then he leans into me, so I lean into him.

"You sign with me," he says, "and I'll get a pair of those for *you*."

I look at him. Smile. "Promise?" I say.

★

It's 9 A.M. and we're sitting at a table in the Four Seasons with Lance, an A&R guy from Interscope. He's like an L.A. ski-slope dude with his orange skin and white hair. He tells us to order whatever we want. Buck and Robby open the menus and begin to laugh.

"Natural goat milk yoghurt-with-an-h, with berries," says Robby, looking up from the menu. "Twenty-eight dollars?"

"But don't forget it also comes with low-fat banana bran muffins *and* apple butter," says Buck.

"Charcuterie of cured meats and select cheeses?" says Robby.

"Ah," says Buck, leaning back in his chair. "I love a good charcuterie."

"A glass of orange juice is twelve bucks," says Robby.

"I'll take ten," says Buck.

"Settle down, cowboys," I say.

We've all heard the stories. How bands order caviar and $300 bottles of wine and stub their cigarettes out on the plate. How record companies put them up in swanky hotels where they order thousands of dollars of room service and throw the TV out the window. I want

these industry fuckers to know what my dad wants them to know—
that I'm not like that, that I'm not here for the free lunch, that I
know that we're *really* here to talk about, well, you know, whatever it
is we're supposed to be talking. About.

Lance orders coffee and smiles like he's trying to smile, like someone told him to smile, told him to be here, told him to let us order $50
breakfasts. He tells me how he "digs" my record, even the "mellow
tunes." After a little while of this, Lance and Buck spend most of the
rest of the time talking about golf.

At Mercury, Merv Csisik is still wearing his trench coat and scratching
his head. He leads us into a crowded conference room where everyone's smiling at us and a piñata is hanging from a light fixture. Merv
hands me a baseball bat and says, "Take a whack." When I do, a bunch
of large gumballs fall to the ground and everyone claps. On each gum-
ball is printed JENNIFER COME WITH US! Then I'm presented with a
"Mercury's Marketing Plan for Jennifer Trynin" pamphlet with my
picture on it.

Our lunch meeting is at the Mark Hotel, which happens to be owned
by a friend of my father. When I've come here with my dad, I've
fretted over what to wear, what to say, how to act. But today I'm here
as me, dressed as me. Old cords. Big boots. Cool sweater. White
leather jacket. And yeah, people are staring. Go ahead. Knock your-
selves out.

We're meeting with the president of Hollywood Records, a newly
established subsidiary of Disney. I've heard exactly two things about
this guy: (1) he used to be in some "cool" band and still likes to be
called Shredder, and (2) he went to Harvard.

Shredder is dressed like a college boy in an old sweatshirt and
fraying jeans, like he's hoping no one's noticing that he's older than
he likes to think he is. He's probably forty. His thinning hair is
whipped around the top of his skull, very Donald Trump. He's telling
us what it takes to Be A Star.

"It's when the chicks wanna be you and the guys wanna fuck you," says Shredder, smiling at Buck and Robby, then looking at me. "I can say that, right? Or does that offend you?"

"Does that mean guys wanna fuck Bono?" I say.

Robby laughs.

"I'd do Bono," says Buck.

The guy seems like a dickweed, but Neil's told me how much he wants to sign me, which can only mean Shredder must think I have what it takes (*girls wanna be me, guys wanna fuck me*), which is fitting in nicely with the new self-image spinning inside me like a web.

I'm pulling my sweater up over my head and I can feel my T-shirt riding up my back. Normally, I'd stop right here, rearrange myself, make sure my T-shirt isn't showing any skin. But nothing's normal anymore and I'm sick of being the kind of girl who pulls her shirt back down. I want to be the kind of girl who just lets things happen. So I keep going, my head deep in my sweater, and that's when I feel his fingers. Up my back. Grabbing hold of my T-shirt. And tugging.

When I emerge from my sweater, Shredder is still holding the bottom of my shirt. I can feel his fingers against the small of my back. He's smiling at me, open-lipped, with a ray of light glinting off his big left tooth.

"You all set?" says Shredder.

"Yeah," I say.

"You sure?" he says.

"Positive," I say.

He finally lets go.

Buck and Robby order everything under the sun. I order a bagel and coffee before excusing myself to the bathroom.

I stand in front of the mirror, lifting my T-shirt and bending over, turning myself this way and that, trying to see what Shredder saw of my back, my side, my stomach. The image of Shredder and me kissing flashes through my mind before I can stop it.

I laugh.

Hey, I'm Jen, I say to the mirror, smiling. Maybe this really *is* me now, the Extra-Strength, Super-Deluxe Me. But in my eyes, around the corners of my mouth, I can still see it. I'm afraid that this is really the Super-Fake Me and that the Super-Real Me—the CouchPizza Reruns me—is huddled somewhere deep inside, just waiting to take back over and ruin everything.

Fuck you, I say to the mirror.

At Randy Sway's office at Vibetone Management, everything is blond— the furniture, shelves, desks, even the assistants, like Kavallah, who is so beautiful I have to sit down. She's the kind of girl whose neck goes straight into her legs. She's wearing a tight T-shirt that says WOWEE in such a way that a vowel accents each of her breasts. She tells us how Courtney Love called their office last week looking for Liz Phair because she wanted to kick her ass.

"So what'd you say?" I ask her.

"I hung up on her," says Kavallah.

"Awesome," says Robby.

"Wowee," says Buck.

Randy trips on something coming into the room, then looks behind him and says, "That first step's a doozy," laughing perhaps nervously but I don't think he's nervous. I just think he's a bit of a goofball. But I like him. I can't help it. But I'm afraid I like him because he looks like Jerry Seinfeld and I like Jerry Seinfeld.

I meet Neil for a drink a few blocks away in a dark sparkly bar where women with straight blond hair and long legs crossed at the ankles are perched on stools, stock still except for their eyes, which move toward the door whenever someone enters. At this moment it's Neil, waving at me, waving to someone else, hurrying toward me like a train.

"Look at this," he says. "I'm not even late."

We hug hello and he orders us martinis, straight up with olives.

"Just got off the phone with BigWig and he's in up to his ears. He wants this fuckin' bad, which is fantastic."

"He's a little scary," I say, as the bartender puts down our drinks in front of us.

Neil cradles his glass in his palm. "Aw, come on," he says. "You're a big girl."

"EdR says if I sign with Geffen, he'll get me tits just like Courtney Love's."

"Wow," says Neil, raising his glass to toast. "Well then. To Courtney's, uhh, talent."

We clink glasses.

I take a sip of my drink and can feel it slithering slowly down the lining of my stomach like a cold snake.

Neil takes a gulp. "Aaaahhhh," he says. "Good. Jesus." Smacks his lips together, puts the glass back on the bar. "So," he says, "how goes the dog and pony?"

"Do they call it that because they're supposed to be strutting their stuff for us or something?"

Neil stands and holds his hands in front of himself like he's a dog on his hind legs. He barks. "But of course," he says. He sits back down. "Don't tell me you're getting tired of this already. Because if things keep going the way I think they're going to, you're gonna be doing a lot more of these, like a *lot* more. I want everyone who *wants* a shot at you to *get* a shot at you. Hell, we haven't even gotten you to the West Coast yet."

"What do you think of Almo?" I say.

"Well," says Neil. "As far as who runs the place, you can't get much better than Herb Alpert and Jerry Moss, who used to be the *A* and *M* in A&M Records, but are now the *Al* and *Mo* in Almo. Get it?"

"I get it."

"But they're under Geffen, and with Geffen proper already after you, I'd say not to worry about them."

"And Maverick?"

"Same deal. Under Warners. Who wants a satellite when you can be on the mother ship, right?"

"What about Atlas?"

"Same deal again. Under A&M. If we can get A&M proper interested, then we'll talk." Neil takes the stirrer from his glass and slides the olives back into his drink. Plop plop. "Okay. Let's bring you up to speed," he says, and begins listing all the labels and publishers and managers who've "weighed in" so far, tapping the stirrer on the bar with every name. Then he decides "there's no time like the present," and launches into a high-speed account of various aspects of "your basic record deal," talking faster and faster until the jargon is whipping around my head like a tornado—*record cycles, recording funds, royalty rates, full rate, three-quarter rate, less applicable reserves, mechanicals, indemnify, irrevocable, exploitation, exclusivity, net receipts, top line net sales, foregoing, notwithstanding, notwithstanding the foregoing, in perpetuity.*

"Wait," I say.

"Question?"

"What's 'in perpetuity'?"

"It means forever."

"Oh," I say, trying to remember anything at all about my one-page contract with Pathfinder Records, for which I'd received no money at all.

Neil takes a deep breath, lets it out, swigs down the rest of his drink. "What a fucking day," he says, rubbing the back of his neck, rubbing his eyes, and something in me turns, quick and quiet as a ball in my hand. I notice for the first time a small mole below his left eye, and that his shirt is missing a button on the right cuff. For a moment, I see Neil as himself, not as my lawyer or as my coach, but as a man here with me having a drink alone.

"I have to go," I say, sliding off the stool. "I'm meeting my family for dinner."

"Oh," says Neil. "Okay. I gotta go anyway."

I know that Neil doesn't see me that way, but I'm tired and already drunk, and suddenly everything is feeling terrifyingly possible. I reach for my wallet but Neil insists. As I stare at the mole on his cheek, I get the strange sensation of being very small and very big at the same time, as if I'm looking up at myself like a building, and down at myself from the sky.

★

By the time I find the restaurant, my mother and Tim+1 are already in a booth, with martinis all around. The place is creepy and dark, with mirrors everywhere and hanging lights slowly spinning from the ceiling. I slide in next to my mom while my brother and his latest girlfriend take a break from falling all over each other.

"Hey, it's Kiki Dee," says Tim.

"You gotta stop calling me that," I say, even though I don't want him to.

My mother looks at me and smiles, gets tears in her eyes.

"Come on, Mom," I say.

"I just feel like I haven't seen you in a long time," she says.

"You must be so excited," says Plus One, fiddling with her earring. "Tim's been telling us the whole music business is after you! That's *so* cool," she says, removing her earring, looking at it, putting it back in her ear. "This thing keeps coming loose."

Tim leans into her, holds her by the arm, blows into her ear. She giggles. He puts us through the new-girlfriend dance every year or two. This one won't stick either. Or maybe it's that I don't want her to stick, that Guy is right, I want my brother all to myself. But not tonight. Tonight I don't care that he's fawning over yet another silly girl who irons her hair or thinks I'm "neat" or eats chocolate pudding for breakfast with her finger.

My mother pushes the hair from my face, and asks me why my hair is always in my face.

"I'm not twelve," I say. "This is my hair. This is how I wear it."

"I'm sorry," she says, and puts her hands in her lap. "It's just that I'm worried about you. You look so drawn, and tired. You're too skinny," she says, which makes me laugh.

"Are you kidding me?" I say.

"I know," she says, "but you are."

My mom never thinks anyone's too skinny, especially me. At least she's not worrying about what she's usually worried about, which is that I'm wasting my life. She never says this outright. She just tells me how hard her friend's kid is working at Goldman Sachs or *The New York Times* or teaching at Harvard, or what a wealthy guy another friend's daughter is marrying. Or she says she's afraid I'm depressed, as evidenced by my delusions of grandeur, of which this silly pursuit of being a rock star is simply a symptom. My mom's a psychologist.

"I'm not trying to be a drag," she says, touching the stem of her glass between her fingers, looking beautiful, like she always does. And I don't mean to be difficult, like I always seem to be with her. "So tell me," says my mom, "what's going on? Tim says he went to one of your concerts and all kinds of people were there to see you. And you have a lawyer now? Do you like him?"

"Do I *like* him?" It annoys my father that my mother and I always make everything "personal." But I'm not making things personal this time. I'm all business. "Sure, I guess, but what's important is that he's like a big-time guy. He works at the firm that does Springsteen."

My mother raises her eyebrows.

"As in Bruce Springsteen," I say.

"I know who Springsteen is," she says. "The Boss."

I laugh. "Very good."

"You think your old ma is so out of it," she says, smiling, winking, raising her glass to me.

"Well, so, yeah. It's unbelievable. I don't even know for sure at this point how many labels are in but I think like at least ten."

"In?"

"In like are going to make me an offer."

"Are you going to get money?"

"Well, yeah. Of course."

"Do you know how much?"

"Not yet. See the thing is, with so many labels coming after me, they're all going to be bidding against each other. So Neil—that's my lawyer—Neil says that in this kind of situation, it can only mean more money up front and better terms in the contract."

"Gosh," says my mom, "it almost seems too good to be true. Have you seen anything in writing? Can you trust these people?"

"Mom, this is just the way it is. This is the way these things happen. This is like the real world."

"Is there a time limit?"

"What?"

"I mean, maybe you should strike while the iron's hot. Take advantage of everyone being so *enamored* of you at the moment."

"Oh, because you think it's all just gonna go away?"

"I just don't want you to miss this opportunity."

"What, because they're going to change their minds?"

"The whole thing just seems very nebulous to me. First they don't love you, now they do love you. What if tomorrow they don't love you again?"

"Thanks for the support," I say.

"Jen. I'm your mother. I love you no matter what. I could give two hoots about your music—"

"That's always been obvious."

"Stop that. That's not what I mean and you know it. Criminy," she says, taking a deep breath and letting it out. "I'm happy for you, I don't want you to think I'm not," she says, touching my jacket sleeve with the tips of her fingers, then putting her hand back on her glass. "It's just that I barely recognize you anymore," she says, and that's when I feel it. The slipping away. My mother is afraid she's losing me.

FOUR

I'm bending low over my red ten-speed, chin on the handlebars, cold wind in my hair. Plane after plane, flying low in the sky. The road, straight and black, rushing to a point. Then a thud. Another thud. A truck barrels toward me, bumping hard against the road. A crate flies off the back. Then another. Then a wheel, a headlight—

"Hello!"

Someone is yelling.

"Hello! Anyone there?" POUND POUND POUND.

I'm sitting up, feet swung to the floor before I'm awake.

POUND POUND. "You in there?"

Guy is beside me, blanket over his head, dead to the world. We've been out here for a week, sleeping in the living room on my shitty futon couch ever since the leak over my bed started up again. It's 8:27 A.M.

POUND POUND POUND.

I grab my jeans from the floor, weave my way to the door.

"What in mother of God is going on in there?" It's Ellie, a Comfort Care worker, in overalls, with a pick sticking up from the back of her Afro like a feather. She's trying to see behind me and into my apartment, where, clearly, all hell must be breaking loose. Behind her is Vincent, old, skinny, retarded, with gray hair and big teeth. He's waving at me with one hand and pulling on his tongue with the other.

"Jen," he's mumbling. "Jen Jen Jen."

"Look!" says Ellie, pointing down the stairwell toward the first-floor landing, where water is gushing down from the ceiling.

Vincent begins to laugh, clapping his hands.

"Hold on," I say. I hurry back to my bedroom and open the door, where the cold pushes past me like a ghost. Inside, I can see my breath. I squeeze between the bed and the wall, where I can see the radiator spewing water into a shallow puddle around its base and down through a hole in the floor.

Shit.

I go back to the kitchen, where Ellie's standing with her hands on her hips.

"So?" she says.

"Hello?" someone yells from downstairs.

Ellie turns. "Good mother of Jesus," she says, and slowly clomps her way down the stairs to Ray, the maintenance man, who almost never shows up. Vincent is still standing outside my door, smiling.

"'Blowin' the Wind,'" he says, clapping his hands again.

"I can't right now, Vincent," I say.

"Vincent!" yells Ellie. "Get down here."

Ray ends up having to shut down the entire heating system to stop the water.

I didn't mean to live here. Windows that won't shut. The rotting bathroom floor. The retards everywhere with their accompanying spittle and mayhem. Not that I knew there were mentally retarded adults living in the rest of the house when I moved into my little 2+ rm apt, sunny, on st prkg, shops, util incl, $/mo. Perhaps the wheelchair ramp leading to the porch and the hand-painted WELCOME sign with smiley face above the front door should have given me at least a moment's pause, but they hadn't. I figured I'd just lucked out to find a place I could actually afford, and along with my first month's rent I'd even sent a note expressing my gratitude to the landlord:

Dear Mr. Leahy,

I'm sure you could get a lot more for this great apartment and I just wanted you to know how much it means to someone like me that there are compassionate landlords out there like you.

Sincerely,

During my first volatile encounter with Ray, who'd taken his time getting around to fixing my toilet, he'd told me what a laugh the entire motley crew that was Leahy Associates Realty Co. had gotten from my note.

"Leahy read it to the whole office, *twice*," he'd said. "People were hollering. *Hollering!*"

Ray tells me he'll be back in a few hours to fix the radiator and the roof. I crawl back under the covers next to Guy, shivering, mouth like sand, head pounding.

Riiiing!

Beeeep. "Kiki, it's your brother. So guess what? I was just takin' a drive, top down—which was stupid as hell because it's fucking freezing out—and what comes on the radio but *one of your fucking songs*! On XPN! And then they said your name and everything! It was very cool, man. So I started thinkin' like, hey! Why don't *I* be Jen's manager? How fuckin' awesome would that be? So I got subscriptions to a bunch of music magazines, like *Billboard* and that *CMJ* thing. I'm gonna keep tabs on what's happening out there, you know, as research. Awright. Gotta go. I'm a busy guy, Jen, I mean Kiki. Can't keep my public waiting." *Beeeep.*

I roll over, smiling, imagining me and my brother, together again, Batman and Robin. Except this time, I guess I'm Batman, which feels weird.

Riiiing!

Beeeep. "Yello. Guy? Hello hello? An-y-bod-y there? Okay. It's Aimee." She sighs like she's the tiredest person on earth. "We got the studio for tomorrow night. So just go straight there from the airport. Over and now out." *Beeeep.*

I put my hand on Guy's back. "Did you hear that?" I say.

"Sleeping," says Guy.

"She sounds kinda bummed out."

"Her deal fell through."

"Again?"

My Squint line rings: *Ring-ring!*

Beeeep. "Hey, Jen. It's your pal Jim, your favorite rock-and-roll journalist. I'm doing a piece on what's happening on the ever-loving Boston music scene, and since you seem to be the main thing happening right now, I thought I'd get a quote or two, cuz with your mouth, well, 'nough said. Aw, c'mon. You know I love you. When are we gonna have sex anyway? Call me." *Beeeep.*

"I wish you'd turn those things off," says Guy.

Ring-ring!

Beeeep. "Yeah, hey. It's Neil. So, I'm faxing you a list for tomorrow tonight and so far it's a bunch of the usuals and some new faces. Warners is sending some more of their top brass and a chick from *Hits* magazine. And, so, a bunch of managers have been checking in. The Q Prime guys said they're planning on making it and I just heard from Aimee Mann's manager who says he knows you. And I just got *another* call from Sway who's still in England but he's like, Neil, make sure she knows I'm serious, and I'm like, Randy! She knows, she knows! But I'm tellin' you, this is all good. Aaaaall good. So, have a great show." *Beeeep.*

"That Randy guy used to manage Mark Sandman, when he was with Treat Her Right," I say.

"Mmmmm," mumbles Guy.

Ring-ring!

Beeeep. "Hey chickadee. It's Billy here from Gimmee and check check and double-check. Everything is super-fine and getting finer all the time. Let's see. Your 'Everything' single is smokin' at college radio and we're jacked to push your disc just after the new year, and—you still wanna do that, right? Cuz, I mean, it's great that all the majors are comin' outta the woodwork at ya but I'm just hopin' you and I can have a real sit-down cuz, like I keep tellin' you, you gotta be thinkin' long-term, cred-wise, you know? I just wanna give you a total heads-up about this kinda *thang*. [*disgusting slurping sound*] "Oh shit! *Fuck*. Total brain freeze. Sorry, man. Sipping some slush. Gotta motor." *Beeeep*.

"Is that guy an asshole or does he just sound like an asshole?" says Guy.

"I can't tell yet," I say. "He just keeps saying how I'm gonna, like, lose my cred if I jump to a major too fast."

Guy rolls over and looks at me. "Cred? What cred? You don't *have* any cred. You made up all that Squint Records bullshit to get a deal, remember?"

"How come you always hate cool people?" I say.

"I don't hate cool people," says Guy, shutting his eyes, pulling the blankets to his chin. "I hate assholes."

My home phone rings again and my machine picks up in the middle of some girls giggling and singsonging "Jennifer, Jennifer, Jennifer." More giggling, the muffle of hands over the mouthpiece, then, "We were just wondering if you, if you're"—fit of laughter—"if you're still a crazy old hag"—more laughter—"who's gonna die alone on the *toilet*!" CLICK. *Beeeep*.

I put my head under the covers.

"Who the hell was that?" says Guy.

I poke my head out. "It's that make-a-love-connection service." "What?"

"Every day they were fucking calling me and I'm like How'd you even get my number? And then, I don't know, I kinda ended up yelling at them. They're like harassing me now."

Guy laughs and rolls onto his side. "Less talking, more sleeping," he says.

I close my eyes but I can't sleep. When I open them again, I'm looking straight into the spooky diamond eyes of Ranger, who is, as usual, staring at me like he's about to tell me something.

I finally fall back to sleep, dreaming of an overflowing toilet on top of my bed, the water streaming from my bedroom into the rest of the apartment. There's banging as I slosh my way through the kitchen.

When I open the door a man's standing there, holding a pad of paper and a pen. He's naked (of course).

"I'm your favorite rock-and-roll journalist," he says. "Where's Guy?"

"Who?" I say.

"I know he lives here," he says, cold and slippery as he pushes past me and splashes his way into the living room, where he points at Guy, still asleep. "There!" he says, scribbling on his pad, which I'm trying to yank from his hand when I realize that I'm naked too as people are wading from the bedroom into the living room—Buck, Robby, Neil, my brother, that guy Johnny, and finally Mr. Tetrocelli, my high school principal. The naked journalist laughs and says, "I knew you had to be sleeping with someone."

YEEEAAAAAAHHHHHH!

BAM BAM BAM BAM.

YAAAAAAAAAHHHHHH!

BAM BAM BAM BAM.

BOOM boom BOOM boom BOOM boom BOOM boom.

Electrotube is soundchecking and the lead singer is stomping all over the place, making rock faces.

Tonight's gig is at the Frontload, a sprawling club with a restaurant and three bars with stages spread out into four different areas on two levels. It's Boston's premier place to play and to see and be seen. Our guest list is ridiculous: eight A&R people, two label presidents, five managers, three booking agents, four journalists, and eleven people I don't know who the hell they are.

It's finally our turn to check. I lean over to adjust a knob on a pedal and when I stand back up, I can feel it happening again—my blood falling through my body like hot, dry sand. And now come the stars, swirling and blinking in the corners of my eyes. My heart, knocking like a car about to stall. I shut my eyes. Take a deep breath. Another. Put my hand on my chest. *I'm okay. I'm okay.* About the last thing I want to do is die of a heart attack in the middle of a show.

"You're being crazy," Guy always tells me.

"Just because I'm crazy doesn't mean it's not gonna happen," I always tell him back.

Soundchecking, I'm trying to come to terms with two things: (1) everything sounds like shit, and (2) I'm not going to be able to hear myself singing at all. When I lean into the mic, it smells like beer and breath, and when my lips actually touch the metal, I get a shock that blasts me backward about three feet.

"*Ow,*" I yell, then wish I hadn't. House soundmen are notoriously touchy about this kind of thing and if they think you're being a baby, they're going to do an even worse job than they normally do.

"Is your amp grounded?" yells the soundman.

People are always asking me this and I never really know what they mean. I do know that there's some switch on the back of amps that you can flip, making all the rampantly coursing current go in some direction other than from the socket to the amp to the guitar strings and up from your fingers through your body and out through your lips connecting to the microphone, sending the jolt whipping its way back through the mic cord to the sound board and into a second wall socket, thus completing the circle and causing semi-electrocution for, in this case, me. I reach behind my amp and flip that switch. Touch my lips back to the mic. Get zapped again.

"Fuck!" I yell.

"Just keep your lips away from the mic," says the soundman.

Thanks.

We're playing through one more song as another band, dressed generic college-style in ripped jeans and T-shirts, loads in their gear. Each guy is cuter than the next, and they have girls with them—pretty girls, like the kind you check out at football games in their tight sweatshirts cut off at the bottom. The kinds of girls who clean up nice with their dyed blond hair and buffed fingernails. But the guys aren't looking at their girls. They're looking at me. Especially the big guy with the bandana. It's like he can't take his eyes off me.

"JEN!" yells Buck, pulling his finger across his throat. I'm the only one still playing. I stop.

We're loading our gear offstage as quickly as possible, lowering everything from the side of the stage onto the floor and shoving it into Instrument Alley by the bathroom. Suddenly, a hand grabs the back of my belt and gently tugs. Then Buck's leaning over me from behind, his chest against my back, his mouth at my ear.

"Your pants are falling off," he says. He stays there a moment, just breathing, and something spreads through me, soft and slow as fur. I let my breath out for the first time in what feels like days. Weeks.

Buck stands back and whacks me on the ass.

I turn and give him a shove. "Don't touch the merchandise unless you're gonna buy it," I say.

"How much?" says Buck.

"Too much for you," I say.

"How do you know?"

"I got a feeling."

Buck mumbles something, smiling, looking at the floor.

"What?"

He looks back at me. "What?"

"What did you say?"

"What did you say?"

"Stop *doing* that!" I laugh.

"Stop *doing* that!" He laughs.

"Are you *kidding* me?"

"Are you *kidding* me?"

"What are we, *twelve*?"

"What are we, *twelve*?"

"*Stop* it!"

"*Stop* it!"

"Buck! Fuck you! I'm not kidding!" I yell, pushing him again, harder this time, and he stumbles backward over a road case and falls on the floor. "Oh my God," I say, laughing, trying not to laugh. "Are you okay?"

"Wow," says Buck, rolling onto his back. "I think you killed me."

I offer him my hand. "Sorry," I say, pulling him up. "Really."

"Sorry?" he says, standing, still holding my hand, pulling me in to him. "Let's do it again."

Welcome to the dead zone—post-soundcheck, pre-show. I'm standing at the little bar at the side of the room with a cup of coffee because it's too early to start drinking, though all I want to do is drink. My blood still feels like hot, dry sand, though it's no longer falling. Now it's just gathering, at the tips of my fingers, in the middle of my head.

"You wanna grab a bite?" says Robby, hitting his drumsticks against his thighs. "We're gonna head next door."

"Naah," I say, "I'm not hungry." I can feel my stomach gurgling, but it doesn't feel like hunger. It feels like pain. The truth is, I'm so hungry, I'm not hungry anymore. At first I was trying to lose weight, back during my Squint Records, When In Rock plan. But at this point, I seem to have lost track. I'm afraid my head's looking too big for my body, like one of those spooky-eyed anorexic girls. "You guys go ahead. I'm just gonna hang here and take care of the list and whatever. And Neil told me some people will probably be showing up early, so I should probably stick around."

Robby does a drum roll on his thighs. "All right. We'll be back."

I keep standing there, feeling the emptiness in my stomach, relieved that I won't have to eat, that my tight blue cords are loose, that I won't have to worry about any of the pesky flab that used to edge out over the snap. Being this thin makes me relaxed. At least I keep telling myself that, ignoring that it also makes me exhausted, on edge, suspicious, lonely.

The college-boy band and a bunch of girls are against the other wall, laughing and smoking. The guy with the bandana is looking at me again. He's tall and handsome, with one of those bodies you can see hulking right there under his clothes. He smiles at me. I figure he must know who I am because guys like him don't smile at girls like me.

He walks over. "Hey," he says, "I'm Dave," and he puts his arm down along the bar, his hand resting on my cigarettes. "I love your record. I already figured out 'Everything's Different Now.'"

"Wow. That's amazing. Thanks," I say.

"We're working with Guy. You got some cool guitars," he says, picking up my cigarettes, wiggling the pack in the air. "May I?" he says.

"Sure," I say.

"Thanks," he says, and removes a cigarette with his teeth, pulls a silver Zippo from his pocket, brings it down against his thigh and back up, opening and lighting it in one fluid motion. He lights his cigarette and takes a big drag, then blows the smoke out in perfect circles, circles within circles.

Dave buys me a beer and after a few sips I feel better. This is what helps. Alcohol. Alcohol and cigarettes. Alcohol and cigarettes and boys.

A couple of hours later, the Frontload is beginning to fill up. I'm sitting drinking at a table against the wall. People keep coming over, saying hi, sitting down, getting up, coming back, bringing drinks. It's all very whirligig, with dishes clattering and people laughing, and sudden blasts of music coming through the door in the back. *So this is what it's like to be me now,* I keep thinking as the same cooler-than-thou music types who've been completely ignoring me for years are now waving to me, rapping their knuckles on my table, giving me things: cassettes, 45s, flyers. But mostly, it's eyeballs. Big and white and slanting in my direction.

I can see Mark Sandman sitting at the bar, just like almost every other time I've come in here. He isn't the most gorgeous guy, nor is he the best singer or songwriter or guitar player, so I can't say exactly why he's the coolest guy in the world, but he is. I stopped trying to chat him up a long time ago, figuring I'd rather he think of me as the annoying chick who at least knew enough to stop bugging him instead of as the annoying chick who was bugging him all the time. I haven't said more than an across-the-room "hey" to him in years. But tonight, I actually have something to talk about.

I get up. "So," I say, when I'm right up next to him.

"So," says Mark.

"I've been talking to your old manager," I say, trying to speak slowly, like he does, but it's coming out fast anyway.

"Really," says Mark.

"Randy Sway," I say.

Mark looks at me with his I'm-seeing-right-through-you eyes. "Ah, my good friend Mr. Sway," he says and takes a drag from his cigarette.

"Yeah," I say nonchalantly, as if Mark's the one who brought it up. "I'm talking to a bunch of different people," I can't help but continue, just in case Mark doesn't know about my newfound rock-star-to-be status. "So I was just wondering what you think about him, you know, as a manager."

Mark grins. "So you're talkin' to Randy," he says, raising his eyebrows.

My heart is pounding. Finally.

"I have six words for you," says Mark. He ticks them off on the fingers of his nonsmoking hand. "Hard. To. Get. On. The." He puts the cigarette in his mouth and sticks out his thumb. "Phone," he says. Then he takes the cigarette out of his mouth.

I return to my table and sit down again, staring at Mark's back.

"Jennifer Trynin," says a man with 70s-style brown hair and a nice smile. He pulls a chair over from another table and sits down. "Your record is awesome." He's wearing an upscale army-type jacket, tan pants, and sneakers. He says he's from Warner Bros.

"I hear everything's all fucked up there," I say.

He smiles. "Everything is not all fucked up, as you put it," he says. "We're just going through a little reorganization."

From what Neil's told me, the two guys who've been running Warner Bros. forever—Mo-and-Lenny, he calls them, like they're one person—are being forced out. Neil's told me how beloved they are in the industry, and how he wants to wait a few weeks before I go out to L.A. for a meeting there because he wants Danny Goldberg to be "in place."

The Warner Bros. guy tells me how he used to be in marketing, but since joining up with The Bunny, he's become the general manager in the new regime.

"So you're like a head honcho?"

"Basically," he says.

Head Honcho tells me I have two choices: I either sign to Warner Bros. as an artist, or he's going to hire me in the marketing department because he thinks I'm a marketing genius. Then he laughs. Then he says how sorry Lola is that she couldn't make it tonight, how he hopes he'll do in her stead, and how he's feeling a little whacked because he just flew in from L.A.

"And boy are your arms tired," I say.

Head Honcho smiles at me. "I've heard about you," he says, and excuses himself to make a call. He gets up and goes to the bar where he stops and claps some red-haired guy on the back. Then the red-haired guy turns toward me, waves, smiles his big smile, and begins walking over.

Well well well. If it isn't my old pal, Howdy Doody.

"Jen!" he says when he gets to my table, bending down for a hug, or maybe a hug and a kiss, but I turn my head and end up with a peck on the neck.

We untangle.

Howdy Doody sits down across from me. "How wild is this? My favorite record of the year and *you* made it! Guy's girlfriend!"

"I'm kinda trying to keep the 'Guy's girlfriend' thing on the down low for right now, okay?" I say.

I've met Howdy Doody a number of times over the years because he used to manage Skivvy back when Guy was working with them. I remember sitting at this very table with Howdy Doody a couple years ago. Three times I asked him to pass me my beer, before I finally reached over and snagged it myself. But these days, as Howdy Doody explains, he's at Warner Bros., working as a product manager—someone responsible for shepherding records through the production stage after they've been recorded.

"Where is Guy, anyway?" says Howdy Doody.

"L.A.," I say. "Working with Aimee Mann."

A chick with shiny jet-black hair, dressed in a flowing black outfit, sits down next to Howdy Doody and kisses him on the cheek. Then she smiles at me. "It's our little rock-star-to-be," she says. It's strange, but I keep thinking I see a stud in her nose, or her eyebrow, or her lip, but I don't. She leans across the table, putting her chin on her hands, and smiles at me. "Yeah," she says, and sits up. "You're you."

I laugh. "Well that's good to know."

"I'm the one who does that column at *Hits.*"

"I vanna be adored," says Howdy Doody.

"What?"

"That's the name of her column. Ivana B. Adored."

"Oh," I say. "Sorry. I guess I haven't really seen it."

"I've been faxing your mentions to Guy," says Howdy Doody. Then he puts his finger to his lips. "Sorry," he says softly. "You've been in the column a lot lately."

"Oh," I say. "I hate to be, like, totally clueless, but I don't really know what *Hits* is."

Ivanah and Howdy Doody look at each other.

"*We* should live in Boston," says Ivana.

"It's one of those glossy music industry rags," says Howdy Doody, "full of radio play lists and who's liking what and what's cool and what sucks and basically, you know, gossip."

"I've been putting you in, in that one-to-watch sort of way," says Ivana.

"You gals need drinks?" says Howdy Doody, and he heads to the bar.

Ivana is smiling, looking at me funny. "So," she says, "do you remember me?"

"Sure," I say, because I feel like I've met everyone in the world.

She squints at me.

"Not really," I say.

"We went to college together," she says.

"We did?"

"We had a class together."

I only remember about six people from college, and Ivana isn't one of them. "Which class?"

Ivana mimes picking up a phone. "Hello, Oberlin Travel," she says.

Oh. My. Fucking. God.

Ivana grins. "Electronic Music 101 with Mr. Standish."

I put my head down on the table. "Tell me this isn't happening," I mumble.

Of all the artsy-fartsy things I've done in my whole life, "Hello, Oberlin Travel" has to be the artsy-fartsiest. It was a "spoken word piece" based on my going to the local travel agency to buy a plane ticket home so that I could go see my high school boyfriend, Joe. Oh-so-cleverly interspersed among the exchange between Becky the travel agent and me—over the clacking of computer keyboards and the whirring of printers—were my thoughts about me and Joe having sex.

> BECKY: And what day will you be departing, Jennifer?
> ME: Wednesday afternoon the third would be great.
> WHISPERED THINKING: *Oh please, yes, yes—*
> BACKGROUND NOISE: *CLICKETY CLACKETY WHIRR WHIRR*
> BECKY: Would you like a window or an aisle seat?
> ME: Window please.
> WHISPERED THINKING: *Yeah, window, please, just like that—*

The piece droned on, with the "whispered thinking" growing throatier and more desperate-sounding—*Yes, yes, Joe, I'm coming, I'm coming*—and Becky's *Hello, Oberlin Travel* becoming louder and louder, until the piece abruptly ended.

Get it?

My head's still down on the table, face against my arms. "I think I'm gonna kill myself," I say.

"Kill yourself?" says Ivana. "I loved that piece."

I pick my head up.

"Hell," she says, twirling her black hair in her fingers. "At least *you* were getting laid."

We tear through the show. This song! That song! Feedback! Wah-wah! More feedback! More wah-wah! I'm sweating and panting as we pull into the last song and by the end, there's a big fucking roar of applause, enough to warrant a big fucking roar of an encore.

Dave and his college band are at the lip of the stage, pounding and clapping. I push my hair out of my face, wipe the sweat from my brow, and dive into "If I Had Anything To Say (Don't You Think I Would Have Said It All?)." Way back against the far wall of the room, I see them: Cliff and Peter from Q Prime, smiling, nodding, leaning into one another and pointing up at me.

That's right.

I'm a crazy-ass motherfucker.

At 1 A.M., I'm scurrying through the bowels of the club, edging my way down the rickety stairs, peeking behind drop cloths and knocking on creepy doors.

"Yeah!" someone yells.

I open the door into a small cluttered room with a strip of fluorescent light beaming from above and some fat guy with long thinning hair sitting at a desk covered by a dirty towel. He looks at me only long enough to see I'm some chick, the kind of chick he has no use for (i.e., not a chick he wants to fuck), and that I'm not a threat. Then he removes the dirty towel from the desk and continues what he was doing, which was counting money.

"Whaddaya want?" he says.

"I played here tonight," I say.

"And?"

"I just wanted to get paid."

He exhales, sits back in his chair, paws around on his desk for his cigarettes, takes one out, and lights it. "Really," he says. The right half of his neck is covered with a tattoo that's bending into the folds of his flesh. He takes a drag from his cigarette and blows the smoke out through the large gap between his two front teeth. "Which band?" he says.

"Jennifer Trynin," I say.

"Whadja do, open?" he says, reaching for a piece of paper with tonight's band names and set times and percent signs scrawled on it.

"We played third," I say, pointing to my name.

"Hmmm," he says, picking up a few bills from his desk. "Here's fifty bucks," he says.

"That was our guarantee," I say, my heart beginning to race. "We also get twenty-five percent of the door."

"Yeah, well, I don't know anything about that," he says, crumpling up the piece of paper with my name and "25%" written next to it.

I splash my way through the slush to my car, where Buck is listening to the radio full blast, waiting for a ride home.

"Will you turn that fucking *down,*" I say, switching the radio off and slamming my door.

"Sor-*ry,*" says Buck, wiping his hand across his mouth, drunk. He sticks his beer between his legs, rubs his hands together. "So fork it over, baby," he says.

"I could only get fifty bucks," I say, starting the car, not really wanting to talk about it because I'm embarrassed and mad and just want to get the fuck out of there.

"What? That place was fuckin' *packed*! What about our fucking *percentage*?"

"He wouldn't give it to me. He wouldn't listen to me," I say, pulling out into the street.

"He wouldn't *listen* to you? What the *fuck* does *that* mean?"

"Don't yell at *me,*" I say.

"I'm *not* yelling at you!"

"Yes you *are*!"

"Well what the *fuck*? Is it cuz you're a *chick* or something? I'm mean, Jesus, that's so fucking *unacceptable*!" Buck pounds his door with his fist.

"Cut it out!" I say.

"And you're just gonna *take* it? I mean, you should go back in there and tell that douchebag you want your money! It's fucking *yours*! He doesn't have any fucking *right*!"

"No fucking kidding, but *whaddaya want me to do*?"

"Don't get mad at *me,*" Buck yells. "Jesus *Christ,* that's *so* fucked up! That's *so fucked up*!" He slumps down in his seat, stares at the floor, and shakes his head.

It takes me a few seconds to realize he's crying. I pull over to the curb.

"Hey, don't worry about it," I say. "It's not that big a deal."

"Everything's so fucked up," he says, looking at me with his nice eyes and the streetlight shining on him. "Sorry," he says. "Sorry I yelled at you."

I smile at him. Hit him gently on the arm. "Sap."

I drop Buck at Laura's and watch him walk up the front steps. I don't know why I'm hoping he'll turn around. When he gets to the door, he puts his hands in his pockets, finds his keys. He turns around and gives me a small wave.

I'm sitting at my desk, designing my monthly mailer—a postcard that lists upcoming gigs and local radio appearances with computer scans of the covers of any new stuff I've recorded that's for sale. People sign up to get the postcards at shows. The first time I ever sent it out, two years ago, the list had seventeen names on it. Today's list has over six hundred. It takes me the better part of a day to do the whole thing, and it's expensive. As of this month, all told, it comes to about $160, mostly for postage.

I keep track of all my expenses in a book, as if I really have my own business. And it's looking like this year, for the first time, I'm going to break even—that is, if you only look at what I pay to musicians and soundmen, for rehearsal space, and the mailer. I've been meaning to "fold in" the manufacturing costs for the two 45s and *Cockamamie,* but then I'd have to admit to myself that I'm still losing money, and who wants to do that?

My fax machine begins to whir, and I grab the slippery fax paper and sit down in my old gray chair with the springs poking into my ass.

It looks like some kind of contract.

I can't make out much because the whole thing is smudged, and what I can is full of legal mumbo jumbo, but it's from Sony Publishing, where Cinda Weinstein works, and I can definitely make out the number, the cash, The Advance: $80,000.

I turn the sheet of paper over and look at the back. Then I look at the front again and it's still there: $80,000.

I've ferreted out advance numbers from other wanna-be big-time songwriters, and I've never gotten wind of more than $30,000, which to me is more money than God.

I'm figuring and refiguring how long $80,000 could last me.

I picture walking into Doyle's and flinging my apron across the bar. "That's right, you heard me," I'll say to Jimmy the bartender—the guy with the wicked-good mullet and a handlebar mustache, the guy with whom you do not fuck—"I quit!"

Yeah!

And then I'll go over to the parenting publication and tell them where they can stick their "What's Happening?" section.

YEAH!

Ring-ring!

Beeeep. "Jen, it's Neil. So we just got our first official publishing offer and—"

I leap across the room.

"Neil!"

"I got you!"

"Eighty thousand dollars? This is fucking great! I can't believe it!"

"So you got it. Okay, well, I don't even really know where these guys are coming from on this cuz it's way too early for actual offers, but here we are, so, so there you go. And it's not bad, but I mean, I don't know. I'm thinking, in this case, they're shooting kinda low, you know?"

"Low?"

"Like I think this offer's a little under."

"Under? Like how under?"

"Like at least a hundred thousand under."

I'm staring at one of my dirty curtains thumbtacked above a window.

"You still there?" says Neil.

I'm lying in bed, slowly petting Ranger and staring at the water marks on my ceiling. I called Guy at his hotel and at the studio where he's working with Aimee but there was no answer. Then I tried Tim but couldn't get him either. *A hundred thousand under. A hundred thousand under.* I can't understand a hundred thousand dollars being under anything.

Ding-dong!

Ranger leaps off the bed.

Ding-dong ding-dong ding-dong!

Downstairs, Buck's standing on the front porch, making faces at me through the window. *Ding-dong! Ding-dong!*

I open the door. "Cut it out already," I say.

"You look like you just woke up," he says.

"I was just taking a breather."

"You should never get out of bed on my account," he says.

"Ha ha," I say. "Hey, do you see the paper out there?"

"I don't think so," he says.

Buck follows me into the stairwell, where I stop at the door to the first floor and knock. The TV's on full blast, *The Price Is Right.* The door opens slowly and a short, plump girl with beautiful wide eyes is standing there smiling.

"Good morning," she says.

"Hi," I say. The room smells like burnt rubber.

"Good morning," she says to Buck.

"Hey," he says.

"Good morning," she says again. Then she sticks a finger up her nose.

Ellie appears, clapping her hands together near the girl's head. "Stop that," she says. "What?" she says to me.

"I was wondering if you've seen my paper," I say.

Ellie shakes her head. "Don't think so," she says.

I look over Ellie's shoulder into the room where Vincent is on the couch, clapping his hands and bouncing every time Bob Barker spins the wheel. At his feet is a newspaper spread out on the floor like a mat.

"What about *that* paper?" I say, pointing at the floor.

Ellie turns. "Oh," she says. "Vincent!" she yells, crossing the room and gathering the paper in her hands.

The plump girl touches a finger to the tip of her nose. "Nose," she says, looking at Buck.

Buck taps a finger on the tip of his own nose. "Beep beep," he says, and the girl giggles.

"Jen," says Vincent, and he waves at me. "Jen Jen Jen Jen Jen."

Ellie is back in the doorway with my paper. "Here," she says.

Up in my apartment, we're laughing.

"'What about *that* paper?'" says Buck, pouring himself some coffee.

"You were sweet to that girl," I say. "I think I've been living with these people too long or something. I used to be nicer to them."

"There but for the grace of God go I," says Buck, raising his cup of coffee to the ceiling.

Buck's school schedule leaves him with a lot of free time and it's the third day in a row that he's been sitting on my couch, reading a book or watching TV, while I'm "doing business." Today he has *The Sun Also Rises* open in front of him when my Squint line rings.

Buck looks up. "You gonna get that?"

Beeeep. "Hey, this message is for Jennifer. It's Jessica from Newbury Comics, and I just wanted you to know that your CD is kicking ass at our stores. We already need more, maybe like fifty so we can put ten in each store. You can pick up your check for the first batch when you drop off the next load. All right. Take it easy." *Beeeep.*

"That's awesome," says Buck.

"You wanna come with me and drop some CDs off for her?" I say.

"Sure," he says, standing up, stretching, walking across the room and standing behind me.

"You're making me nervous," I say.

"What're you doing?" he says, leaning into me, putting his hands on my shoulders.

"I just need to fix one thing on the mailer and I can print it out and then we can get it copied and put it together."

"Whaddaya mean 'we,' Kemosabe?" he says.

"You said you were gonna help!"

"I'm just kidding," he says. He squeezes my shoulders. Keeps squeezing my shoulders.

"Cut it out," I say. "You're distracting me."

"From what?"

"From everything."

Buck slowly turns my chair until I'm facing him. He squats down and puts his hands on my knees. "From what everything?" he says.

"I don't know," I say, feeling suddenly exhausted, like I'm about to fall asleep.

Ring-ring!

Buck jerks his hands from my knees.

We head to Bertolli's Print Shoppe, where Mr. Bertolli, as usual, can't understand what I want.

"Slow down," he says.

"Red card stock. Medium grade. Two hundred copies, cut twice," I say, tracing the crop marks with my finger. "So I'll get four cards per piece." I've only done this here about a million times.

Mr. Bertolli brings the sheet of paper right up to his face like he can't see it. He puts it back down and begins punching numbers into his calculator. "That's gonna be, that's gonna be, wait." He starts again.

"We got a plane to catch, dear," says Buck, pointing at his watch, tapping his foot.

"You know, if you did it on regular paper, it'd save you two cents a sheet," says Mr. Bertolli.

"I know, but we need the card stock," I say. *Every time* we go through this.

Standing in line at the post office, I drop my wallet. Buck picks it up and puts it in my back pocket. In the car on our way across town, Buck pulls out the stamps, rips one off, licks it, and sticks it on my cheek.

He also smacks my thigh with a CD. At the Newbury Comics head-quarters, he pushes me gently into a wall. By the time we get back to Bertolli's Print Shoppe to pick up the mailers, Buck has touched me twenty-six times.

When we get back to my apartment, the phone's ringing.

"Why don't you ever answer your phone?" says Buck, putting the box of mailers on my kitchen table.

Beeeep. "It's me again," says Guy. "So, we're taking a break. Every-thing's going great. Aimee says hi. Where are you?"

Buck and I look at each other.

"All right. Whatever. I'll try to call again later." *Beeeep.*

Buck and I are sitting on the floor putting the mailer together, assembly-line style. Buck holds the Squint Records stamp up in the air. "Very professional," he says.

Ring-ring!

"I'm not even gonna ask," says Buck.

Beeeep. "Hey Jennifer, it's Cinda calling, Cinda Weinstein. Just checking in, wanted to say hey, and so I was catching up on some of my reading and *Music Week* is like the equivalent of *Billboard* in En-gland and there's a column here called 'Ones to Watch' and you're listed in it. It says, 'Jennifer Trynin is currently courting the major la-bels in the U.S. This lady from Boston recently released the stunning album on her own Squint Records label. She creates a sound like a more mainstream Throwing Muses.' So, you're definitely *one to watch* in the U.K. Uhh, anyway, how are you? Did you get a fax from us today? So just call me, okay? When you can. I know you're busy. Okay. Bye-bye." *Beeeep.*

"Wow," says Buck. "You're famous!"

"I don't think I sound like Throwing Muses," I say.

"What fax was she talking about?" says Buck.

I glance over at the fax lying face down on my desk. "Nothing," I say. "I don't know."

Buck stands, yawns, then lies down on the couch. "Break time," he says, reaching for the remote and clicking on the TV.

I stand and stretch.

"This sure is comfortable," he says, staring at the TV. "Wanna join me?"

Up this close, the hair on Buck's jaw could almost be tree trunks. He's flat on his back, staring at the TV. I've somehow ended up on my side, with my head in the crook of his arm. He asks if I ever watch this one, this soap. I say no, never got into soaps. He smells like burlap, or burlap is what his smell makes me think of. His hand is pressing on the small of my back, and when I touch his face to calm myself, I only feel scared. My mind is gray as slate or as the sky or like I've been dunked in water as we lean into each other and kiss.

On our way to the rehearsal space, Buck keeps pulling things from my glove compartment and holding them up to me one by one—a pack of cigarettes with one cigarette left, a pair of sunglasses missing a lens, a lighter, another lighter, a shoe horn.

"Do you need *this*?" he keeps saying, and then he laughs. "Do you really need *this*?"

I keep laughing along, trying not to look at him, because every time I do, I feel like someone's blown a hole in my chest.

We meet Robby at the space and grab our gear, which isn't much because tonight's gig is the WBCN Holiday show at the Frontload, with a million bands only playing a couple of songs each. With this kind of show, there's usually a backline (amps and drums for everyone to use) so that there's minimal set-up time between bands. We got added to the bill last minute, so no one really knows we're playing tonight, and I'm glad. I never even told Neil about it, because I knew he'd tell people and then they'd come but I just want to play. I don't want to talk.

When we pull up in front of the club, Laura's standing on the corner, waving at us, blowing another hole in my chest.

"I didn't know Laura was coming tonight," I say.

Buck looks at me. "Yeah," he says.

"Hey you guys," she says, as we're getting out of the van. Buck grabs her around the waist, bends her over backward, and gives her a loud, smoochy kiss on the cheek before he stands her back up.

"What was that for?" she says, wiping her face with the back of her hand.

The show's sold out and the room is packed. Christmas spirit is on full blast, with lights hanging in strings along the walls and some sort of eggnog drink for sale at the bar. We've been drinking for hours and everyone's being very chummy. Robby's flirting with every girl who's flirting with him. Buck and Laura are being very huggy and silly. The farther we get from this afternoon on the couch, the easier it is for me to convince myself that maybe it never really happened at all. And even if it did, so what? No harm done, right? It was just kissing. And it's never going to happen again anyway.

I raise my beer to Buck and Laura. "Happy holidays," I say.

I'm watching the show from offstage because the floor's too crowded. We're up after the next band. Suddenly, Buck's beside me, with his hand on my arm. He leans into me. "I thought we'd never be alone again," he says, hot and wet and right into my ear. "And I want you to know that there's nowhere else I'd rather be than here with you right now."

For a moment, everything goes dark and quiet, like I've been shoved in a pocket.

I lean back into him and hear myself say, "Me, too."

The following night, we're wandering around downtown. Me and Robby and Buck and Laura. Robby's girlfriend was supposed to come with us, but they're fighting. The street is wet and shining with head-lights. Buck knocks into me with his hip.

"Hip check," he says.

When I get home, I feed Ranger and grab a beer. I sit at the kitchen table in the dark, staring at my guitar, at my tape recorder. When I used to come home, before all this, sometimes I wouldn't even take off my jacket. I'd just sit down here and pick up my guitar. The aloneness wouldn't make me feel fidgety or empty. Or if it did, I'd fill myself up by taking everything out and looking at it, breaking everything apart, then putting it back together in some song.

Who knows how many hours I've spent sitting at this table with my guitar in my lap, drinking and smoking, staring out at that tree across the street, through the snow and the rain and the sun like white against the bark. *If it snows for one more day, I may just have to get my shovel from the shed, or maybe I'll make me an angel instead, think I'll dig a great big old hole in my head.* I'd be worrying, planning my escape, wondering how many boxes it'd take to pack everything up, wondering how much it would hurt to just pack it in. *If it snows for one more day, I just may up and roll my life around the yard, putting two of everything in my car, and dream of driving away someplace far, singing Yay. Yeah.*

In the summer, the tree would sprinkle the ground with little red berries whenever the wind blew, while I was rifling through rhymes: *sight, blight, flight, right, kite.* But sometimes I got really sick of rhyming: *If I kiss you, will you turn your back on me? Or will you come through? Or am I just too blind to see people for what they are, you you you especially?* The only reason "come through" was ever there in the first place was to rhyme with "will you"—and the only reason "will you" was ever there was to rhyme with all the "yous" that came before it. I mean, "Come through"? Come through what? Where? What was I saying? In the end, I never got anything else to fit there quite so snug, so I let it go. But every time I sing "or will you come through," I can't help but wince.

That tree across the street has never even blinked, though. It just stands there, through every moment of all the days and nights and beer and coffee and cigarettes and excuses and crying and throwing stuff—as if it's saying, "Don't sweat it, Jen, cuz some of us just don't give a shit."

My Squint machine is blinking. The last message is from Johnny.

"Hello, Princess," he says. "How goes the war? Just want you to know I'm thinkin' about you."

The machine clicks off.

Headlights move across the walls.

My home phone begins to ring and I wonder if it's Guy. Hope it's Guy. Hope it's not Guy. I put my head in my hands.

Beeeep. "Jennifer, Jennifer, Jennifer . . ." Girls giggling. Dial tone. *Beeeep.*

I light a cigarette and call my brother.

Ring.

Ring.

Ring.

"Hey, this is Tim. Leave me a message." *Beeeep.*

"Hey. It's Kiki. Ha. Just kidding. I just got in. I was out with Robby and Buck and Buck's girlfriend, and did I tell you Guy's away? He's been gone like forever. But, so, Buck's been helping me out, and we've been hanging out a lot lately, and I don't know. Do you like him? Oh, and I got my first real offer yesterday. From a publishing company. For like eighty thousand dollars and Neil's saying how he thinks that's like *too low,* like a *hundred thousand dollars* too low. Can you believe that? That means your manager's cut is already like twelve thousand bucks. Not bad, right? Ha ha. But really, I'm, like, I don't know. I just can't believe it. Anyway, so now I'm home and I was just wondering what you were doing, but I guess you're doing it. So, whatever. I'll see you later."

Guy finally comes home. He kisses me in the dark and I start to cry.

"I missed you, too," he says.

We're back at Brownie's and it's only eight o'clock but the show's already sold out. Neil's strutting around in a paper crown someone gave him because it's his birthday. He seems to know everyone and everyone seems to know me. I can't think of anything to say but it doesn't matter because no one's listening. BB and my dad are here again and so are Tim+1 and a bunch of their friends. Every time I look at anyone, they're already looking at me. Smiling. Waving. *Hi Jen!* It's like I can feel layer upon layer holding me in, like I'm one of those Russian dolls that are just shells of doll after doll, each of them painted and fitted perfectly into one another. I know my real self has become small as a pea. Neil is standing with Tim and my father. He claps my dad on the back, and the three of them look over at me. Smile. And I wish I could stop this moment forever, that the future would just be now, just be this—Tim and my dad looking at me the way they are.

I'm out on the sidewalk taking a breather, smoking a cigarette, when Johnny walks up.

"Well hello, Princess," he says.

"Hey," I say. "You know, I wish you'd cool it with the Princess thing. Do you even know my name?"

"The question is, do you know my name?"

"Asshole?"

"Close."

We hug, and when we pull apart, one of Johnny's hairs is sticking to my lips.

"Are all your fans lining up inside?"

"Basically," I say. "I just can't keep doing it, you know. The thing."

"Poor little Princess," he says.

"Can you cut the shit for like one second?" I say.

"I know," he says. "It must be tough being you."

"You're a dick," I say.

"Hey," he says. "I'm not the one stringing *you* along."

"That's the way you see it?"

"I think that's the way it is."

I sit down on a low wall just behind me. Johnny sits down next to me.

"Listen," he says. "Not to be just another person kissing your ass, but I really mean this. I really think you should come with me. I know

what to do with you, with your whole thing. I mean, okay, at the beginning, everyone was going so fucking crazy over you and I was like,
what? I mean, I really like your songs and everything, but I just didn't
see the whole sexy thing. I really didn't. But then I did. Now I do.
Now I totally get it."

I look at Johnny. "You're so full of shit. My sexy thing? Are you
kidding me? You're like a model-fucker. I know guys like you."

"You think you know me?"

"Be honest. Model-fucker or not model-fucker?"

Johnny smiles. "All right. Model-fucker. But hey, I mean, I'd be
with you," says Johnny, not looking at me.

I stand up. "What is that supposed to mean? Like you're so deep
or something, you'd even fuck some dog like me? Is that what you're
saying?"

"What?"

"Because that's what it sounds like."

Johnny stands. "You're like cracked in the head, you know that,
Princess?" He pulls out his wallet and looks inside. "I gotta hit a cash
machine," he says.

"Great," I say.

Johnny smiles at me. "You don't want me to go, do you?"

I smile. "You're fucking unbelievable," I say.

He kisses me on the cheek. "That's what the girls tell me," he says.

After the show, a bunch of us gather at the bar. We meet Sarah and
Lathem, two A&R chicks from Atlantic. Sarah is heavyset and young—
maybe younger than I am—with brown curly hair. Lathem is tall and
pretty, with her hair swept up in a light blue silk scarf.

"What kind of name is Lathem?" I say.

"My parents are freaks," she says.

A woman from Warner/Chappell Publishing is there. When she
gives me her card, I see that her name is Scarlett O'Harron. I say that
must kind of suck and she says it does. Her boss is there too, Kenny
O'Harron—no relation.

"But that's weird," I say to Kenny.

"Oh, lassie, life's weird all right," says Kenny in a thick Irish accent.

Buck and Robby come over, silly and happy and drunk.

"You guys were great, but the sound system sucks!" says Kenny, holding out his beer for a toast when he realizes that only he has one. "What?" he says. "Barkeep!" he yells. "Drinks!"

Tim comes over with BB and my dad, who're dressed to the nines and smiling like crazy.

"This is so exciting!" says BB.

"It really is, kiddie," says my dad, "but the sound system seemed to be a little," he says, and he holds his hand out, moving it like a scale, "mezzo-mezzo."

"Right you are, sir," says Kenny, extending his hand toward my father. "Kenny O'Harron," he says.

"Ah," says my father, shaking Kenny's hand. "An Irish fellow."

"Born and bred."

"Hard to tell from the accent," says my father, and everyone laughs.

A chubby rock chick wearing a black leather vest with nothing under it grabs me by the arm. "I'm doing a rockumentary," she says, slapping her hand against the big bag over her shoulder. "I want you to be in it."

"Sure," I say, and as she walks toward the stairwell to the basement, I quickly grab Buck and Robby. "Come on."

The rockumentary chick is already at the bottom of the stairs, camcorder on her shoulder, shooting us as we're coming down. We're goofing around, pushing each other, trying to grab each other's beers.

"This is great," she says. "Very natural."

Buck snags my beer and holds it over his head.

"Okay," she says. "I got enough of that stuff. So now I just want to focus on Jennifer, you know, for the actual interview."

"Oh," says Robby. "All right. Well—"

"*Fine,*" says Buck, cramming my beer back into my hand, taking the steps two at a time back up the stairs, and slamming the door behind him at the top.

Robby and I look at each other.

"What the hell is his problem?" asks the rockumentary chick.

"He's just drunk," says Robby.

"No worries," she says.

When I get back to the bar, Buck and Robby and Tim are yukking it up with Kenny. They all turn to me with their beers in the air and yell together, "YOU GUYS WERE GREAT, BUT THE SOUND SYSTEM SUCKS!"

Late, back at BB's, Buck tiptoes into my room, lays his sleeping bag on the floor next to the bed, sits on the bed next to me.

When we kiss, it's all I can feel.

The alarm clock goes off. My head is pounding and my eyes feel like they're filled with Vaseline. I hear a groan. Buck's on the floor in his sleeping bag and the sight of him fills me with a peculiar dread. We tell Robby that Buck slept on the floor in my room on account of Robby's snoring.

We head out into a sunny cold day filled with handshakes, smiling, small talk and more smiling, with more record company people, publishing people, booking agents, and business managers.

Finally, we go for drinks with Scarlett and Kenny O'Harron, who introduce us to some manager named Frankie B., whose hair is dyed white and sticks straight up, à la Johnny Rotten.

"And the 'B' is for . . ." I say.

"Just Frankie B.," he says.

By eight o'clock, my lips feel like I've been sucking on a hot pipe. We pick up some Chinese takeout on our way back to BB's.

Robby drums his chopsticks on the coffee table. "Got any forks?" he says.

I go into the kitchenette and rifle through the drawers.

"I can't fucking believe BigWig called me Bob again," says Buck.

"Here," I say, handing Robby a small spoon. "Best I could find."

"He doesn't call *you* Bob," says Buck.

"I don't think BigWig has ever said anything to me," says Robby. "But even if he did, there's no way he knows my name."

"Doesn't that bug you?" says Buck.

"No," says Robby.

"They're all just such self-serving assholes. Do you think they really give a shit about any of us? About you?" says Buck, looking at me. "All they want is this record and then they're gonna do exactly whatever the fuck they want. You can't trust any of these fucking people. They're just a bunch of sycophants."

Robby raises his eyebrows and smiles. "Sycophants?" he says. "Very fancy, Bob." Then he waves his spoon in front of my face. "Earth to Jen," he says.

I look at the fried rice in my chopsticks and put it back on my plate. I can hear my father walking around upstairs. "I gotta go check something," I say.

Climbing the stairs, it's like I can't breathe. I knock on my father's door and he opens it, eating a piece of cheese.

"Ah, kiddie," he says. "What a nice surprise. Cheese?" He's in his usual attire—tweed sport coat, colorful handkerchief sticking out of his breast pocket, loud socks. "How were the meetings today?"

"Fine," I say. "Where's BB?"

"She's down at the corner picking up ribs. Where're the boys?"

"They're eating Chinese downstairs."

"How's my good friend Kenny O'Harron?"

"Fine."

My dad bends over the coffee table, picks up his glass of wine. Takes a sip. Puts it back down. Takes another piece of cheese.

"Dad?" I say.

"Mmmm?" he says.

"I'm, well, I'm feeling, like, I don't know. Scared, or something." I stop talking because my throat clamps up and I'm afraid I'm going to cry, which is the last thing I want to do in front of my father, because he told me once how he thinks crying can be a ploy. A ploy for what, I'm not sure. But being a crier from way back, I just know I don't want to do it right now.

I rub my eyes like I'm tired.

"Scared?" he says.

"Yeah," I say.

"Of what?"

"I don't know," I say. I feel a tear fall down my cheek before I can stop it.

My father takes a few steps toward me and for a moment, I think he's actually going to lean down and hug me, which makes another tear fall down my cheek. But he stops at the coffee table and takes another piece of cheese, this time on a cracker.

I swipe the tears away. "It all just feels different now. Like it's not fun anymore."

"Fun?" says my dad.

"It's just, I don't know if I want to give them my music anymore. Like, once I take their money, it'll never be the same. It'll never be my thing again. And it feels, like, dirty or something. Evil."

"Oh, come on," says my dad. "That's ridiculous. This is the way life is, my girl. Nothing stays the same. You're in the big leagues now. You're playing with the big boys. Isn't that what you wanted?"

I go back downstairs with a buzzing in my ears. I walk through the little living room, past Buck and Robby, into the bedroom, and close the door. I stare at the phone. Think about calling Guy. Or Tim. But all I do is fall onto the bed. Then I get under the covers. Then I put the pillows over my head.

★

Eleven A.M., and Guy and I are in bed, drinking coffee and reading the paper, when the phone rings.

Beeeep. "It's Buck, pick up," says Buck's voice on my machine. "I know you're there."

"It's Buck," says Guy.

"I'm not deaf," I say.

Buck sings, "Je-en, Je-en."

Guy looks at me.

I don't look at him.

"Okay then," says Buck. "If you really think you can live without me." *Beeeep*.

"What's that supposed to mean?" says Guy.

"What's what supposed to mean?" I say.

"If you can live without him."

"How the hell am *I* supposed to know?" I say, too loudly.

"What's the matter with you?"

"Nothing," I say. "I don't know."

Guy folds his paper, puts it in his lap, looks at me again. "You know, I ran into Kramer the other night and he told me how he knew Buck back when he was in some other band and how he was a great bass player and everything, but that he could be a real handful. Like, trouble."

"Trouble?" I say. "What the hell is *that* supposed to mean?"

"He didn't elaborate," says Guy.

Guy keeps looking at me.

I don't look at him.

The Squint line rings.

Beeeep. "Hi Jen, it's Neil. So, yeah. I got a deal memo this morning from Merv at Mercury cuz they're jumping the gun even though I *told* them we're not really taking offers yet but they're going like *crazy* over there and they just want to make sure that they're getting in there and making an impression. So they're talking like one twenty-five and I'm like, Merv, tell me you're joking, but he's crying poor-mouth at the company but how that doesn't mean they're not one hundred percent committed to you and yadda yadda yadda, and I'm like, Merv. Come on. So, just wanted you to know, you know? The race is *on*! I *love* it!" *Beeeep*.

Guy laughs. "One twenty-five. In their dreams one twenty-five."

I slam the paper down on my legs. "*What* is so fucking *funny* about one twenty-five?" I say.

Guy looks at me again. "Maybe you should go back to sleep or something," he says.

"I'm getting these offers that sound like a shitload of money to me and Neil keeps like *scoffing* at everything!"

"Listen" says Guy. "Mercury's starting at a one twenty-five advance is ridiculous. That's what you offer some baby band that doesn't have shit going on, and as we all know, you have a *lot* going on. Same thing on the publishing side. Sony's eighty thousand is a lowball offer, and besides, I'm sure Neil's gonna wait till you've got your record deal to make a publishing deal because publishing advances are somewhat dependent on the record advance and the kind of deal you're able to get from the record company. Publishers offer more or less based partially on how likely they think it is that they'll make their money back. I doubt Neil's gonna consider anybody offering less than two or two-fifty for your publishing. All Neil's doing is sending a message to everyone out there that they're gonna have to put up some serious bucks if they even wanna start talking."

"But a hundred and twenty-five thousand is a lot of money," I say.

"It's not," says Guy. "Especially not in this case, like I said. And you have to remember that the record advance isn't cash you can just put in your pocket. It's a fund that the record company fronts you to make your record. In fact, you don't ever even see that money. The record company pays it directly to the producer and the studio for time and all that. *If* there's anything left over after the record's done, that's the money that you can actually put in your pocket."

"But *Cockamamie*'s already done," I say.

"I'm talking about usually. In your case, yeah, *Cockamamie*'s done, but you still have to pay back for your studio time and I have to be paid too. That was our deal when we made the record, remember? Spec time?"

"Right," I say. "I remember."

"Anyway, so after *all* your recording costs are paid for, whatever's left of your record advance—*if* anything's left over—that money plus your whole publishing advance gets commissioned by your team. As payment for doing your initial deals, Neil will take, ballpark, ten percent. From there on out, from every dime you take in, your manager will commission fifteen to twenty percent and the business manager takes around five percent. I mean, that's one of the reasons so many managers are beginning to sniff around. Not that they don't love your music, but they also smell a bidding war coming on. Bidding wars spell big advances spell big commissions for them."

"But don't I just have to pay those advances back at some point?"

"Sort of," says Guy. "But bigger advances are always better."

"And do I have to pay back the money that I lost to my *team's* commissions?"

Guy tosses his paper on the floor. "Okay," he says. "You finally in the mood to listen to how it all works?"

"I guess," I say.

So here's what Guy explains to me about how it all usually works.

Say you're me, so you're both the recording artist and the song-writer who writes all the music that's going on the records. The first thing that happens when you sign your deals with the record company (as the recording artist) and the publishing company (as the songwriter) is that you get an "advance" from each. Advances are simply money given to artists against future earnings. These advances must be recouped by each company from your earnings before they pay you another dime. (Though if they don't recoup, you don't have to pay the advances back.)

Publishing companies are supposedly responsible for "helping your music get out there" by trolling around and trying to get your songs onto TV and into movies (but for the majority of artists, your publishing reps usually just sit around and wait for things to take off so that the TV and movie people come to them).

Record companies are responsible for everything else. So, in addition to the advance/recording fund, record companies put up lots more money for marketing-related activities (like creating artwork, arranging photo shoots, shooting videos, providing tour support, placing print ads, and hiring independent operators like Gimmee to promote your songs to radio stations). Much of this additional money must also be recouped by the record company from you before they pay you another dime.

How you repay each company is where things get complicated. It's not, as you might think, at the rate of how much they take in for each record sold. Instead, you're turning over to them the ownership and control of your songs in exchange for contractually agreed-upon royalties that come from three sources (not counting touring income and merchandise revenue, which are other things altogether). As a recording artist, you receive *record* royalties from your record company, which are (typically) a percentage of the suggested retail list price (or SRLP) you receive for each record sold. As a songwriter, you receive *mechanical* royalties from your record company and *performance* royalties from a performing rights organization (such as BMI, ASCAP, or SECSAC) with whom you've registered your songs.

In a standard deal, record royalties begin at 12 percent (or 12 "points"), but a quarter of that is usually given directly to the record producer. From your remaining 9 points, the record company typically deducts 25 percent for "packaging" and another 15 percent for "free goods," "breakage," and so on. This leaves you with an actual record royalty of 5.74 percent (or about 86¢ on a $15 CD), which you'll only receive if the record company manages to recoup your advance plus all applicable marketing-related expenditures from your royalties at such a piddling rate. In other words, in order for you to recoup a typical record-deal advance of $175,000, plus the (easily) $500,000 spent on your behalf for applicable marketing-related activities, you'd have to sell 784,884 records. In other *other* words, even if you end up selling 784,883 records, you won't see another dime from your record company. (Keep in mind that only about 10 percent of all records released by major labels each year sell more than 10,000 copies.)

Mechanical royalties are the fee the record company pays you as the songwriter for the right to sell recorded versions of your songs. These royalties are typically based on the statutory rate (set by Congress) for the year in which the record is released—in 1995, 6.6¢ per song. In theory, this means that for an eleven-song record like *Cockamamie,* the record company should be giving you 72.6¢ per record sold. However, it's standard (if mysterious) practice for the record company to get you to agree to be paid 75 percent of the current statutory rate on a maximum of ten songs per record (regardless of the actual number), which reduces the mechanical royalty to 49.5¢ per record sold. This means that from a theoretical sale of 10,000 records (the most likely scenario), you'd (as the songwriter) receive $4,950 from the record company in mechanical royalties.

Now, if you *didn't* have a publishing deal, you'd get to pocket that $4,950 (less your team's commissions). But you're me, so you *do* have (or will have) a publishing deal for which you've received an advance, which must be recouped before you can pocket dime one of said mechanical royalties. Your mechanical royalties are split 25/75 with your publishing company in the following way: 25 percent of your mechanical royalties (or 12.375¢ per record sold) is considered the publishing company's and goes directly into their pocket, while 75 percent (or 37.125¢ per record sold) is considered yours but is collected by the publishing company until they've recouped your advance. So say your publishing advance is also $175,000. To recoup this advance through mechanical royalties alone, you'd have to sell 471,381 records.

In reality, the publishing company also recoups your publishing advance by taking half of your *performance* royalties, which are simply the fees paid by anyone who's using your music to enhance their business. These royalties are tracked, collected, and distributed to you by performing rights organizations, which make licensing deals with everyone from radio stations to restaurants to jukebox businesses. Theoretically, performance royalties are based on the combination of the actual number of ears hearing your music and the money being earned by whoever is using your music. In reality, it's impossible to know exactly how many people are hearing your songs. Therefore, performance royalties are determined by a complicated mishmash of guesstimations, taking into account where, when, and how your music is being used. What it all comes down to is this: If you have a top-10 hit, you might receive $500,000 in performance royalties. If you have a minor, short-lived hit, you might receive $15,000. If you get a song used, say, in a commercial or as a sitcom theme, you might be raking in the dough without ever getting your song on the radio. Short of these scenarios, you ain't gonna see much of anything at all.

Your performance royalties are split 50/50 with your publishing company in the following way: Your publishing company pockets 25 percent of these royalties and puts their other 25 percent toward recouping your advance, while you get to keep your 50 percent from the get-go (less commissions).

In the end, if you ever recoup at your record company, you'll begin receiving about 5.74 percent of the SRLP of each record sold (less commissions), while your record company, the distributor, the retailer, and your producer receive the remaining 94.26 percent of the same. If you ever recoup your publishing advance, you'll be able to keep 75 percent of your mechanical and performance royalties (less commissions), while your publishing company pockets the other 25 percent.

"So, in a way," I say, "the higher the advances the companies offer, the more confidence they're showing in the artist's ability to sell records."

"Pretty much," says Guy.

"But on a practical level, if I understand this right, the whole advance thing is just them giving you money now so they can have a piece of the pie later, right?"

"Right," says Guy. "A big piece of the pie later."

"But if it's just your money anyway, what difference does the initial advance make?"

"It makes a big difference. First of all, cash you have in your hand now is better than theoretical cash you may never get later. And the bigger your record advance, the better your chance of having some money left over after you've paid for the actual making of your record. Also, the more money the record company advances you, the more likely the company will be to spend more time and money on trying to make you successful."

"But the more money the record company spends on you, the more money you owe, the less likely it is that you'll ever recoup."

"You're thinking too small," says Guy. "The way it really works is the more money they spend on you, the more likely it'll be that you'll cut through in the marketplace and really begin to sell records, at which point everyone will begin to make some real money."

"Like Michael Jackson," I say.

Guy laughs. "Well, he's an extreme example, but sure. Here's the thing. There are a lot of facets to every record deal. The advance is just a part of the negotiation. If this turns into a full-blown bidding war, you're gonna be getting way more than twelve points on the record. Neil's gonna be trying to get you all kinds of things."

"Like?"

"Like full rate instead of three-quarter rate on your mechanicals. Like guaranteed tour support and marketing funds. Like negotiating to make some costs only half- or nonrecoupable."

"You're kinda sexy when you talk like that," I say.

Guy smiles. "I am?" he says.

"Yeah," I say.

"Recoupable," says Guy. "Negotiable. Marketable. Mechanicable."

Beeeep. "Jen. It's Neil. So. I was just wondering. Can you say bidding war? I love it! *Love* it! Call me, okay?" *Beeeep.*

It's finally Christmas and my phone stops ringing for a few days. Extensive and complicated holiday baskets keep appearing at my door from everyone and their brother in the music business. I get a holiday "bucket" from local rock station WBCN, filled with green and red M&Ms and a gigantic canister of white Tic Tacs.

Guy keeps telling me to relax, to try to enjoy this vacation from all the craziness. But every time he kisses me or hugs me or even smiles in my direction, Buck's face flashes through my mind and I get mad at Guy for reasons I make up on the spot.

Just before New Year's, I throw a party. It's my birthday, but I don't tell anybody. It was two years ago today that I lost my luggage and my life was full of shit. And now here I am, 730 days later, getting more attention from the music industry than anyone really deserves to get.

The party is an all-you-can-eat sushi dinner, my treat, and everyone is there. Buck and Laura and Robby, some of the Flint Raft guys and some of Shineaway, and tons of other people. Even Tim and my mom. We meet at my favorite restaurant downtown, where Guy and I only go once a year because it's so expensive.

We stuff ourselves into one of those private rooms where you sit without your shoes in a hole in the floor and I start ordering: four "Pleasure Extreme Boats" (just sashimi), six "Rock 'n' Roll Boats" (just sushi), and order upon order of tempura, gyoza, oshitashi, edamame. Everyone's toasting everything and downing sake bombs, which are basically boilermakers with sake instead of whiskey.

I'm sitting in the middle of the table between Teddy Z. and my mom, and Guy is down at the far end, laughing it up with a bunch of our friends. And even though everyone's leaning toward Guy like they always do, I can feel them staring at me when they think I'm not looking.

At the other end of the table, Robby is sitting next to Tim, who's next to Laura, who's next to Buck.

Buck smiles at me.

I smile back.

He shrugs.

I shrug.

He smiles.

I smile.

My mom taps her glass with her chopsticks. "Jen," she says, and motions the table to settle down. "Well," she says, and she winks at me. "You did it. You hung in there for, what has it been? Seven years? Eight? Whoo. A long time. And now, finally." She picks up her white wine with ice cubes in it and holds it in the air. "Go get 'em," she says, and I feel like a ball in the sky, everything still and quiet below, my friends, my family, watching me disappear into the sun.

Then, "Way to go, Jen!" says Tim, and everyone begins dropping more sake into more beer, laughing, raising glasses. "Go get 'em," everyone's saying. "Congratulations! To *Cockamamie*! Good job! Great record! Only a matter of time! Only a matter of timing! This is rockin'!" With every new toast comes another drink, and with every drink I feel smaller and smaller and farther and farther away. I know I should make a toast too, but I don't know what to say.

"To the good old days" is what I say.

"*Good* old days?" says Tim.

"Jen," says Guy. "Easy with the morbidity."

"Morbidity?" says Teddy Z.

"Morbibity?" says Robby.

"To more morbibity!" says Buck.

"Hey, Harvey!" says Guy.

Everyone turns toward the door and it's Harvey, one of my old drummers, showing up with a gift—a mechanical parrot on a perch. There's a little tape recorder in the thing's head that lets you record whatever you want into its beak. So everyone begins passing the parrot around, saying *Merry Christmas! Happy New Year! Go, Jen! Thanks for dinner, Jen!* By the time the parrot gets to me, I try to record "I'm really drunk," but it doesn't take. Instead, it just plays back the last thing recorded into its beak, which is "Jen's a lucky dog."

Jen's a *lucky* dog?

Suddenly, Buck's fingers are around the back of my neck. "Nice parrot," he says, and he kisses me on the cheek.

Four sake bombs later, I awake with my head on my knees in the bathroom and someone knocking on the stall door.

"You okay?"

It's Laura.

"Fine," I manage to say. "Thanks."

"You sure?"

"Positive," I say.

I wait to hear the outer bathroom door click shut before I retch into the toilet.

By the time I get back to the table, the party is breaking up and I tell myself that nobody's really noticed how drunk I am, and even if they have it doesn't matter, because I'm no longer me.

FIVE

★

"Ibth thith a cooooookie?" says Buck.

Robby's cracking up, tears in his eyes. "Lave me a-looooooooone!"

We're up in first class, snuggled beneath blankets, munching on steaming-hot chocolate chip cookies while we watch the in-flight movie. Buck and I are together on the left; Robby's across the aisle. Beneath the blankets, Buck's hand slips into mine.

I know I shouldn't be doing this. I should never have accepted the second and then the third sickly sweet mimosa from the flight attendant, even though each has hit the spot as only perfectly timed alcohol can. I should be poring over my notes about the people we're going to be meeting in just a few hours. Or I should at least be catching up on my sleep, or reading, or thinking, anything instead of what I'm doing, which is laughing. Buck and Robby are cracking wise about *Nell,* in which Jodie Foster plays a jungle girl Liam Neeson falls in love with and tries to civilize. Even in my this-is-the-life stupor, with Buck's constant thumb on the back of my hand, I can't help but notice the unfortunate affinity between me and Nell, who's been thrust into a strange land where she doesn't even know how to talk.

"Thooz go on my fet?" says Buck.

"I want *new* thooz," says Robby.

When the stewardess comes by with yet another round of drinks, she asks us what we'll be doing in L.A.

"We're going to pick up our record deal," says Buck, rubbing his chin with his hand as if he's about to give a long interview.

"Going to be big rock stars, huh?" smiles the stewardess.

"Well, *she's* going to be," says Robby, pointing at me. "We're just tagging along."

"That's right," says Buck. "Don't mind us. We're just pieces of shit."

By the baggage claim, a guy in a black jacket and cap is holding a piece of cardboard with my name on it. He leads us out to a shiny, sprawling black limo and tells us he'll be taking us around during our stay.

"This'll do," says Buck, patting the top of the car with his hand. "I think I can ride in this." Inside, he goes straight for the minibar.

"We have meetings today, you know," I say, sounding like a schoolmarm even to myself.

"Oh, good to know, boss. I thought we were just here to like, whistle Dixie," says Buck. He grabs a Coke.

Robby's smiling, absent-mindedly flicking the electric door lock back and forth, locking and unlocking the doors with a click-click-click. He turns to me. "This is very cool," he says.

Buck is thumbing through a fat, glossy magazine when he says, "Holy shit" and points to a page. I lean over and read, . . . *and who's in Lala land this week to meet with the big wigs? None other than Beantown's own Jennifer Trynin* . . .

I rip the magazine out of Buck's hand, flip to the cover, then back to the column.

"This is *Hits,*" I say. "This is that chick Ivana's column. Holy shit!"

"Here you are again," says Robby, holding open another *Hits* magazine right under my nose.

. . . *Trynin and her clan are being wooed coast to coast* . . .

"And here!" says Buck, holding open another issue and then another and then one more.

I sit back against the seat, feeling like someone just threw a bucket of water on me.

Buck and Robby are laughing and high-fiving each other, singsonging, "We're gonna get a record deal, we're gonna get a record deal."

"Whaat eeth thees ting wey cull da mooooozik bidineth?" says Buck, moving his fingers as if he's handling money.

★

We're staying at The Mondrian, which is made of shiny black marble with sparkles in it. We're each getting our own suite, and when I put my credit card on the counter for the concierge, he tells me it's all being taken care of.

"Everything?" I say.

"Everything," he says.

"Sweet," says Robby.

"Since when do you say 'sweet'?" says Buck.

When I get to my room, there are flower arrangements and bowls of fruit from all kinds of record companies, and a faxed itinerary from Neil's office listing all the meetings we'll be having during our stay.

The message light on the phone is blinking with *Hey there!*

messages from Ivana, Drake, Lola, Preppy Boy, and then Johnny, telling me how he won't be there for the Almo meeting because he's in England, but how Jerry Moss, the head of Almo, loves my record and can't wait to meet me.

"Just be your charming self, Princess," he says.

★

We meet with Irving Azoff, the president of Giant Records, about whom people seem to delight in telling me scary things. How Irving once put a snake in some guy's briefcase. How Irving is the guy who said, "I never met an asshole in the record business I didn't like." How Irving has managed some "little bands," like the Eagles. Irving's nickname? The Poison Dwarf.

Having heard all this, when we walk through the door I'm not surprised to discover that he's short, but I *am* surprised when he gives us a big smile and claps his hands together, saying, "Oh goody."

Irving tells me how impressed he is with my entrepreneurial spirit and that he's been thinking about offering me something much more ingenious than a "regular old record deal," that he's prepared to make Squint a "subcontractor" of Giant—to enter into what would be, in essence, a licensing deal, thereby leaving me at the helm of "my company."

All I can think of is my answering machine and my mailer, my little rubber stamp with the Squint Records return address.

At Interscope, we follow ski-bunny Lance down a hallway as he takes swipes at the carpet with a golf club. We have an awkward meeting with the two guys who run the place, who keep asking us questions that reveal they don't know dick about me or my record.

Who plays the guitar?

Who writes the music?

I can't help but get the feeling that the only reason Interscope's coming after me is that everyone else is, and that's just the kind of guys they are.

———

Later, we're sitting jammed around tables in the back of some club with Ivana and a bunch of her friends, all of whom seem to work in show business of one kind or another. They're all dressed very trendy in cords, T-shirts, jeans jackets, and big shoes. They look pretty much like the same kinds of scenesters back east except with better skin and more precise color coordination. And whether they work as stylists or grips or video directors, what they all want me to know is that *really* they have a band and are just wondering if we're playing in L.A. anytime soon and can they open for us.

Billy from Gimmee shows up and everyone knows him. He's short and stocky, in green work pants and a gray T-shirt. He tells me for the millionth time how he's really worried about me, how he's seen this kind of shit go down before, how the second a major gets ahold of us, they're just going to do their "usual major label asshole move" by "jumping the gun" and "slamming" one of my songs onto commercial radio before they've built up my "true fan base" on the indie scene.

"Like they did with 'Seether,' that Veruca Salt song," says Billy. "Man oh holy fuckin' man, was it everywhere or what? And I'm just sayin' the *last* thing you wanna do is lose your cred before it's firmly established. Veruca Salt totally sank in that arena and it's really burnin' 'em, cuz the *true* fans don't take to that kinda super-quick jumpin' ship to the majors. You gotta be keepin' your disc on an indie for as long as possible, building your thing word-of-mouth, you know, grass roots. So I was thinking that we could put you on Sad Sack—"

"Sad Sack?"

"That's our new label. You know, so we could be gettin' your record to all the coolest indie stores—stores like *our* store—"

"You guys have a record store too? *And* a label *and* you do promotion?"

"We're also a floor wax," says Billy. "We just want the kids to be able to buy your record while it's still playin' on their fave college stations, cuz that way, when *Cockamamie* finally hits the commercial airwaves for real, the kids'll be okay with it cuz they'll feel like they discovered you for themselves first, you know? And, so, like, you can avoid the Seether Syndrome cuz the overall impression'll be that you started out right, you know, paid your dues and everything."

"But I *have* paid my dues."

"Well, yeah. But just for insurance, we think it'd totally be in your best interest to have your official indie release be on Sad Sack, instead of Squint, cuz like Sad Sack has a track record."

"A track record with what?" I say.

"Oh, you know, with some cool stuff, like Rabbitting and Cake Savvy."

"Who?"

"They're still building," says Billy.

"How'd you even know I was gonna be in this bar?" I say.

"Scary, isn't it?" says Billy.

After I don't know how many drinks, a bunch of us end up back in Buck's suite. Immediately, everyone's in the minibar, grabbing beers and Toblerone bars and cans of nuts. I sneak out to the terrace for a smoke, because I just can't talk about bands anymore.

The night is warm and twinkling with the city lights below. I can almost see the faces of all the people who I believe are thinking of little else besides me, and it's like I'm being lit up by a searchlight. But then comes the nagging feeling, the little-voice feeling, telling me that it's only a matter of time before someone kicks me over like a bucket.

When I go back inside, it's just Buck sitting there watching TV. I sit down next to him.

"Everybody split?" I say.

"Finally," says Buck.

"Where's Robby?"

"I don't know," he says. "I think he went to make a phone call or something."

"The to-be-ex?"

"Probably."

"It's kinda late to be calling, isn't it?"

Buck shrugs.

"I'm exhausted," I say, letting my head fall onto the back of the couch.

"I guess it's just you and me, kid," says Buck, and I feel his hand on my leg, then on my arm, and as many times as I've promised myself I wouldn't do this anymore, we begin to kiss. Then my eyes go open for a second and I can see out the big glass door leading to the terrace and across the way into the glowing stairwell on the other side of the hotel where someone is standing, looking out. When I close my eyes again, the person in the stairwell looks like Robby.

A few moments later, there's a knock on the door and I push Buck away.

"Settle down, Jesus," he says.

"Who is it?" I yell.

"It's Robby."

"Fuck," I say.

"What's the matter with you?" says Buck.

It must have been Robby in the stairwell. Now he's going to quit the band and tell Guy about me and Buck kissing, and then Guy will leave me and my whole life will come crashing down.

I open the door and Robby's standing there, looking upset and staring at me funny.

Fuck fuck fuck!

> *Dear God,*
> *If you let me out of this one, I'll never kiss Buck again.*
> *Sincerely,*

"Are you okay?" I say.

Robby gets teary and looks at the ground.

> *P.S.: And I'll cut down on the smoking, too.*

My heart is pounding.

"It's just that," says Robby, looking back up at me, "I had to call her. I know I shouldn't have, but I did, and it really sucked."

I let out the breath I didn't know I was holding. "I'm sorry," I say.

"That's rough," says Buck. "Come on in. Have a seat."

"Naah. I'm gonna hit the hay. I just wanted to apologize to you guys for being such a drag sometimes."

"You're never a drag," I say.

"I mean, on the one hand, this is like the greatest thing in the world with you guys and everything. But on the other, my whole life's kinda falling apart."

"Yeah," I say. "Girls. You know. Can't live with 'em—"

"—can't shoot 'em," says Buck.

All I know is that I'm suddenly awake, with my heart pounding. I'm terrified, cold, and confused. Not about where I am—I'm all too aware of exactly where I am: in Buck's room with him asleep next to me, both of us in our clothes on top of the still-made bed that I wouldn't get into with him. It's 4 A.M.

I sit up.

"What's the matter?" says Buck, half asleep.

"I gotta go," I say, swinging my feet to the floor, rubbing my face.

"No, stay," he says, his fingers pulling at my sweater.

"I can't," I say, standing up, yanking my sweater out of his hand. Buck opens his eyes. "What's your problem?"

"I gotta go back to my room."

"Why?"

"Just cuz," I say, grabbing my jacket from the chair.

"What? Someone's gonna find out?"

"I guess," I say, but that's not the only reason I have to get the hell out of here. It's like the walls are trembling, closing in on me, like the building is about to crack and fall into a smoking heap, crushing me alive. This is what can happen to you in L.A.

Back in my room, I lie down on my own still-made bed and stare at the ceiling with its beige stucco swirling around a light in the middle like a nipple. I imagine Guy and Ranger snuggled in our bed and all I can think about is how long it would take for me to walk home.

★

Beep. Beep. Beep. Beep.

I hit the clock until it stops beeping. The sun is shining through the windows. When I realize I'm still dressed and on top of the covers,

I remember last night, and a feeling of doom washes through me.

The phone rings on the night table.

"Hello?"

"You're not dead," says Buck. "Just checking."

"Thanks," I say.

"What the hell was up with you last night?"

"I don't know," I say. "I just, you know. I—"

Beep. Beep. Beep. Beep.

I hit the clock again. "I don't know how to fucking shut this thing off," I say. "Hey, could you give Robby a call and make sure he's up?"

"Whatever you say, boss," says Buck.

The bathroom is huge and gold, with tons of little lotions and millions of towels and a phone on the wall above the toilet. The shower is enclosed in glass with a marble ledge where you can sit.

The phone above the toilet rings and it's Buck again, asking for Robby's room number.

In the shower, I make the water hot as hell.

I'm rubbing my hair dry with one of the millions of towels when the phone rings again.

"What now?" I say, still rubbing my hair.

"Oh. Umm, I'm looking for Jennifer Trynin," says a man with a reedy voice, New York-y, slightly whiny.

"Oh. Sorry. I thought you were—anyway, this is Jen," I say.

"Oh good. This is Danny Goldberg."

I drop my towel. My heart begins to pound. "Danny Goldberg?"

"From Warner Brothers," he says. "I'm not disturbing you, am I? I didn't wake you, did I?"

"No, no. I'm—" I say, looking around. "I'm just drinking coffee."

"Well, I wanted to check in and see how you're doing. You got a minute?" he says.

"Absolutely," I say, because for Danny Goldberg, I got all the minutes.

"Good," he says. "Do you know who I am? Did Neil tell you about me?"

"Yeah," I say. "Of course."

"Good. Okay. Well, I'm just a little concerned, you know, that maybe *you're* a little concerned about what's going on with Warner Brothers. I mean, everyone knows it's a little crazy over there these days with all the changes and reconfiguring, but everything's gonna settle down soon and it'll all be fine. I just want you to know that if you *do* end up wanting to work with me, with us, you've got nothing to worry about."

"I'm not worried," I say, and I'm not. So the famous Mo-and-Lenny are history. What do I know from Mo-and-Lenny anyway? All I know is that Danny Goldberg is the new commander-in-chief and that he used to manage Nirvana and that any connection with Nirvana is a friend of mine.

"Well, good. I'm really glad to hear that. Because, it's just that, you know, I used to be a manager," he says.

"I know," I say.

"Yeah," he says, like he knows everyone knows. "And I really miss it. I miss that personal connection, you know? That's really what's it's all about for me, and ever since Kurt died—"

"Yeah," I say. "I'm really sorry about that. Everyone's sorry."

"Yeah," he says. "Thanks. But I love your record. It's really a great record, and I was just thinking how if you go with Warner Brothers, that maybe I'd have a chance to have another relationship like I had with Kurt, you know, with you."

I'm staring at my thighs, my stomach, my bellybutton. "Wow. I don't know what to say."

"You don't have to say anything," he says. "You just relax. Take a deep breath. You've already done the hard part. Now I can only hope you'll let me help you."

"Thanks," I say.

"So I'll see you later," says Danny Goldberg.

"Absolutely," I say. "Three o'clock, right?" As if this appointment isn't burned into my skull like a cross.

"Three o'clock," he says. "Looking forward."

We hang up.

The bathroom hums quietly with the water flowing through the building. Steam is still fogging up the room. I stand and stare at myself in the mirror. I look soft and smooth, with everything I've ever doubted about myself blurred to perfection.

We meet Drake and his boss for breakfast at our hotel. They ride in our limo with us over to the A&M offices, which are housed in this little Seven Dwarfs–like town, with little walkways and colorful signs. We meet A&M's president in his big gray office with big gray furniture. He asks Drake and his boss to wait outside, which makes me feel weird and bad. Then he goes on and on about "other female singer-songwriters" and "the waves" they're making. The room smells like tomato sauce.

Warner Bros. is in Burbank, about which I know nothing except that a lot of TV game shows are brought to you live from there.

The Warner Bros. building looks like a ski lodge, with wide front steps, where Lola and Howdy Doody are sitting. They stand when they see us, yelling "Yay!" and clapping their hands.

Lola takes us to meet the head of radio promotion, whose office is filled with basketball jerseys, basketballs, and pictures of basketball players.

"I'm a nut," says the head of radio promotion, "but you can call me Wags."

"Wags?" I say.

"It's a long story," he says. Everyone sits and for a while, Wags and Buck go back and forth about all things basketball, until Wags turns to me and says, "But we're here to talk about *you!*" and claps his hands together. Then he cups his chin in his hands. "How do you write music?" he says.

You'd think I'd love this question, but you'd be wrong. How do I write music? I sit down with my guitar and screw around until something sounds remotely intriguing which I try not to forget before I push "record" on my tape player and play it again.

"Oh, you know, I shoot a little heroin and take it from there,"

I say, like I always say, as if I have any idea what I'm talking about. Not only have I never done heroin, but I don't even know if it's a solid or a liquid or a powder or what. I thought you could only shoot it, but then I saw people on TV "snorting smack" and I'm like, *Is that heroin?* but I've never asked because I'd rather die stupid in a ditch than be revealed for the sheltered little fuck that I am.

"You're kidding, right?" says Wags. "Because drugs are nothing to fool around with."

Lola is leaning in the doorway with her arms crossed, smiling at me. Something about her makes me feel calm.

Next, we meet this guy with Einstein hair who's sitting behind a desk on which there's a Rubik's Cube, a Slinky, and a deck of cards. He seems irritated as he explains that he does A&R, like Lola, and that if we end up signing there, she's asked him to look out for us at The Building since she lives on the East Coast. Then he plays us a cut off a CD by some band called YouAmI, who're from some city where music is much more *real* than it is in L.A. Or New York. Or Boston.

Out in the hallway, Lola says how much Einstein loves us, that it's just not his style to come out "guns ablazing." She tells me not to be afraid of him.

"Do I seem afraid?" I say.

"A little," she says.

I excuse myself to go to the bathroom, not because I have to go but because I need a break. But Lola tags along, so instead of getting a moment to myself, I'm sitting on the toilet in a stall making small talk with my eyes shut, trying to conjure images of water fountains, oceans, other people peeing.

Next is lunch, and we all head down the street and take a left into "The Lot," where we're suddenly in the middle of someone's idea of a small town circa 1950. A white cart goes whizzing by with a guy in the passenger seat who looks like he just got his head blown off. There's blood all over him, and bandages. He waves to us, yelling, "Pizza with everything!"

We gather around a table in the nicest cafeteria I've ever seen. Everything is white and clean and the food looks great: poached salmon, poached eggs, all kinds of sandwiches on fancy breads. The place is bustling and everyone looks familiar. Like that guy over there in the surgeon's smock. Or that pretty woman sipping soup. All of a sudden I realize that the entire cast of *ER* is at the next table. And over there is that mean guy from all the cop shows. And that old lady eating a hamburger—wasn't she just raped and pillaged on *NYPD Blue*?

After lunch, we head back to The Building for a meeting with Head Honcho, the new GM with the 70s hair, who's sitting behind a big desk in a sunny office. He gets up and hugs each of us, then sits back behind his desk. "So," he says, smiling at us. "I really loved your show at the Front Mode."

"The Frontload," I say.

"I like the Front Mode better," says Buck.

Hanging behind Head Honcho's desk are a bunch of gold and platinum records in frames with A&M logos on them.

"What's with the A&M logos?" I say.

"That's where I used to be," says Head Honcho. "I was director of marketing. I just started here a few months ago. Just before Mo-and-Lenny left."

"Are people around here happy that Mo-and-Lenny left?" I say, as if I have any idea what I'm talking about.

"Happy?" says Head Honcho. "I can't say anyone's particularly happy about it, no."

"Then why'd they leave?"

"It's a long story," he says. "Nothing for you to worry about. When," he smiles at me, "*when* you come here, you'll be the first act signed under the new regime. Great, right? Doesn't that sound great?"

Finally, Lola leads us into a big room with nothing in it but a bare desk and a few chairs. There are a bunch of boxes piled in a corner. Finally, Danny Goldberg comes bounding in the door in khakis and an untucked button-down shirt, his hair everywhere. He plunks his bursting briefcase on top of the desk and doesn't sit down.

"Hey," he says, sounding winded. "How you guys doing?"

"Fine," we say.

"Like my new office?" he says.

"Sure," we say.

He apologizes for being late, for not being able to stay, and for how crazy everything is for him right now. "But don't worry," he says. "We're gonna do right by you guys. You're gonna be at the top of the line, the head of the line, and, you know, we'll talk more when I'm a little more settled in." He tries to close his briefcase, apologizing for the plane he has to catch, but all I'm thinking is, *Me and Danny Goldberg. We'll talk. Later. There'll be plenty of time.*

We meet Preppy Boy at the sprawling Geffen building, where everything is white, and behind every reception desk is a person in his or her twenties, well-coifed and smartly dressed. There are posters of the Geffen bands everywhere: Aerosmith, Guns N' Roses, Sonic Youth, Beck, Soundgarden, Hole, Nirvana. I still can't believe these guys want to sign me.

"Everyone can't w-wait to m-meet you," says Preppy Boy, as he leads us into a small room jammed with a million people—the entire marketing staff, all the radio promo guys, plus various A&R people. They tell us how much they love the record, how cool we are, how much we'll love being part of the Geffen family (because that's what they're like, they're like a family).

Preppy Boy leads us down another long hallway for our meeting with EdR, the president of Geffen, the guy who's going to buy me new tits. Outside EdR's office is a poster of another Geffen band, Veruca Salt, the Seether-Syndrome band.

EdR is sitting behind his desk with me in a chair to his left and Buck and Robby slouching on a couch to his right. He doesn't look at them.

"You already know everyone here loves your record," he says, "and the radio guys are raring to go with some of your songs, especially that 'Feelin' Good' song. That thing could really go like *go.*"

"God, thanks," I say. "And I'm really glad that you guys are so psyched about the record, but I don't know. I mean, we don't really want to be that way, like one of those bands that's ramming their music down people's throats, you know what I mean?"

EdR leans forward, puts his elbows on his desk, clasps his hands, and makes a teepee with his fingers. "Do I know what you mean?" he says. "Yeah," he says. "I know exactly what you mean."

"Good," I say, "because it's really important to us that this whole thing unfolds naturally, like grass roots. We just don't want the big push."

EdR sits back in his big chair and takes a deep breath. "Listen," he says. "I'm a little confused. As far as I've been led to believe, you're asking for a lot. A lot of money. Complete artistic freedom. All kinds of contractual shit. You want *us* to do the dance, but *you* don't wanna do the dance. And I gotta tell you, that's not gonna fly with me. I don't care who you are or who wants to sign you, but if you sign here, we're gonna do what we think gives us our best shot. Capisce?"

"But I—"

"Because what have you proven so far? Very little actually. We're taking a big gamble on you and I gotta tell you that I don't appreciate your attitude, which is, well, how about unrealistic. I don't know what kind of smoke the other labels are blowing at you, but I'm not gonna do that. Slow build and grass roots and indie-shmindie. That's nice. But I run a business here and I don't know what it is with you people. The whole grunge thing."

"We're not grunge," I say.

"Whatever. You know what I'm talking about."

Back in the limo, Buck slides his hand under my butt. I can't get EdR's voice out of my head. *Indie-shmindie. Indie-shmindie.* I'm feeling sick and tired, from too little food, from too much Buck, and maybe most of all from my own indie-shmindie shenanigans.

I'm trying to pay attention during our meeting with Jerry Moss (the old *M* of A&M, and the current *mo* of Almo), but I'm powering down.

He's tall and slender, with thick white hair and a broad smile. He speaks slowly, as if he doesn't want to scare us, offering us tall glasses of iced tea, as the late-day California light washes through the room like film noir.

It's finally time for dinner and we head to The Ivy to meet with some older manager guy who has a gold pinkie ring with a diamond in it. His longish gray hair is matted to his skull with some type of product that's making my eyes water. Or maybe it's his aftershave that's making me weak—the aftershave I can see him reaching for in his splendid bathroom with marble everything and brushed nickel faucets, steam still billowing from his shower, as he stands with a towel wrapped around his big bald stomach, slamming the tip of the aftershave bottle into the center of his fat palm, rubbing his hands together, inspecting the pale mottle of his skin in the mirror, then smack smack smack goes the aftershave against his cheeks, one of which is leaning into my ear at this very moment.

"Sit here," he says, motioning toward the table, his fat palm on my shoulder. "Sit next to me."

The Viper Room. Outside, everything is black. Black walls. Black canopy. Black door. Black. Johnny Depp owns it and River Phoenix died outside of it. While we're waiting in line to get in, I look up and down the street, where tons of people are milling around in suede jackets and cool shoes. I have no idea where we are or how I'd get back to the hotel, even if my life depended on it. If River Phoenix could die out here on the sidewalk, so can I. I flick Buck on the arm.

"Hey," I say.

"Hey," he says.

Inside, it's also completely black, but otherwise, it's just another club. There are a bunch of chicks onstage, scantily clad, singing and doing dance moves to backing tapes booming through the house system. They look like men in drag.

We're here with Drake, who's beginning to wear me out. He wants to know how we think the A&M meeting went, how our other meetings are going, if there are any questions he can answer, if we'd like more drinks.

"Yes to more drinks," says Robby.

Buck slides his arm around my back in the dark. "Jen's dead," he whispers in my ear.

I push him away. "Shut up! Why the fuck did you say that?"

"Hey," says Robby. "I think I just saw Johnny Depp."

★

I'm back in New York at Neil's office.

"So," says Neil. "I just got off the phone with BigWig and the thing is, he says he's not happy with your meeting there this morning, and he's wondering if maybe you guys could come by one more time before you leave town. Like maybe at the end of the day today."

"What?" I say.

"I know, but I swear, he's going crazy. He keeps feeling like you're not really *getting* the company, you know?"

"Neil. I swear. I *get* the company. And anyway, I have that meeting with Atlantic."

"Maybe you could just swing by Columbia afterwards."

"I can't."

"But—"

"No."

"So whaddaya want me to tell him?"

"What do I need, a fucking note from my mother?"

Neil keeps tapping what looks like a really expensive pen on his desk.

"Tell him it's the weather," I say.

Tap tap tap.

I hook up with Buck and Robby, and we spend the next few hours meeting with managers all over the city who work with bands like The Cranberries, Counting Crows, Soul Coughing.

"Bands that begin with C," says Robby.

I tell the manager of Soul Asylum how much I like their song "Fast Car."

"What?" he says.

"I mean 'Fast Train,'" I say.

"You mean 'Runaway Train,'" he says.

"Yeah, 'Runaway Train.'"

Buck looks at me like I'm an idiot.

We end up at the Atlantic offices for our meeting with Sarah and Lathem and the president of Atlantic, who looks like an older Epstein from *Welcome Back, Kotter.* Then we pile into a limo with Sarah and Lathem and head for some crowded club where some "really super-cool band" is playing really super loud. Sarah pushes a fifty into my hand and tells us to get drinks while she and Lathem go and find us a table in the back. Buck grabs the fifty, and he and Robby head for the bar.

"Well hello there," says a chick sitting slumped on a bench against the wall with a million bobby pins in her hair, making it stick out like a scarecrow. "Long time no see."

She looks familiar, or at least I'm telling myself she does. "Oh!" I say. "Hi!"

She leans into her friend and points at me, saying, "This is the chick I was telling you about." The friend gives a weak smile.

"Remember me this time?" says the chick.

I'm trying to smile as my mind is running through faces and names like flashcards. Alice? Barbara? Cathy? Dorothy? The chick is tapping her foot. Finally, "Of course I remember you," I say.

"So what's my name?" she says.

My right big toe begins to cramp.

"Cheryl," she says, and writes her name in the air. "Let's see," she says, "I met you at Brownie's and then saw you again at Ludlow and twice up in Boston. MCA? Ringing any bells?"

Right. Cheryl. From MCA. The company that dropped out a while ago because, according to Neil, they felt they couldn't compete.

"Hey," I say. "I'm sorry. I really do remember you. It's just, you know, all these new people. It's been weird."

Cheryl hits her friend on the arm, saying, "Yeah, it must be really rough." Her friend rolls her eyes.

Buck's back and hands me a beer.

"And here's the boyfriend," says Cheryl.

"Whoaaaa," says Buck. "I'm no boyfriend. Just a friendly bass player at your service."

"Hey you losers," yells Sarah from the tables in the back where she and Lathem are waving us over.

Cheryl cranes her neck to see who's calling to us, then cups her hand around her friend's ear and whispers something. The friend looks at me, then back at the floor. "Whatever," she says.

Buck and Robby head over to the table. I decide to hit the bathroom, and as I'm wending my way back to the table, I hear him.

"These guys are unfuckinbelievable!" he says. "Let's sign 'em up! Where's my pen?"

I duck down behind some girl, then peek out over her shoulder, where standing not five feet away are BigWig and Marketing Maven, who's next to Captain Talent, who's next to Philippe. Far as BigWig knows, I should be heading east on 84 right about now. But wait a minute. What the hell are they doing here drooling over some other band?

"Jennifer!" yells BigWig.

Shit. For a few irrational moments, I stay crouched behind the girl, eyes shut.

"Jennifer!" says BigWig again, and I open my eyes and stand up straight. "I thought you went back this afternoon." The entire BigWig posse is staring at me.

"Well, that was the plan," I say.

"The weather and everything," says BigWig.

"Exactly. The report was for, you know, snow, and we wanted to beat it back but then we were running late and—but what a coincidence that we're all here, right?"

"Sitting over there?" says Philippe, cocking his head toward the table where Buck and Robby and Sarah and Lathem are suddenly yelling and laughing and slamming their fists on the table. "Switching teams in the last quarter, are we?"

★

I wake up with Ranger's tail on my lips.

"Hey," says Guy, standing in the doorway, holding roses. "Happy record release party."

"Oh no," I say. "That's tonight, isn't it."

Guy sits next to me on the bed and puts the roses down on my stomach. "Listen," he says, "I'm really sorry."

"About what?" I say.

"Just the way things have been. I know I've been really busy, and with you traveling all over the place all the time now, I know things are feeling a little distant. What I'm saying is that I can feel it too."

"Oh," I say.

"It's just that—" says Guy. He puts his hand on the rose stems. "It's just that, whatever's going on, you know, between us, I just want to see it through, you know? Whatever it is. Whatever's gonna happen, we can live through it, right? I can live through it. To get to the other side, I can live through it."

My throat clamps up. He knows. Does he know? He knows but he doesn't want to know.

I sit up. Hug Guy. Hard. Really hard.

A record release party is just a gig that you call your record release party in hopes that it will draw the attention of press people and the local radio stations. I'd booked this gig back in October before all the craziness started, as part of my plan for releasing *Cockamamie*. Back then I was still too concerned with my draw to risk competing with Christmas-type events, so we'd ended up pushing the gig all the way to the end of January. Who'd have guessed everything would be going so boffo?

The gig's at my favorite club, TT the Bear's, and by eight o'clock, big black limos line the street outside. The place is already packed with tons of friends and Tim and Dad and BB and just about everyone I've met in the entire music industry. My friend Gayle is scurrying around with a video camera on her shoulder and Neil's walking around the way Neil always walks around, which is like he owns the place. The joke throughout the club is that if a bomb went off, the record industry as we know it would cease to exist. The second part of the joke is how that wouldn't be the worst thing.

Tonight is the deadline for any labels who want in. This is the plan, according to Neil. As of tomorrow, I've got to narrow the list down, way down. Probably to my top three.

"Another festive shindig," says my father when I finally go to say hi. "Tell me," he says, "don't you think it's interesting that a man as small-statured as Irving would name his company Giant?"

"What the hell," says Mikey Dee, with his crazy grin and Marty Feldman eyes. Mikey's like Mr. Rock and Roll, a genuinely rabid fan of the local music scene. He's the guy you always see down front at your shows, air-drumming like a wildcat. He hosts a local radio show called "On the Town" and writes for the cool music rag *The Noise*. He was the first person of his ilk to give me and my music the time of day, and has been supporting me since my twelve-song cassette days. "I'm hearing you have like five label presidents here. Is that true?" he says.

"I don't know," I say. "Something like that."

"Fuckin' wow is all I can say," he says.

"Hey," I say, "remember that time I played that song at that cookout and you came up to me afterwards?"

"Of course," he says. "'Slab on a Rack,' right?"

"I can't believe you remember the name of that stupid song."

Mikey points to his head. "I'm insane is why I remember."

"Thanks for helping me," I say.

"Hey, you make the music. You don't need to thank me."

"No, I do need to thank you," I say. "You liked my music when no one liked it. You're one of the main reasons everything started going better for me around here."

"Oh, stop."

"I'm not kidding."

"Just don't forget me, okay? And that 'Better Than Nothing' song," says Mikey, winking at me, "that's the pick to hit. You can quote me."

By the time we take the stage, I'm drunk, but I figure so is everybody else, so fuck it. Cameras are flashing. Buck gives me a loud smooch on my cheek and says, "Take that!"

We start to play and everything feels ten times too fast but I just don't care. About four songs in, a bunch of guys begin pushing and yelling just in front of the stage right at my feet.

"Hey," says Buck. "Hey, come on!"

More pushing and more yelling until CRASH, a bottle shatters and then another, and I yell, "Hey, cut it out!" but really I'm like, Now *this* is what I've been talkin' about! People at *my* show being *loud* and *drunk* and *sick of it all*!

As we're playing the last song of the set, I open my eyes and look out at everyone. My family. My friends. Guy. All the industry people. Everyone lined up in rows. Like a class picture. Like it's the last day of school. Like it's good-bye.

"You're alive," says Guy. He tosses a videotape onto the bed. "Your record release party."

"That was fast."

"Gayle says she's sorry, the tape's a little fucked up. She was kinda drunk."

Ring-ring!

Beeeep. "Hey, girl! It's Billy here from your friendly Gimmees. So the first batch of discs went out to radio last week and it's goin' full-on gangbusters! We'll be gettin' you your reports in a couple days. And it's like time time *time* to focus in on our Sad Sack *thang,* okay? We don't want you screamin' out into the stratosphere without a lifeline, right? See ya." *Beeeep.*

"You told that guy to take a hike about your record coming out on Sad Sack, right?" says Guy.

"Only like a million times, but it's like he's deaf or something."

"You better watch out for those guys."

"And so now he wants me to supply them with five thousand *Cockamamies*—"

"*What?*"

"—to distribute through Sad Sack to a bunch of mom-and-pops."

"Balls of fucking *steel*," says Guy. "And they make a profit of *what* on every single CD *they* sell?"

"Well, we're talking about them reimbursing me for manufacturing and then splitting whatever profit there is."

"If you ever see one fucking dime from those scumbags, you can shoot me," says Guy.

I wait until Guy leaves for the studio before I call Neil and tell him it's down to Columbia, Warner Bros., and Geffen, just as everyone had been predicting.

I lie down on the couch with my record-release-party tape in the VCR and the remote in my hand, but I can't seem to push play.

My Squint line rings again.

Beeeep. "Hello, Princess."

I pick up the phone. "Hey," I say.

"Well knock me over with a fucking feather," says Johnny. "You picked up."

"Where were you last night?"

"What do you mean?"

"I had my stupid record release party and you didn't even show up."

"Of course I did."

"No you didn't."

"Well maybe you were just too busy flitting around like a debutante to notice poor li'l ol' me."

"You're so full of shit."

"So I hear today might be the day. Are we going to the prom or are you dumping me?"

"I don't know what I'm doing," I say. "Are you still gonna be my friend if I don't go with Almo?"

"Who says I'm your friend now?"

I'm staring at the TV between my fingers like I'm watching a horror movie. Without a light or a proper microphone, the images are dark and the sound is garbled, and the camera's tilting and dodging all over the place because I guess Gayle was drunk from the get-go.

"Say hi to Jen," she tells everyone, and everyone says, *Hi Jen, Congratulations Jen,* waving, smiling.

Gayle approaches a bunch of musicians sitting around a table and asks their names. *President Clinton,* says one. *O.J. Simpson. Kurt Cobain.* When she asks them why they're here, one of them says, *Free beer!* and the rest of them say, *Yeah, free beer.*

Neil and Irving Azoff are standing against the wall eating chicken wings. "Who're you guys?" asks Gayle. They look at each other and laugh. Neil says, "I'm a bloodsucker." Irving says, "I'm a bank." They laugh again.

The singer from Shineaway comes into the frame blowing a big bubble, which breaks when she laughs. She's standing next to Theo from Flint Raft. Gayle says, "Say hi to Jen," and Theo says, "Hello," while the Shineaway singer makes a silly face. "Hi Jen," she says, and sticks her tongue out.

"And who're you?" Gayle asks two guys.

"We're from Mercury Records," says one of them.

"And what're you doing here?"

"We're here because we think Jennifer's *great!*"

"Yeah," says the other guy. "What he said."

The camera darts to Guy's silhouette, with glaring lights behind him. Aimee's next to him. "I don't wanna be in the video," says Guy.

"You can watch me wait on line for the bathroom if you must," says Aimee.

Lola walks through the frame and Gayle says, "Hi, what's your—" but Lola's already gone.

The camera goes wobbling toward my dad and BB and Tim. My dad turns and smiles. Gayle says, "Wish Jen well," and my dad raises his glass. "Safe home, Jen," he says.

Buck and Robby fill the frame. Together they yell, "YOU GUYS WERE GREAT, BUT THE SOUND SYSTEM SUCKS!" Then they laugh.

"Hey," says Gayle. "Sing us a song."

"What should we sing?" says Buck.

"How about 'I Got You Babe'?"

Buck and Robby look at each other, then back at the camera, and begin singing, arms around each other, wrong lyrics. They stop after a few lines and take a bow.

Behind them, I can just make myself out, sitting in a chair against a wall, smoking a cigarette and looking at the floor.

Robby's voice is talking on my machine, sounding weirdly drunk and going on and on about something I can't understand. I pick up. He's calling from the hospital, delirious with painkillers, alternately laughing and crying as he explains how he was out partying with some friends and "wasn't even wasted" when he slipped on some ice. Then he tells me how bad the break is, how the cast goes from the tip of his toes to the top of his hip, but that he won't be bedridden for more than two months, three at the most, and that he's sure he'll be okay by the time we go on tour. He asks me to hold on, puts the receiver down, and for the first time in my life the sound of someone blowing his nose nearly breaks my heart.

I tell him not to worry, that we'll find a sub for the upcoming shows, and that we'll wait for his leg to heal before we head off on any kind of tour. No one has ever been so grateful to me in my whole life, which makes me feel good for about two seconds. By the third, I'm already feeling like a calculating scumbag. Because while there are many reasons I wouldn't simply replace Robby—including my fear that it would kill him, and my genuine affection for him—the biggest reason is that I'm afraid no one would even notice, thereby revealing me as the solo-artist-in-band's-clothes that I am.

Buck is in Mexico with Laura on a long-planned vacation. The day before he's due back, he calls me collect to say he misses me. I tell him about Robby's leg. Neither of us mentions that this means our next trip to L.A. will be alone.

I run into this guy Chase who used to be in some band with Buck. Chase asks me how it's going with Buck.
    "Fine," I say.
    "Hmm," says Chase. "He still with Laura?"
    I look at him. "Yeah," I say. "Why?"
    "She used to be with me," says Chase.
    "Oh," I say.
    "But then Buck joined the band and the next thing I know, you know, poof."

Beeeep. "Jen, hi, it's Neil. So we're still at the meat-and-potatoes stage in the memos but the money's getting up toward the three hundred mark and Columbia's starting at fifteen points, which is beautiful. So I'm just going back and forth with everybody. Oh, and Sway's really beginning to feel the heat, so he was thinking about coming up and making a sort of social call, have a little sit-down, okay? Anyway, so I'll check in again soon to tell you where we are, but wherever it's gonna be is gonna be good. WOOHOO!" *Beeeep.*

Randy and Buck and I are in Robby's living room, which isn't a whole lot bigger than the pullout couch that Robby's laid up in. We sit crammed around the perimeter of the bed, eating pizza from the box and trying to avert our eyes from Robby's swollen foot, which is sticking out of the end of his cast like a dead fish. Randy's mumbling on and on (. . . *airplay* . . . *maximum spins* . . . *call-out* . . . *BDS* . . .), shifting his gaze from his pizza to the floor to the ceiling. I look at Robby, who's suddenly smirking, and then at Buck, who begins to grin. That's when I start to giggle, really giggle, like the kind of giggle you can't stop at a funeral or during a test, and then Robby breaks out laughing, and then Buck is cracking up so hard that a drop of saliva goes down his chin and falls onto Robby's cast, sending us into the next stratum of hilarity while Randy keeps droning on (. . . *demographics* . . . *indie promo* . . . *foreign markets* . . . *Triple A* . . .).

★

Buck and I head back out to L.A., alone. It's our final round of meetings with Warner Bros. and Geffen. As we lift off and my ears begin to pop, all I can think about is the plane falling quick and straight as a pumpkin smashing to the ground. I can't help but reach out for Buck's hand.

When we land, we go to a few meetings with potential managers that whip past as if I'm watching them from a speeding car.

We check in to the Sunset Marquis, where every room has its own veranda, and my room overlooks the pool.

Billy from Gimmee stops by, going on and on about his Sad Sack *thang,* while Buck and I drink beer and kick each other under the table.

By the time Billy leaves, the sun is setting through the open door leading to the veranda and the wind is blowing warm. I fall back onto the bed and say I'm exhausted. Then Buck falls onto the bed next to me, where we stay, rolling around a little, until someone screams down by the pool and I open my eyes and push Buck away.

He swings his legs to the floor and sits up, saying, "*Jesus,*" rubbing his face in his hands. Then, "*Fuck,*" he says, and stands up, his back to me.

"I'm, I'm sorry," I say.

"Don't *say* that," says Buck, almost in a yell. "I'm not gonna, like, *force* you. Jesus." He grabs his jacket from the floor. "Sometimes, it's like, I don't know." Buck moves toward the door, opens it, looks back at me. Then he shakes his head, steps into the hall, and closes the door behind him.

Later, we're sitting out on the patio having drinks with Allan, an old friend of mine from Boston who lives in L.A. now, making videos. He's talking about wanting to do our first video and I'm excited because he's become a pretty big deal in the video world. We're on our third martini when the conversation takes a weird turn and Buck and I are suddenly arguing. I look at Allan and say, "*You* know what I mean, don't you, Allan?" and Buck says, "Oh, so you're gonna listen to *him* instead of *me*?" which is when he stands and his chair tips backward onto the patio. Then he stomps away, hands in his back pockets.

"What the fuck was that?" asks Allan.

"I, I, I," I stammer because there's a lump in my throat like a boulder. "I, I don't know. He's —"

Suddenly all I want to do is tell Allan, someone, *anyone,* about me and Buck, how I have *no fucking idea* why I ever started kissing him and betraying Guy and how Buck's beginning to freak out on me. But I can't tell anyone. I won't. Because if no one else knows, I can keep telling myself that it's not really happening.

I stand and right Buck's chair, trying to laugh the whole thing off, when Buck is back, his knuckles going white around the back of another chair.

"Can I talk to you?" he says.

"Buck," I say, trying to smile like nothing's going on here. "Let's talk later."

Buck glares at me. Purses his lips. Looks at Allan. Back at me. "Fine," he says. He lets go of the chair and takes the steps two at a time back down to the lobby.

I'm sitting alone on my veranda, drinking and smoking and watching the people by the pool below. There's talk and laughter and wind in the trees, and everyone is beautiful.

From the far corner beyond the pool, Buck emerges. He crosses the patio slowly, looking at no one, hands in his pockets. He disappears into the lobby on the other side.

I sit and watch for a long time, but he never comes back.

★

In the morning, I can't swallow.

Buck and I have an 8 A.M. pickup for our appearance on KCRW, this area's NPR affiliate, for a show featuring new, "smart" popular music.

I go down to the lobby, wondering what in the world I'm going to say about Buck's disappearance and how one goes about filing a missing person report.

But then—there's Buck, sitting in a chair, reading a book.

"Hey," I say.

"Hey," says Buck, standing and shoving the book into his back pocket.

"Are you okay?"

"Yeah," he says, looking at the ground, looking up over my head.

"I'm really glad you're here," I say.

"Just doing my job," he says. He takes the book out, fans through the pages, puts it back.

We both stare out the limo windows all the way to the station.

At the studio, we're sitting in the control room on stools, with headphones on. The red ON AIR sign lights up and the DJ gives us a nod.

"Welcome to 'Morning Becomes Eclectic,'" says the DJ. "We're here this morning with Jennifer Trynin, to talk about her new record, *Cockamamie.*"

"And Buck" is the first thing out of my mouth.

"What?" says the DJ.

"And Buck, my bass player. He's here too."

"Oh, of course. Sorry. And Buck."

Buck still hasn't even looked at me.

After a little chatting about The Bidding War, the DJ says, "You guys feel like playing one?"

I look at Buck. "You ready?"

"Sure," says Buck.

I play and sing through the first few lines of the song, my head dizzy with worry that Buck's not going to sing when he's supposed to, that he's just going to sit there, silently sticking it to me on National Public Radio. My hand slips to the wrong chord just before Buck's supposed to come in and—there he is. Singing.

It sounds great.

We play through five songs all told, with a lot more chatting, during which Buck finally chimes in and is his usual charming self.

Before we head over to Geffen, Buck tells me how sorry he is about last night, about losing it the way he did, how he doesn't know what comes over him sometimes but that he really doesn't want to screw this up for me, for himself. Then he says he thinks he should cut back on the drinking, and maybe cut back on the kissing thing too.

"I think it's making me crazy or something," he says.

"God, yeah," I say. "Me too."

We shake hands. Smile at each other.

"Okay then, buddy," says Buck.

"Whatever you say, pal," I say.

★

At Geffen, Preppy Boy and EdR lead us into a spacious office with lots of open windows and the sun outside. We sit down on a long white couch as some guy comes buzzing in with a nice smile and very short hair, dressed neatly in white slacks and tan shoes, everything cuffed and tucked.

"You must be Jennifer Trynin," he says, as he's shaking my hand. "I'm David Geffen."

I pull my hand out of his, laugh, say *Sorry,* take his hand back, and begin shaking it again. "You're, umm, David Geffen?"

"Last time I checked," he says. Then he takes a painting of a ship from the wall and holds it up right in front of me. He tells me it's an illustration from the *Iliad* and how strongly he feels that in life, it's the

journey that's the real reward, more valuable than the actual arriving—
how life's about the doing, not the getting. And I'm thinking, *Yeah,
I totally understand. Me and David Geffen, we get it.* And even though
Neil's told me that Geffen Records has been sold and that Geffen himself is moving on to other things, I convince myself that he still has his
finger on the pulse over here, that if I come here he'll have his finger
on me.

And at the same time, his *Iliad* story is ringing that unfortunate
bell in my chest, the one that's telling me that maybe I've already done
what I'd set out to do, that I'm afraid I don't have the energy or where-
withal—no less the talent—to maneuver my way through this new land
of major-label artist. I wish I could ask David Geffen if there's a way
for me to quit while I'm ahead, to take the money and run.

We have our final meeting at Warner Bros., where we laugh and drink
bottled water and talk about everything under the sun except for anything to do with whether we're going to sign with them.

Then Head Honcho, Howdy Doody, and Einstein take us to a
sushi place in a strip mall, where the sushi chef yells at me for using
soy sauce. I keep looking over at Buck but he's not looking back, and
I get the feeling that all he's thinking about is anything that has nothing to do with me.

When we get back to the hotel, Buck goes right to his room and I go
to mine. My message light is blinking red.

"Jen, hi, it's Neil. So now we're cooking. We've got three firm at
three-fifty per record, plus an option for two more at four-fifty. We're
at plenty of half-recoupables with guarantees for tour support and
promotion and I'm trying for nonrecoupable on that stuff but don't
hold your breath. Oh, and we're up to eighteen points for *Cockamamie*
and full-rate on twelve songs for mechanicals. Fuckin' *unreal!*"

I hang up and get myself a vodka from the minibar. I lie down and
channel surf, drinking from the bottle.

———

On the plane back to Boston, Buck mostly reads. But when we hit some turbulence, I reach out and squeeze his hand and he squeezes back. So I squeeze it again, and he squeezes again. By the time we land at Logan, we're laughing it up like this is still the funnest thing in the whole world.

★

I'm down at the rehearsal space, running songs with our new fill-in drummer, who's about twelve and plays like a motherfucker.

We take a break and I go to check my messages. As I'm walking down the hallway to the pay phone, I run into Bisbo, Mr. Art For Art's Sake, with his shaved head and teardrop tattoo on his cheek. He has a rainstick tucked under his arm.

"So," he says, as he nods his head. "I hear you're giving in."

"Bisbo—"

"You know they're gonna kill your music." Bisbo's maybe twenty and went to Australia once (he'll tell anyone willing to listen or caught in a corner), where he learned The Meaning Of Music: that it should only and always be played from pure emotion and that one should never accept payment for sharing it.

"I can't get into this right now," I say.

"There's always time to discuss the important things," says Bisbo.

"You wanna discuss how your fly's down?"

Bisbo looks down at his fly. "Oh," he says, zipping it up with re-markable dexterity considering the rainstick.

"Gotta run," I say.

"See ya in purgatory," says Bisbo, turning the rainstick upside down and sending all the little whatever-they-ares inside the tube falling from one end to the other, making the thing sound, as you might expect, like rain.

Beeeep. "Hi Jen, it's Neil. So it's looking like not only are we gonna be able to carve out Australia, but Warners conceded to a reversion clause for *Cockamamie.* Not totally solid on the specifics yet but it'll be something like the rights revert back to you X years after the release date. This is un-fuckin'-heard-of, so if you're still wondering if these guys really want you, rest assured, okay?" *Beeeep*.

★

I'm watching TV, half asleep, when my Squint line rings.

Beeeep. "Yes, this is David Geffen—"

I leap off the couch, accidentally kicking Ranger and falling to the floor, so I'm on my knees when I pick up the receiver.

"Hello?"

"Jennifer?"

"You're calling me?"

This is when David Geffen tells me how I remind him of Linda Ronstadt. How she'd come into his office crying when he was trying to sign her, saying how she didn't think she could compete with the other great artists he was already working with. Then he says how unfortunate it is that so many artists are driven to unleash the very inner demons that always seem to sink them in the end.

★

"You can't keep jerking 'em around like this," says Neil.

I'm sitting at my desk, staring at a Polaroid of me and Buck and Robby way back at the beginning, about four months ago. We're laughing, arms around each other. I'm pointing at the camera.

"It's time," says Neil. "You gotta decide."

At this point, all three labels have agreed to basically the same advances and contractual terms. I've paced and smoked, made pro-and-con lists, flipped coins—two out of three, three out of five.

"And then we gotta move on like pronto," says Neil. "Publishing. Booking agents. Managers. Everyone's breathing down my neck."

When I tell Neil how I'm thinking about hiring my brother as my manager, how he has *real* business experience and is smart as hell—Neil says, "What you need is a *real* manager. You hire your brother and you can kiss this whole bidding war goodbye." Then he tells me to try to relax, that we have to take things one step at a time, and that it's time to decide on a label. Now.

We hang up.

I stare at my guitar.

The truth is, I don't want to decide. Because as long as I stay here in The Before, I can continue to be as great as everyone imagines.

I smoke another cigarette, wishing Guy were here to talk about it one more time, but he's working. And besides, I don't want to go with some label just because Guy thinks I should. This is my thing. My music. My life.

Two hours later, I'm standing alone on a balcony above the stage at the Paradise, watching Shineaway, and it's done. I'm going with Warner Bros., with Lola, with Danny Goldberg. I'm sure Neil has already made the calls.

I can see Guy standing down on the floor next to Kramer. Arms crossed. Swaying to the music.

I keep thinking of this book from when I was young. Or maybe it was a movie. A little girl is walking around a city, Paris I think. She's happy and holding a red balloon at the end of a long string. Then the wind picks up and the string is suddenly running through her fingers until she's just standing on this bridge, watching her balloon floating up and up into the blue sky and it's gone.

SIX

The following day, I get phone calls from lots of people at Warners telling me how happy they are. Danny Goldberg never contacts me directly, but I hear through Neil that he's "totally excited." I get a fax from Howdy Doody, which is just one page completely filled with the word YAY! Like:

YAY! YAY! YAY! YAY! YAY! YAY! YAY! YAY! YAY! YAY! YAY! YAY!
YAY! YAY! YAY! YAY! YAY! YAY! YAY! YAY! YAY! YAY! YAY! YAY!
YAY! YAY! YAY! YAY! YAY! YAY! YAY! YAY! YAY! YAY! YAY! YAY!
YAY! YAY! YAY! YAY! YAY! YAY! YAY! YAY! YAY! YAY! YAY! YAY!
YAY! YAY! YAY! YAY! YAY! YAY! YAY! YAY! YAY! YAY! YAY! YAY!
YAY! YAY! YAY! YAY! YAY! YAY! YAY! YAY!

Lola, Howdy Doody, and Einstein are sitting across the table at this mangy club in Worcester called Pete's, where we're playing tonight. They're making notes and talking all over one another, telling me there's so much to do and so little time, that I should step it up on picking a manager and a booking agent, and don't forget about the photo shoots and the videos and the tour.

"So," says Lola. "Thoughts on the first single?"

"I think we should just go with 'Better Than Nothing' straight outta the box," says Einstein.

"What?" I say. "What happened to doing this low-key and putting out 'Happier' on Squint and hopefully building a little intrigue and *then* coming out with 'Better Than Nothing,' or maybe even saving 'Better Than Nothing' for the third single?"

"The *third* single?" says Einstein.

"Jen," says Howdy Doody. "Unfortunately, in today's radio climate, you don't always get a third single."

"Your best bet is to lead with your strongest commercial song," says Einstein.

"I want to start with 'Happier,' low-key," I say.

Einstein and Howdy Doody exchange glances.

"Just one problem," says Lola.

"What?" says Einstein.

"Fuck," she says.

"What?" says Howdy Doody.

"'Aren't you the guy who robbed the Store 24?'" says Lola. "'Maybe *the fuck* who tried to jimmy my door?'"

I'm touched she knows the lyrics by heart.

"She's got 'fuck' in the chorus," says Lola. "Can't be a single."

"We can bleep it out," says Einstein.

"Can't do that," says Lola. "It compromises the artistic integrity of the song."

"It does?" I say.

"Yes," says Lola. "It does."

"So let me get this straight," Guy says later, with his best Spinal Tap inflection. "You're saying that you *don't* think that bleeping out the 'fuck' would compromise your artistic integrity, and therefore *not* going with 'Happier' just because *Lola* thinks the bleeping would compromise your artistic integrity really *would* be compromising your artistic integrity. Will someone check me on this?"

I get a call from Head Honcho, who says he heard from Lola who heard from Howdy Doody that Einstein thinks I should stop making so many faces when I play guitar. I tell Head Honcho to tell Lola to tell Howdy Doody to tell Einstein that I think he should stop being so fat.

"That's not very constructive," says Head Honcho.

"Well, what the fuck is he talking about? What does that even mean?"

"We're also kinda wondering if your bass player could maybe not wear that baseball hat all the time."

Somehow, by the time we hang up, Head Honcho has agreed to everything I want to do—service an initial run of five thousand Squint *Cockamamie*s to mom-and-pops in the key college markets through Sad Sack's distribution system; make "Happier" the first single and "Better Than Nothing" the second, with accompanying low-budge, indie-style videos; release *Cockamamie* as is (just with an additional Warners logo on it); start off touring in small clubs; and create Squint 45s of "Happier" and "Better Than Nothing" to sell at shows, perpetuating the Squint Records indie-shmindie shenanigans.

★

I'm kneeling on the floor of a Tweeter in downtown Boston, fiddling with this teeny-weeny travel clock radio, when something falls against my back. It's a little girl. She hugs my neck.

"Sorry, sorry, sorry," her dad says, pulling the little girl off of me. He's handsome, with dark hair and nice teeth. He looks about my age, maybe younger.

"That's okay," I say, as the little girl reaches toward the teeny-weeny travel clock radio in my hand. I smile at her. "Let's listen to it, okay?" I turn it on.

"*I'm feelin' good, I'm feelin' good, I'm feelin' good, for now . . .*"

"Holy shit," I say, and the dad shoots me a look. "I mean, that's me." I hold the radio up toward him, as if he could see me in there if he just got a little closer.

"What's you?" he says.

"That's me singing," I say, "on the radio. That's my song. That's me."

The dad cocks his head, looks me up and down, picks up his daughter, and walks away.

★

More manager meetings, publisher meetings, meetings with business managers and booking agents.

The best moments of my days are when Tim calls to talk about some new thing he's learned about the way the music business "really works." He keeps faxing me articles from *Billboard* and radio playlists and anywhere he sees my name mentioned. We've deferred our Tim-as-my-manager plan from the present to the future, figuring I'll hire a "real" manager for now, become a huge success, then fire that guy and hire Tim.

I'm leaning toward Q Prime as my "real" managers, because Cliff keeps calling me and we're getting rather chummy—until he says, "What can I say to make you come with us?" and I say, "I don't know, it's just—" and that's when he says to hang on for a second and puts his hand over the receiver, *muffle muffle,* and when he comes back, it's like he's someone else. Someone I don't know. Some dickhead.

"Forget it," he says.

"What?"

"It's not gonna happen. Doesn't feel right."

"But it felt right before," I say, like he's breaking up with me.

"Well, that was before."

"But—"

"You're too unsure."

"But—"

"You don't know what you want."

"But—"

"Good luck." Click.

Dial tone.

Fuck!

He's *so fucking right!*

I shut off the lights, turn on the TV, curl up on the couch and cry.

For about a minute.

Then I sit up.

WHAT THE FUCK AM I DOING?

I can't pull this kind of crap anymore!

I'm a fucking rock star!

Or, I'm *gonna* be a fucking rock star.

Soon.

Or something.

Right?

There's no time for this shit.

I start making decisions all over the place: NO NO NO YES! NO NO NO YES! Even though people are under the impression that I'm some level-headed chick who knows how to make the *tough decisions,* the truth is my process ends up being a whole lot more Duck-Duck-Goose than I'd ever admit.

I pick Randy as my manager, not only because he has a great reputation for representing "real talent," but also because he's cuter than any of the other managers I've met. I know that's a stupid reason, but everyone keeps telling me to "go with my gut." I can't help it if my gut goes for cute guys. I hire Erika, a short chick with blond hair, as my business manager for no reason in particular but, truth be told, she's also cute. I decide to go with Scarlett and Kenny O'Harron and Warner/Chappell Publishing because all the bigger publishing companies are offering basically the same deal and Neil says it couldn't hurt to "keep it all in the family." And I hire my booking agent, Roy, *not* because he's cute (though he's not bad), but because the ringing phone wakes me from one of my falling-from-the-sky dreams and the sound of his voice on the other end makes me feel safe. And also because, frankly, I'm just sick and tired of talking to people.

"You *what*?" says Neil.

"I hired Roy as my booking agent."

"Without talking to me?"

"What do you mean 'without talking to you?'" I say. "You're the one who told me how great he is."

"But, Jesus," says Neil, who I guess is mad though I'm not sure, since I've never heard this tone of voice from him before. "I have a ton of other people waiting their turn to talk to you, and now—*ay*."

I can hear him tapping his expensive pen on his desk.

★

I go to a flea market and spot some old juice glasses with 70s smiley faces on them and a metal dollhouse with windows and a fireplace painted onto the walls. I pack everything up and send it to the Warner art department with instructions on how I want everything photographed. Voilà, covers for the "Happier" and "Better Than Nothing" 45s, respectively.

Head Honcho tells me I'm a genius.

In fact, I'm such a genius that he encourages me to submit a "treatment" for the "Happier" video.

"What's a treatment?" I ask him.

"It's a written description of your vision for the video," he says.

"Like, a general vision?"

"Whatever kind of vision you want," he says. "It's your vision."

So here's my vision: super low-budge (vibe-wise, because I don't have even an inkling of how much it costs to make a video, low-budge, hi-budge, or any-which-way-budge). Slapdash. Black and white. Shot in a convenience store (*Aren't you the guy who robbed the Store 24?*). No story line, just the random machinations of your average convenience-store patrons. We, the band, appear only on surveillance monitors placed strategically about the store.

There. Very indie-rock (if I do say so myself).

Ricky, the Warners video department head, tells me I'm a genius.

★

Robby's finally back in business (sort of) with a new "walking cast," which only goes up to his knee. We're all down at our rehearsal space, loading gear into the van to go play some stupid benefit gig that I couldn't say no to because all our friends are playing at it and I was afraid that if we didn't do it, we'd look like the major-label assholes that we are, in all likelihood, becoming. Robby has the radio tuned to WBCN.

Just as Buck and I are hoisting my amp into the back of the van, a beautiful girl and two beautiful boys go wafting by and disappear down into the rehearsal complex. My stomach clamps.

"Wasn't that Juliana Hatfield?" says Buck.

"Yeah," I say.

"Don't you guys know each other?"

"Kinda," I say.

After trolling around in her shadow for years, I was ecstatic when Juliana Hatfield's people contacted Roy last week about our opening for her on her next tour. But in a fit of I'm-the-future-she's-the-past bravado, I'd turned it down.

Suddenly "Everything's Different Now" comes blaring from Robby's speakers.

We all look at each other and crack up.

"This is so weird, you know?" says Robby. "Like that singer from my old hardcore band called me up and he's like congratulations and everything, but then he's like, But do you really like her music?" Robby shifts his weight from one crutch to the other.

"Oh, so what's *he* doing these days?" says Buck. "Parking cars?"

Juicy, the singer from Supa Juice, comes bounding out of the rehearsal complex. "Hey!" she says. She and I hug. "So," she says to me, smiling, nodding. "I hear things have been raging."

"Yeah," I say, not wanting to elaborate, not wanting to rub it in that here I go getting a record deal while Juicy, a far better singer than I, is still dragging her ass around the local scene.

"You know, a very very like super-weird thing happened the other day," she says.

"Yeah?" I say.

"Yeah," she says. "We were down in New York, talking to some management possibilities, and we have this meeting with Becka Stein and when we walk in there, it's like, holy shit, cuz on the wall is like this dartboard with darts all over it and it's a picture of you. On the dartboard. A picture of your face. Like a big picture."

★

Beeeep. "Hey, Jen." It's Howdy Doody. "So, uhh, I was just talking to Billy at Gimmee, and I don't know what's up with that guy. I mean, we're doing everything you and I talked about, like keeping them on at full pay for promo and passing along five thousand of your Squint *Cockamamie*s for them to sell, but he keeps telling me how they're going to release a run of *Cockamamie* on their Sad Sack label and, I mean, where's that coming from? *You're* the one putting out the pre-Warner discs on Squint, right? I'm just confused. I think they're still smarting from the whole Veruca Salt thing, like they feel that they dis-covered them and did all this work and then some big label swoops in and makes all the money. I just think they're trying to get their own label jump-started by riding your coattails, you know? So I'd say hold off on dealing with them and I'll take care of it from here." *Beeeep.*

★

Beeeep. "It's Billy from Gimmee. So we talked with some of your Warners people today who're being the typical major-label assholes and are trying to muscle us outta the picture just like we thought they would. So if I were you, I'd get it straight with them what you're tryin' to do, you know? Don't let them fuck this up for you." *Beeeep.*

Suddenly, everyone's taking our picture—on my roof, in a hockey rink, down a million streets. We do a long shoot for a full-page picture in *Interview* magazine, about which the Warners crowd is very excited. I don't let on that I'm not sure what *Interview* is. We spend a couple of hours under a highway overpass in downtown Boston on a level bit of ground by the Charles River where it's hot and dank and loud, with cars barreling along above us. Then we shoot in a studio. The photographer's kind of cute and we're kind of flirting and I keep think-ing Buck's giving me the evil eye.

"Think we could have a few shots without the hat, Buck?" says the photographer.

"I don't think so," says Buck.

I look at Robby, like *You ever notice this?* Robby shrugs his shoulders.

"Could we just try it?" says the photographer.

"Gotta have the hat," says Buck.

At 6 P.M. exactly, Buck says he has to go.

"But we're not done," says the photographer.

"I was told we'd be done at six," says Buck.

"Buck," says Robby.

"Buck!" I say.

Buck looks at his watch, purses his lips, says ten more minutes, then he's outta here.

When Buck leaves, the photographer tells Robby that he can go too, that he'll finish the shoot with some solo shots of me.

"But why would we have to do any solo shots?" I say.

"I was told to get some," says the photographer.

When we're finally done, I don't have a ride because I'd come with Robby, so the photographer offers to take me home on his motorcycle. I climb on the back and put my arms around his chest.

As we're speeding down the road, he yells, "You okay?"

"Sure," I yell.

"So, do you have a boyfriend?"

I don't know why I hesitate. It's not because I really like this guy. I think I don't want to tell him I have a boyfriend because it will disturb the picture I have of myself at this moment, speeding down the highway on the back of some photographer's motorcycle, wind in my face, sun setting like there's no tomorrow.

I'm screening video directors' reels, reel after reel after reel. Alt-rock bands playing in attics, in fields, underwater. Heavy metal bands with fake blood on their teeth. A Christian band standing in the rain.

I pick the most low-budge-looking video of the bunch, directed by some chick named Milly who Head Honcho tells me is "totally stoked."

Milly begins faxing and calling and sending me Polaroids of convenience stores all over L.A.

I get our travel itinerary for the video shoot from Kavallah at Randy's office. I notice that we're flying coach for the first time since all this began. No hot cookies. No sweet mimosas.

I call Neil.

"You're already married," says Neil. "The Bunny doesn't have to bring you flowers anymore, okay? Everything spent on you from here on in has to come from one of your budgets, in this case your video budget. They're not gonna go wasting cash on things like flying you guys first class. And at the end of the day, it's all your money now anyway, because everything is ultimately recoupable to you. Do you follow?"

"What about when Howdy Doody and Einstein flew out to see us play at that stupid club in Worcester? Who pays for that?"

"Well, The Company pays now, but at the end of the day, it's still going on your tab."

"And their hotels?"

"Your tab."

"But I didn't even ask them to come!"

"Dat's bidness," says Neil. "And by the way, not that I don't love you to death, but you gotta start bothering—I mean calling—Randy with this kind of stuff."

"Okay, Mizz Trynin. Ready for the next section?"

I'm on the phone again with the ever-so-patient Daniel Berg, the new lawyer who's just been hired under Neil and has been given the unenviable task of walking me through each of the hundred-plus pages of my Warner Bros. and Warner/Chappell contracts, which have been landing in ever-so-slightly altered renditions—*shwump!*—on the porch for the past three weeks.

"You might have to hang on a sec, Mr. Boyg," I say. "I think my earlobe's asleep." From the beginning, Daniel Berg has called me *Mizz Trynin*, so sometimes I call him Mr. Boyg.

Daniel says he's impressed with my determination to understand my contracts, how usually new artists just sign on the dotted line, take the money, and complain later when something happens that they don't understand. But I feel like it's my responsibility to understand my contracts. I mean, I'm the leader here, right? Buck and Robby are depending on me. Plus, I can't wait to be back at Gino's, sipping a cool martini, nonchalantly answering the myriad of picayune questions I know my father's going to ask.

"Gotta love bidding wars," says Daniel. "I mean, these mechanicals are ridiculous for a new artist."

That's been Daniel's refrain as we approach each new section of the contract.

For example, in a typical deal, the artist is signed for seven records, with advances of between $150,000 and $250,000 per record. This means that the artist is beholden to the label for seven records, while the label is free to drop the artist at any time, without paying him any more money. The label is also free to refuse to release an artist's record while still keeping him under contract for a substantial period of time (again, without paying him any more money). This means the artist can end up in the position of having neither a record in the marketplace nor the freedom to shop his music elsewhere (which is exactly the situation Aimee's been in, on and off, for years). Daniel tells me that landing in this kind of professional limbo is nothing I have to worry about.

I'm getting a five-record, "three plus two firm" deal with advances/recording funds of $350,000 for each of the first three records and an option after the third, which, if exercised, will bring additional advances of between $450,000 and $900,000 apiece for the fourth and fifth records, depending on the sales of the first three records. Getting a "three plus two firm" deal means that the record company must pay me my advances for the first three records, whether they have any intention of going forward or not (i.e., if they decide to drop me after Record One (*Cockamamie*), they're still obligated to pay me my advances for Records Two and Three). After the third record, they are free to drop me and I'm free to shop my music elsewhere. But if they exercise the "option" to keep me, they are once again obligated to pay me my advances for Records Four and Five, after which I'm again free to shop my music elsewhere. This kind of arrangement is only offered to "coveted" artists.

My royalties are "ridiculous" too. Instead of the standard 12-point record royalty rate for a new artist, I'm getting 18 points on *Cockamamie* and 17 points thereafter (with escalations to 18 points, depending on actual sales). I'm also getting paid on 100 percent of records sold (instead of the standard 85 percent). This means that instead of earning 86¢ per $15 record sold, I'll be earning $1.68. Therefore, not only will I make more money than your standard new artist if I ever recoup my advances and expenses, but I'll recoup faster.

Instead of the standard mechanical royalty rate of three-quarters of the current statutory rate on a maximum of ten songs per record, I'm getting "full mechanicals," which is 100 percent of the current statutory rate on a maximum of twelve songs per record. In the case of my beloved eleven-song *Cockamamie,* this means that instead of receiving the standard 49.5¢ per record sold, I'll be getting 72.6¢.

Neil was also able to "carve out" Australia, meaning I'm getting an additional deal from Mushroom Records with an additional $20,000 advance per record.

From Warner/Chappell, I'm receiving a three-record publishing deal with the following advances for each record: $400,000 for Record One (*Cockamamie*); $300,000 to $600,000 for Record Two; and $350,000 to $700,000 for Record Three, depending in each case upon sales of the previous record. However, there are "catastrophe clauses" for Records Two and Three. If Warner/Chappell receives less than $100,000 from my portion of mechanical and performance royalties generated by *Cockamamie,* they'll only have to pay me $237,500 for Record Two. If sales of Record Two do not exceed

$275,000, they don't have to pick up their option for Record Three.

In terms of recoupability, Daniel explains that when an artist goes on tour, if the proceeds are less than the expenses, "tour support" is provided by the label to cover the remaining expenses. In a typical record deal, this tour support is provided at the discretion of the label (meaning they can deny it, thereby potentially prohibiting the artist's touring) and is 100 percent recoupable to the artist. In my deal, I'm getting a guarantee of at least $150,000 in tour support per record cycle, of which only 50 percent is recoupable to me. Also, in a typical record deal, many "third-party costs" (for example, hiring independent promotion companies like Gimmee) are 100 percent recoupable to the artist. In my deal, they're half-recoupable.

"And here's the pièce de resistance," says Daniel. "The reversion clause."

"What's that again?" I say.

"The ownership of *Cockamamie* reverts back to you five years after the termination of your Warner Brothers contract. That means that at that time, you can manufacture and sell copies of *Cockamamie* and keep all the money, regardless of whether you're still unrecouped at Warners. In other words, the record is yours again."

"I like that," I say.

"You *should* like that," says Daniel.

"Let me guess," I say. "It's unheard of for a new artist, right Mr. Boyg?"

"Absofuckinlutely, Mizz Trynin," says Daniel.

★

I get color xeroxes of Head Honcho's top three choices from the *Interview* shoot. He says he's thinking about using one of them for a general publicity shot. It's a picture of me sitting alone on the floor next to a big chair with my hands clasped in front of my knees, looking docile and pensive and, well, folky. Solo-y. Singer-songwriter-y.

"No fucking way," I say, and tell Head Honcho all about my days in the Sunday-through-Wednesday-night-folk/acoustic-chick-band wasteland. I warn him that if Warners is going to market me as some wistful singer-songwriter, they may as well throw their money out the window right now.

Band shots, I tell him.

Rock.

Rock and roll.

Check it out.

We head back to L.A. for the "Happier" video shoot. Our seats are in the last row of the plane, by the bathrooms. As we lift off, I want more than anything to be holding someone's hand, but Buck and Robby are sitting across the aisle.

We're picked up at the airport by a cute guy with long brown hair driving a gold Plymouth Duster from the 70s. He's wearing a skullcap that says "F*ck It" and takes us straight to this dilapidated house in what looks like a dangerous section of town. Evidently, this is where we're going to rent "the coolest equipment" for tomorrow's shoot. Inside the house, it's dark and smells like glue. Everywhere, against every wall, atop every piece of furniture, are amplifiers, drums, guitars, keyboards, all vintage and sparkling. We're introduced to a short Hispanic guy with a shaved head and leopard-print pants named something I don't quite catch.

"Roo-hoo-loh?" I say.

"No," he says. "Rahuelah."

"Rah-hoo-hah?"

"No. RaHUElah."

"Rah-OO-lah?"

"Give it a rest, Jen," says Buck.

We point out all the gear we want for the shoot and Rahuelah makes a list, saying it'll be delivered on site tomorrow morning, 7 A.M., no problema.

We meet the video crew back at our hotel and gather in Buck and Robby's room, where we watch a strange biopic about the Carpenters in which all the "actors" are Barbie dolls.

"How *fucking* amazing is this *fucking* video?" says Milly, who brought it. The rest of the crew, about six people, are lounging all over the hotel room, pounding beers and making small talk and generally just being themselves, i.e., languid and good-looking. I figure they're all out-of-work actors or models.

Around 1 A.M., I'm back in my room, staring at myself in the mirror to try to see what I look like. Really look like—not like in a picture, but in real time. In motion. But I can't really tell, because every time I move, I lose sight of myself.

At 7 A.M., Buck and Robby and I are standing outside a bodega drinking bad coffee from Styrofoam cups while all the good-looking crew people are setting up lights or sweeping floors or slapping duct tape everywhere. Ricky the video guy is sitting on a folding chair, drinking coffee and reading the paper. People on the other side of the street are looking over at us, pointing, whispering into each other's ears.

There's a large folding table out on the sidewalk piled high with an impressive array of food: potato chips, tortilla chips, donuts, bagels, butter, peanut butter, jelly, M&Ms, trail mix, Hershey's bars, Snickers bars, Milky Ways, Twizzlers, Devil Dogs, bean dip, and one lone tray of sweaty sliced vegetables.

Suddenly everyone's eating donuts. Everyone but me. I'm afraid if I eat a single bite, the button on my pants will ping away and my zipper will unzip and my pants will fall off. Then my bra will unhitch and fly away like a supersonic rubber band, ripping my shirt, which will fall to the street, leaving me standing here in nothing but my underpants. Then my hair will fall out and my skin will melt away until I dissolve in a little puddle like the Wicked Witch of the West.

Three hours, six cigarettes, four crappy cups of coffee, and fifty-five wilting carrot sticks later, Buck and Robby and I are finally inside the store, lip-synching to "Happier" and pretending to play Rahuelah's gear that's set up in a corner.

Buck's to my right, swaying from his heels to the balls of his feet, like he always does when he plays. Robby's behind us, swinging his black hair around, his crutches resting on the wall behind him.

At first, I feel ridiculous, like I'm jumping around my bedroom pretending to play guitar on a tennis racket.

"That's not bad," says Milly after the first pass through the song. "But let's all try to loosen up a little, okay? Jennifer? Your mouth's a little tight."

Fuck. Whenever a camera is within a mile of my face, my mouth gets tight.

We jump around through another pass of the song.

And then another.

And another.

There's a camera positioned high above me with an A-frame ladder just beneath it, and every once in a while Milly screams "*CLIMB!*" and I have to scurry up the ladder, still pretending to play my guitar, while making coy faces like three inches from the camera lens. I almost kill myself every time I scurry back down.

The film crew is done with us by around 9 P.M., but we're encouraged to stick around and watch the rest of the action, of which there is plenty because, in the end, Ricky and other Powers That Be at Warners can't live with a video consisting of nothing but people buying gum at a convenience store while a bunch of slackers jump around in surveillance monitors.

So we follow the video crew all over Hollywood as they film the other scenes. A crazy ugly fat guy (an actual actor) with long black hair robs the convenience store (per the lyrics), sticks the surveillance monitor under his arm (with us playing on it), runs out of the store, and rides away on this little banana-seat bike. From there, the monitor gets stolen over and over again and the video follows its journey until the song ends and you see the monitor disappearing down a dark street in the back window of the cute-guy-with-the-F*ck-It-skullcap's gold Plymouth Duster from the 70s.

Beeeep. "You are *never* there. Are you there? Jen? Well, it's your ma and I was just listening to NPR, and I'm always hearing these interviews of all these wonderful artists and *sometimes* I just think, What about Jen? How come I don't hear *Jen* playing her songs on these shows? So I was on my way home and all of a sudden, there you are, on the radio! I almost drove off the road! You were singing that song about the 7-11—oh what's it called? 'Happy'? 'I'm Happy'? And then they were interviewing you, and you were just so, so, I don't know. So *you*! I still can't believe it! I had to pull over. My heart's still pounding. Call me, okay? Call me call me call me!" *Beeeep*.

Everyone's thrilled because the "Happier" video is accepted onto MTV's *120 Minutes* (the show for new cool bands) and will be aired the following Sunday night.

Head Honcho tells me again what a fucking genius I am and wants me to come up with an idea for the "Better Than Nothing" video we'll be shooting ASAP.

I'm lying in bed, staring at the water marks on my ceiling.

How about a video of me sleeping?

How about a video where we're playing in a shitty house and water comes crashing down through the ceiling?

How about a video where we're playing in a shitty house and *people* come crashing through the ceiling?

I KNOW!

We'll make a video that takes place in *the same metal dollhouse living room* that's on the cover of the "Better Than Nothing" 45!

YEAH!

And the room will appear suspended in midair just like it is on the cover of the "Better Than Nothing" 45!

YEAH!

And, and, we'll have all these little kids roaming around on the "ceiling" of the room with, with *pickaxes* like they're trying to break into the room!

YEAH!

And then, and then, we'll have adults *hanging* from the bottom of the room by their *fingertips* and then *falling,* one by one, into The Great Abyss!

YEAH! YEAH! YEAH!

Lola tells me my idea is "inspired."

Everyone else at Warners tells me I'm a genius.

And even though they're worried that Milly's not experienced enough to do the "Better Than Nothing" video (because it's going to be way more involved with way more people and will cost way more money than the "Happier" video), Head Honcho says we should go with my gut and if my gut says to go with Milly, then gosh darn it, we're going to go with Milly.

I get a fax from Vibetone, a black-and-white xerox of a picture of me playing guitar like I'm strangling it, next to a picture of some spiky-haired chick playing a synth and yelling. Or it looks like she's yelling. There's a Warners logo at the top of the page, and underneath, in big blocky letters, it says, "HEAR THEM ROAR!!!"

I call Randy.

"What is this?"

"It's a print ad," he says.

"This is *in* a *magazine*?" I yell.

"Well, I, umm," he stammers, "not yet. It's a proof."

"Hear them *roar*?"

"I did what you asked me to do, Jen, and told those guys not to market you like a singer-songwriter, okay?"

"So instead they're gonna market me like the next Helen fucking Reddy?"

Buck and Robby and I are back down in New York for meetings with who-knows-who about God-knows-what. After drinks and dinner, we head over to Randy's office to watch the virgin airing of the "Happier" video on *120 Minutes.*

COULD WE BE ANY MORE EXCITED THAN WE ARE?

We're all crammed onto Randy's off-white sofa staring at his TV, hearts beating, hands in our laps.

The first video is colorful and features a dog with a big tongue.

The second video is eerie and dark and everyone's screaming on a cliff with fire in the background.

The third video is . . . US!

Third?

THIRD?

WE'RE THIRD???

(How awesome is this?)

But immediately I'm pissed. At the top of the video, you can hear the *boooop, boooop, booooop* that's the count-in for the people who're making the video; i.e., it's not supposed to be there when it's, say, *on TV*!

Second, the soundtrack is off. Not by much, but enough to bring to mind those old kung fu movies where the actors' mouths are completely out of sync with the overdubbed English.

I stand up. "*What*?" I yell (because I'm under the impression that I've hit The Big Time, and in The Big Time, this kind of shit doesn't happen).

"Hmm," says Randy.

"*Call somebody!*" I yell (because now I have a manager to take care of such shit).

"Well," says Randy. "I'm not sure anyone's really there at the studios right now who could really do anything about—"

"*This is unacceptable!*" I yell (because I'm gonna be a rock star any fucking second and will no longer put up with this kind of shit).

Randy calls MTV the following day and they apologize, promising to air the "Happier" video first the following week and for four weeks after, although they maintain that the reel they received from the production company is at fault.

Although I'm pleased with the outcome, I'm not pleased with Randy, who never seems even remotely as irate as I am over the whole thing, meaning either that Randy doesn't really give a shit or that this kind of shit happens all the time.

★

"*We?*" Neil screams into the phone. "*We* just thought *we'd* be splitting the money?"

"It's just that—" I say.

"Over my dead fucking body!" says Neil.

"But isn't that what people do?" I say. "Isn't that what bands do with the advances and stuff? Just split it up?"

Neil exhales into the phone. "Jen," he says. "It's time to wake up and smell the bullshit. *There is no band!* You gotta stop this already. They're *your* songs. This is *your* thing! Those guys didn't even play on the fucking *record*. I mean for fuck's sake, they've been playing with you for what? Like three months?"

"Something like that," I say.

"They're not even signing the deals! And it'd be ridiculous enough if you were talking about regular old advances, but we're talking about, what, like almost a million bucks here, and that's just for *Cockamamie!*"

"But isn't that all the more reason I should share the money with them?"

"Listen," says Neil. "I'm just saying your arrangement with them should reflect reality. I mean, what have they really done besides play a few gigs and get some free meals? And, what. You think they're gonna be playing with you forever? Do you *know* for *sure* that you're gonna want them to play on Record Two? Three? Four? Fi—"

"I get it," I say.

"I'm not sure you do," says Neil. "This whole thing is about *you*. Jesus! They're lucky to be playing with you at all! They should be thanking their fucking *stars!*"

"You already know what I think," says Guy when I ask him what he thinks.

"But all along, I've been talking to those guys like we're a band and like all for one and everything."

"Well, that was stupid of you," says Guy. "You should just pay them when you use them on the road and in the studio, like anyone else on this planet would."

But I can't do that. I can't treat Buck and Robby like hired guns. Both because I see them as much more than that, and because I want them to feel invested in the future.

I decide to pay Buck and Robby an actual salary so that no matter what's going on with me—say I'm taking time off to write new songs—they still won't have to get some crappy temp job. I'm going to offer them $30,000 a year with a $5,000 raise every year that they're still playing with me. They get 1 point each on *Cockamamie* (or, on average, about 10¢ per record sold), 3 points each on every record they play on in the future (or about 30¢ per record sold), and a third of any profit we make on touring and merchandising.

So let's say it takes us four years to complete our first two record cycles. Even if we don't sell a single record, they'll each receive $150,000. If we hit it big and sell two million each of *Cockamamie* and Record Two, they'll each receive an additional $400,000 (which is about what will be left, after commissions, once their advances and portions of various marketing expenses have been recouped). Plus, if we're selling that many records, we'll no doubt be making lots of money on touring and merchandising.

"So," says Guy, "you're giving points to the guys who played on the record *and* to Buck and Robby just for touring? You gonna offer points to your soundman? Or your tour manager? Fuck it. Let's give points to the fucking mailman!"

"You're being a dick."

"You're being crazy!"

"I think my plan sounds fair," I say.

"Fair?" says Guy. "It sounds like some kind of fucked-up guilt thing to me."

"I *knew* it," says Buck, when I tell him and Robby that it's only going to be me signing the deals. "I told you," he says to Robby.

"So you're saying we're gonna be signing a deal with you, not with Warners or Warner/Chappell?" says Robby.

"Yeah," I say.

"Like hired guns," says Buck.

"It's not like that," I say, and then explain the Buck-and-Robby scenario I've concocted.

"Wow," says Robby. "That sounds pretty good."

"Wow?" says Buck. "I think it sounds pretty bad. When I started playing with you, I thought I was joining a *band*. That's what you said. You asked if I'd be in your *band*."

"I know I said that," I say. "But I guess things have changed."

"I guess they fucking have," says Buck.

I tell them I think it's best if they hire their own lawyer. But they say that they don't know any entertainment lawyers, and even if they did, they can't afford to pay one. So I get a name from Neil and pay for their lawyer myself.

"But isn't that a conflict of interest or something?" says Buck. "You find us a lawyer and pay for him yourself to protect *us* from *you*?"

"So sue me," I say.

It's tax time again and I'm late filing, as always, even though I've been using the services of Aaron Polanski, CPA.

I've already told Erika, my newly hired business manager, that I'd just as soon finish the past year's taxes with Aaron because he already knows how to do them. I'm trying to think of a way to tell Aaron about what's happened, how I won't be able to use him anymore, how the next time he'll see me will be on TV. But how do you tell someone that?

When I walk into Aaron's office, smoke is hovering in wisps at the ceiling and the blinds are drawn over a window that I'm sure is shut.

"Jennifer!" he says, tucking in his light blue button-down through which I can see his undershirt. We hug. He's a big man with big hands and a big head. He has a picture of his high school football team on the wall. That and a calendar with a kitten on it. There's a wilting plant in the corner and a dingy couch that looks like it's been slept on.

"How's everything going?" I say.

"Great," says Aaron, falling back into his chair. "I got *lots* of fish in the fryer." Aaron pulls open his bottom desk drawer. "I want your opinion," he says, piling a bunch of balled-up hosiery on his desk.

Aaron fancies himself an importer.

He unballs a pair. "Feel these," he says. "They're from China."

I feel them.

"Do they feel right? Like stockings you'd wear?"

I take them by the ends and stretch them out. "They're a little short," I say.

"I know, I know," says Aaron. "We're gonna have to do something about that. They're shorter there, you know. In China. The women."

I put the stockings back on his desk. "Details," I say.

"Yeah," says Aaron, gathering the stockings and shoving them back into the drawer. "So, how's the music going? Are you a star yet?"

Aaron's been asking me this for six years, and for six years my answers have been pretty much the same: "Okay" and "No."

This year I say, "Things are unbelievable. I was the object of a gigantic bidding war and was flown all over the country and wined and dined until finally one lucky label got to have me."

Aaron laughs.

"And so now I'm getting like a million dollars and we're leaving on a national tour in a few weeks." This is how I'm telling him. "And then comes airplay, TV, you know, the usual star-making stuff." Because I don't know how else to do it.

"Yeah," laughs Aaron. "Well, don't forget me when you're a big star."

"I don't know, Aaron," I say. "I got a whole posse now. Managers, booking agents. I even got myself a big-city business manager to take care of all my money. I don't know if I'll have time for you anymore."

Aaron looks at me. Laughs again. Lights a cigarette. Blows out the smoke. Keeps looking at me. Then, "Holy shit," he says. "You're not kidding."

Bing bang boom.

We're back in L.A. at some soundstage where a crowd of people are gathered for the "Better Than Nothing" video shoot. This time it's a big production, with tons of crew people and lots of extras. There are rows of folding tables for people to eat at and an entire catering crew. The actual soundstage is just a big box of a room, like a huge garage with a wall that slides open. "Better Than Nothing" is blaring from gigantic speakers, and propped about twenty feet in the air is a life-size replica of the living room from my metal dollhouse. Milly tells me to take a look, so I climb the ladder and hoist myself into the sparkly living room. It's been re-created to a T in bright reds and blues and yellows, with a fireplace painted on one wall, a door on another, and the large picture window on a third—just like the real metal doll-house. I feel like I'm six and in the middle of the best pretend moment of my life.

I'm drinking a Diet Coke and smoking a cigarette when a woman approaches in red sweatpants, an oversized baseball shirt, and two long ponytails sprouting from each side of her head like big dog ears. She introduces herself as Patty, Makeup Momma.

"Ready to be transformed?" she says.

"I guess," I say.

I follow Patty into a small room off the soundstage with a couple of chairs and a big mirror.

"C'mere," she says, patting one of the seats with the palm of her hand. "Sit."

I sit.

"Scooch forward a teensy bit."

I scooch.

Patty has on so much makeup, I imagine wedging a fingernail in at the base of her chin and dislodging her entire face like an old scab.

"So, I hear you're not really into the whole image thing," she says.

"Not really," I say, which of course couldn't be farther from the truth. It's just that the image thing I'm into is the anti-image thing.

"Hmmmm," she says, taking my chin gently between her fingers and turning my head to the left, to the right. She smells like crayons.

"I see we have a wee bit of under-the-eye scrunchiness," she says. "Getting enough liquids, are we, or are we not?"

"Does beer count?" I ask her.

Patty laughs. "Of course beer doesn't count. Liquor and coffee are like the primo offenders of dehydration—and from the looks of it, we're a wee bit dehydrated, aren't we?" Patty unfastens her many-tiered makeup kit, which opens not unlike the mouth of that monster in *Alien,* with tiers of makeup advancing like rows of teeth. "Safe to say we don't wear much makeup?"

"I guess I've never really gotten too into the whole thing," I say.

"Good," she says, slapping me on the knee. "Good for you. That's very brave. I really think that. Especially with your coloring."

I decide to take this as an insult. "You mean my paleness," I say.

"No," says Patty. "We don't use words like 'pale.' The washed-out look can be very sexy if you do it right," implying that clearly, I'm not doing it right. "So what're we going for here?" she says, eyeing her makeup kit, picking stuff up, rubbing colors onto the back of her hand and holding her hand next to my cheek. "Should we stick with the wan, washed-out kinda sexy thing, leaning into a tomboyish I-don't-wear-dresses-because-I-don't-have-to look? Or do we want to skew more into a druggy indie-rock chick thing?"

"Have you heard my record?" I say.

"You know, I haven't had the chance," she says, "but word is it's way cool, like a cross between The Pretenders and X or something. And that you play guitar like Keith Richards."

I can hear these exact words coming out of Randy's mouth, like he's memorized them to say to people like Patty.

"So, let's get down to business," she says, coming toward me with a skin-colored sponge, and though I try not to, I can feel myself grimace. She stops before reaching my face. "We're a little on edge, aren't we?" she says.

"What is that?" I ask her.

"This? It's con*cealer,*" she says, as if she were saying something as fundamental as *air* or *water.*

"Concealer?" I say. "What is that, like, rouge?"

Patty laughs. "Are you for real?" she says. "Is this like the first time you've ever had your makeup done?"

"Kinda," I say.

"Wow," says Patty. "Okay. I'll go slow."

For the next hour, I sit in the chair, fighting sleep and breathing through my nose, as Patty carefully applies what I come to learn is pre-application moisturizer, spot concealer, general concealer, two shades of blush, eyeliner, two shades of eye shadow, eyebrow pencil, and three shades of lipstick. Finally, she curls my eyelashes with a silver contraption before coating them with black gooky stuff from a small tubular brush.

"You have to keep your eyes open while I do this," she says.

I force my stinging, tearing eyes open.

"This isn't supposed to be torture," says Patty.

When she's finally finished, Patty spins my chair toward the big mirror on the wall. The most surprising thing is that I don't look all that different, just like a better version of what I already look like, with my "features" (as Patty refers to them) perhaps a little more enunciated.

I smile.

"You likee?" says Patty.

"Yeah, I do," I say.

"This is only the beginning, you know. A few more videos and you're gonna look like me," she says, which totally harshes my post-makeup buzz.

For the next nine hours, Buck and Robby and I jump around, lip-synching to "Better Than Nothing" in the life-size replica of the metal dollhouse, where it's hot as living fucking hell. Randy and Ricky the video guy stop by and wave to us from the ground. By hour ten, someone finally passes a few ice-cold beers up the ladder, and nothing's ever tasted so good in my whole life.

We're walking by a newsstand in LAX when I see it.

My face.

On the cover of *Billboard* magazine.

I stop.

Stare.

"What's the matter?" says Robby.

I point.

Robby and Buck look.

It's the picture where I'm leaning back on the hood of that big, black car and peering over my Peter Fonda/*Easy Rider* sunglasses with Buck and Robby in the background, except that the picture's been cropped. It's just a close-up of me. My face.

"Typical," says Buck.

The caption beside it says, "Warner Bros. Wins A&R War for Jennifer Trynin."

Robby picks it up. "Is this awesome, or is this fucking awesome?"

Inside, the long article is titled "After A&R War, Trynin Eyes Road—Warner To Reissue Boston Artist's Debut," and says, among other things, "Trynin's debut album, *Cockamamie,* released in October on her Squint Records imprint, touched off one of the most frenzied major-label bidding wars in recent memory . . . In keeping with Trynin's wishes, Warners is plotting a low-key campaign for its much-talked-about new artist."

The doorbell rings a quick *ding-dong-ding-dong.* It's Earl the FedEx guy.

The package is from Milly, the first cut of the "Better Than Nothing" video with a note explaining that this is the rough rough *rough* cut and telling me to call her.

The video is very colorful and I'm relieved that I don't totally hate the way I look, but it's not exactly the video I'd envisioned. I'd seen it as a whole lot darker and more ominous or something. But it's actually looking rather cartoon-like.

I grab the videocassette and drive over to Buck's, because we're going to run some errands.

We watch the video.

We look at each other.

I shrug my shoulders. "Ehhh," I say.

"Ehhh," he says.

"You look cute in it," I say.

"No, *you* look cute," says Buck.

"No, *you* look cute!"

"No! You you *you* look cute," says Buck, as he grabs me, twists my arm around my back, and gently pushes me down on the couch. He leans into me from behind, putting his mouth to my ear.

"I want to keep liking you," he says.

"I want you to keep liking me," I say.

"But sometimes I'm really mad at you."

"Sometimes I'm really mad at you, too."

"But I still really want to do this."

"I still really want you to do this."

Buck stands up and pulls me back off the couch by my arm. "Let's get out of here," he says.

Buck whacks me on the ass before we get in the car.

"So we have like thirty thousand dollars to just *spend*?" he says. He reaches over and squeezes my thigh. "Let's say you and me go to Hawaii for the weekend."

"It's not like that, wise guy," I say.

Another fanfuckingtastic thing in our Warners contract is that we have a $30,000 equipment fund, which Neil has advised me to spend as quickly as possible "because you never know what's gonna happen."

"Happen like what?" I'd asked.

"Happen, like, you know. Like things happen."

"Like what things?"

"Say something happens and you don't have a record deal anymore."

"*What?*"

"I'm just saying *pretend*. Like L.A. slides into the ocean. You might as well take what you can while the gettin's good, right?"

I take Buck's hand off my thigh. "It's an equipment fund," I tell him. "Like we buy stuff we need, you know, anything from strings and

cords to new amps and guitars and stuff, and then we submit the receipts to Warners and they reimburse us."

"I always like free stuff," says Buck.

"Well, it's not exactly free," I say. "It gets thrown onto our recoupable pile."

"Which means what again, to me, someone not signed to the
contract?"

I smack Buck's thigh. "It means that, technically—"

"Since when are you so fucking technical?"

"It means that you won't *technically* own whatever equipment you
guys get with the money until that portion of the recoupable stuff has
been recouped."

"Which'll be like when?"

"I don't know," I say. "Just get what you need. We'll worry about
that stuff later."

But the fact is, I'm beginning to get an idea of when we might actually recoup. Ballpark, if you add together the record advance plus
tour support (half-recoupable) plus approximate video costs and various marketing expenses to support three or four singles, *plus* the
equipment fund, our future debt for *Cockamamie* could easily reach
$1,000,000. At a recoupment rate of $1.68 per $15 record sold, we'll
have to sell 595,238 records to recoup.

"Two o'clock," says Buck. "Parking space."

When we walk into Cambridge Music, the blue-haired guy is behind the counter like he always is. He's one of those great guitar players who's been in tons of cool bands and has even been signed a
couple of times, but nothing's ever really worked out in the end.

We nod a quick hello to him and head toward the back of the
store, where they have all the cool vintage gear.

"I'll take one of everything," says Buck.

We both grab a couple sets of strings and head to the counter,
where the blue-haired guy is glaring at us.

"So," he says. "I hear you guys got the big record deal." He's
slumped on his stool, grinning, with his skinny knee bent up to his

chin. "Good luck," he says, but it comes out sounding more like, "See ya later, suckers."

When Buck and I get out to the sidewalk, we're laughing.

"Good luck!" I say. "Good luck! Good luck!"

"Can you say, I'm a jealous bitter asshole?" laughs Buck.

"Fuck that guy," I say. "What does he know."

"He doesn't know shit," says Buck.

When I get home, my message machine is blinking with messages from Head Honcho, Lola, Howdy Doody, Einstein, Randy, and Milly, Milly, Milly.

Everyone hates the "Better Than Nothing" video. It seems they think it's too lighthearted and "goofy."

Twenty-four hours and another rough cut later, Milly's "Better Than Nothing" video gets shelved.

"Like we're just gonna throw it out?" I say.

"It's just not right," says Head Honcho. "It happens."

I call Randy.

"They're shelving the video," I say.

"Yeah, uh huh, I heard," says Randy, who sounds, as usual, as if he's reading something while he's talking to me.

"So now what happens?"

"We make another one."

"Paid for by . . . ?" I say.

"You," says Randy.

This time no one asks me to submit a treatment. So in addition to checking out a million new video directors' reels, I also read through pages and pages of proposed treatments, which range from dressing us up like KISS to shooting us playing in a dungeon where dirty boys are hanging in shackles. After much discussion with Head Honcho, he "suggests" I go with some director whose big idea is to shoot us playing in a gas station. The only thing I'm happy about is that the guy is willing to do the shoot in Boston.

———

When we show up at the gas station for the shoot, it's the usual—Doritos and duct tape, cameras and lots of people milling around. Tim+1 (a new +1) have come up to watch, and I've already talked to the director about trying to fit them into the video somewhere.

We're all standing around in this trailer filled with clothes. Stefan, the wardrobe guy, is encouraging us to be "daring" and "creative." I try on a pair of black biker boots. I take them off.

"You know, Buck," says Stefan. "Not that it isn't like really really cute, but do you think we could try it without the baseball hat?"

Robby and I look at each other.

Buck reaches into his pocket, fishes around for something. "Gotta have the hat," he says.

"But—" says Stefan.

Buck steps out of the trailer.

Stefan looks at me. "What's with him?"

"He just likes to wear a hat," I say.

"Getting a little light on top?" says Stefan.

"No," I say. "It's like that guy in that 80s band with the checked shirt."

"Cheap Trick," says Robby.

"Yeah," I say. "He always wore a hat. Or that rap guy with the clock around his neck. It's like a trademark."

"Doesn't come off that way," says Stefan.

"Yeah, well," I say. "That's just the way it is."

I'm getting my makeup done in the trailer and have been sitting there for about an hour when Robby walks in, looks at me, and laughs.

"What?" I say.

"Oh," he says. "Nothing, it's just—"

Then Buck walks in, looks at me, and says, "Wow."

"Give me a mirror," I say to the makeup girl.

"But I'm not done yet," she says, and hands me a mirror.

My hair's all bouffed up and my face is covered in some kind of slick concealer that makes me look very tan and sticky. My eyes are swooped up to points and my mouth looks like those big wax lips you eat on Halloween. I wash everything off my face and dunk my head in a sink. I ask the makeup girl to redo me, and this time no Bride of Frankenstein stuff.

Tim and I are sitting on folding chairs, chatting and watching the video people shoot "additional footage," which right now is this young, shirtless dirt-biker dude doing wheelies and jumps all over the gas station. Next, Tim+1 are going to be some suburban couple making out by the pumps. They've dressed Tim in a white polyester shirt and blue slacks and slicked his hair back. Plus One is still being made up.

"We're playing in L.A. next week," I say, "for The Company. You should come. You could write it off, like as research."

Tim looks at me. "Write it off?" he says. "Off of what?"

"Off of your investment in your next career," I say. "You know, as my manager."

Tim looks at the ground, then back at me. "I got a job, Kiki, remember?"

"Blow it off," I say.

"Right," says Tim. "So, I keep forgetting to tell you that I got, like, head-hunted."

"Really? For what?"

"To be the head of this huge company," says Tim.

"Wow," I say. "Where?"

"São Paulo," says Tim. "Brazil."

I turn to him. "What? *Where*?"

"Brazil," Tim says again.

"But, isn't that on the other side of the fucking world or something?" I say.

"Sort of," he says. "Don't worry about it. I'm never gonna take it. I mean, come on. Brazil? Do they play golf there?"

I laugh. "Exactly."

"But I'm psyched to have gotten the offer, you know?"

"You should be," I say.

Plus One comes over, giggling. "Can you believe this?" she says, pointing at her face.

We laugh.

"You look like Laverne and Shirley," says Tim.

Buck and Robby and I are lip-synching to "Better Than Nothing" in the garage while we "play" our instruments. I keep telling myself not to act goofy (as Head Honcho told me I'd acted in the first "Better Than Nothing" video), but acting goofy is how I deal with my nerves, and without it, I'm afraid I'm just coming off angry.

In the final scene, this tall, willowy blond drives up in a white car and parks at the pumps. She gets out, looks around for the attendant, sees us playing in the garage, comes in and interrupts us, supposedly asking me to fix the rim on one of her tires. I have to act "irritated" (easy for me) as I walk her to the back of the garage and start fooling with some big machine that fixes rims. All I know is what a fucking brilliant idea it is to end my video with me standing right next to some tall, willowy blond.

★

Four copies each of the Warner Bros. Records and Warner/Chappell Publishing contracts arrive at my door in a big box via messenger. Each contract has multiple pages flagged with those colorful SIGN HERE stickers.

Guy gets out the Polaroid. "Let's document this," he says. "Your first million."

FLASH: Jen signing contracts on her bed beneath the rotting roof!

FLASH: Jen signing contracts in the shower!

FLASH: On the toilet!

FLASH: Next to the kitty litter!

FLASH: Jen signing contracts on the hood of her trusty little red Honda while also making a peace sign at the camera.

★

We're flown out (coach) to do a show at The Troubador in L.A. for The Company.

Here's my list of reasons for being slightly petrified:

In all the time that I've been playing electric guitar, I've used exactly one amp: my Fender Super Reverb with the red grill cloth. But since we didn't want to go to the trouble and expense of flying our gear out with us, we're renting.

It's also only Robby's third gig back since breaking his leg and frankly, he's kind of sucking. Not because he sucks but because he is, understandably, "a little rusty." He's still in his walking cast, but he's moved up from crutches to a cane.

And Buck's acting intermittently weird, maybe because Guy came with us to "tour manage" and Buck doesn't like anyone telling him what to do, especially Guy.

The Troubador is packed with people from Warners. And their spouses. And their friends. And their friends' friends. Buck and Robby and I are standing on a balcony above the stage, pointing out anyone we recognize—Danny Goldberg, Head Honcho, Randy, Lola, Howdy Doody, Einstein, Ricky the video guy.

"I can't believe this," says Robby.

"It's a tough job," says Buck, putting his arm around me, "but someone's gotta do it." He looks at me. Smiles. "How you doin', girlfriend?" he says.

"Swell, boyfriend," I say. "Yourself?"

"It's hard being this cute," says Buck.

When we walk out onto the stage, the place erupts in applause. Deafening. Never-ending. Like we're real rock stars.

We play through our set at what feels like double time, and after every song, the place erupts again. I drop a pick and someone takes it. The second we finish our last song, someone swipes my set list.

Afterward, it's drinking drinking drinking and *Fuck, you guys rule!* Tons of people head over to the bar at the Sunset Marquis, where everyone's ordering martinis. Candlelight flickers against the walls as I run my pinky up and down the chilled stem of my martini glass. Buck and Robby are dying laughing in the middle of a bunch of girls. And through the glass, out on the terrace, I see Guy talking with some chick. Tall. Blond. Aimee.

It's like the Sweet Sixteen I never had only better, much better, because everyone's drunk and good-looking and staring at me. I orbit the bar in a bubble of liquor with random hands turning me in circles, buying me drinks, patting my back, dragging me over here, over there. Buck walks up and says something to me just as someone takes me by the hand and leads me away, over to some guy who's sitting on a couch between two beautiful women. He's a famous photographer who's "just dying to take my picture" and I'm bumbling around, trying not to appear as drunk as I am, when Buck comes stumbling over and screams, "CAN I HAVE JUST ONE FUCKING SECOND OF YOUR PRECIOUS TIME?" He's dousing the room like a rug on a fire.

Buck glares at me, breathing hard.

The famous photographer rolls his eyes, whispers into the ear of one of the beautiful women.

Then someone laughs, then someone else, and as the party din revs back up, I grab Buck and push him out into the lobby.

"Get your fucking hands *off* me," he says.

"What the *fuck*?" I say, with a smile on my face, just in case anyone's watching us.

"What? *I'm* saying what the fuck to *you*! I come to talk to you and you *walk away*?"

"Someone pulled me away! I'm meeting people! That's what we're supposed to be doing at these things!"

Buck is rocking a little, looking down at the ground, wiping his nose with the back of his hand. He's drunk. Really drunk. Drunk like skunk drunk. I try to put my arm around him.

"Get *off* me!" he says again. "God! You make me *sick*!" and he turns away, walks toward the doors, through the doors, and he's gone.

I stand there, wondering if I should go after him. Partly because I'm worried about him, and partly because I'm scared that he's completely lost it and is going to turn up pounding on my door later, confessing all of our horrible sins to Guy and ruining my life as I know it.

I go back to the bar and over to Guy and Aimee.

"Another bass player with issues, I see," says Aimee, without saying hello or hugging me because whenever you talk with Aimee, no matter how long it's been since you've seen her last, she makes you feel as if you're in the middle of a long conversation that never stopped.

"I don't know," I say. "He's just drunk or something."

"Hey," says Aimee, and she laughs, smacking Guy on the arm. "At least *he* has a record deal, right?"

"Well, sort of," I say.

I reach out and take Guy's hand. Smile at him. "Having fun?" I say.

"More fun than you, I bet," he says.

I can't sleep. I keep seeing Buck dead by the side of the road. Or screaming at me on live television. Or slitting my throat.

Guy's snoring softly. I want to wake him up, tell him everything, how I screwed up, how I'm screwed up, how I'm sorry, how Buck's insane and is scaring me to death. How I want so badly to just get rid of him, get another bass player, make everything okay again.

But I just lie there. Because I'm leaving on tour in six days for God knows how long and I can't face being out there all alone. And I know that I could make every resolve in the world to be strong, to be good, to never kiss Buck again, never watch TV with him again, never hold his hand on the plane again—but I know I will. I'll have to. There'll come a time when I'll feel like I don't have a choice.

I wake in the morning with my head pounding in time to the ringing phone. It's Buck, telling me he's sorry, that it'll never happen again, that he understands everything now, how it has to be, that it'll be smooth sailing from here on in.

As I'm hanging up, a piece of paper is slowly edging its way under the door. It's a fax from Randy, a review of last night's show in something called the *Music Connection*. I swallow. Cough. My hands shake as my eyes race through the article:

> *Boston's Jennifer Trynin writes concise, gutsy pop songs which are bound by her knack for memorable, interesting melodies . . . fronts her power trio with marked authority . . . conducted*

herself like a guitar god . . . stage chatter was unaffected and casually funny . . . In a setting less hamstrung by industry presence, Trynin would have undoubtedly brought down the house. Her set was notable for its unflagging energy and freshness.

I look up the ceiling and mouth, *Thank you.*

A few hours later, I'm sitting in a hard plastic chair at LAX browsing through the *L.A. Times,* and BAM! There's my name: "Road Test for Lyrically Smart Trynin." I smile. *Lyrically Smart.*

I read on:

If you didn't know it going into Jennifer Trynin's show at the Troubadour, you could probably guess by the end that she has spent a lot more time writing, recording and playing alone than she has performing with a band . . . Her aggressively casual and chatty manner was perhaps an indie-rocker's way of easing the pressure of an appearance in her new label's hometown, or maybe it was overcompensation for onstage uncertainty . . . Trynin's musical approach was similarly forced, indulging her lead-guitar abilities at the expense of her songs' best qualities.

"What's that?" says Buck.

"Nothing," I say, folding the paper, getting up, and throwing it in the garbage.

SEVEN

"With plenty to say and ample musical gifts with which to say it, Boston newcomer Jennifer Trynin is poised to join the upper ranks of GenX alternative rock queendom. . . . One of the year's best debuts. A revelation."

—Billboard

★

I'm sitting on the edge of my bed staring at my duffel bag, my brain spinning so fast it's like it's not moving at all. This will be my last night sleeping in my own bed for God knows how long, because tomorrow we're heading out on tour and no one seems to be able to tell me when we'll be back.

If I were the person I've been pretending to be, I'd be out drinking. Hell, I wouldn't even be packed.

But I'm packed all right, packed to the teeth. Fifteen T-shirts. Four pairs of corduroys, three pairs of corduroy cutoffs. Underwear, underwear, underwear. Two pairs of big shoes. Three jackets. Toiletries. Tampons. Giant-sized Advil. Plus a ton of other stuff, like my teeny-weeny travel clock radio, a mini tape recorder, a stapler, stamps, Post-it notes, a pad of paper, five black Bic pens, and two rolls of tape, one Scotch, one masking.

Guy steps into the bedroom. "Wow," he says. "Now that's a big bag."

I have another bag too—my "day bag"—a large green backpack in which to carry jacket-o'-the-day, magazines, phone numbers, gum, cigarettes, lighter, water, snacks. I've decided not to bring my journal, because I can't think of anywhere safe enough to keep it.

The truth is, if I could, I'd carry around a third bag the size of my house with my house in it. What I really wish is that I could pivot through this entire tour with one toe on my front doorstep.

Guy leans over, peeks into my duffel. "A flashlight?" he says. "What're you, going camping?" He sits on the bed and puts his arm around me.

"I've never traveled in my whole life," I say. "I've never even been on a fucking teen tour."

"Everything's gonna be okay," he says.

★

We gather outside the rehearsal space to load the van—Robby, Buck, Laura, me, Guy, and the tour manager Randy hired a few days ago, who's short and muscular in a plain white undershirt, black shorts, and black sneakers. He has long, dark sideburns and keys dangling from his neck on a thin rope.

"I'm Burns," he says to me. "Tour manager."

"I'm Jen," I say. "Singer."

"Ten-four," he says.

A car pulls up and out hops SoundBoy, the soundman we hired away from one of the clubs in town. He says, "If it's gonna be this friggin' hot all summer, I quit."

"What's with the leg?" says Burns to Robby, who's leaning against the van, lightly banging his cane against his cast.

"Combat," says Robby. "Shrapnel."

After the gear is loaded into the back of the van, SoundBoy starts throwing all our duffels in one by one. "Jesus Christ!" he says, when he gets to mine. "What the fuck is in here?"

Burns hands out our tour books, which are about the size of a *Reader's Digest,* with a red cover and my name and a black xeroxed image of the chair from the cover of *Cockamamie* on it.

"Nice touch," I say, pointing to the chair.

"I like to be creative," says Burns, and I'm hoping he's just trying to be funny, because otherwise it's going to be a long tour.

There's a page for each day of the tour, telling us everything we'd ever want to know, like name and location of that night's club, load-in time, soundcheck, doors, show time and length of set; hotel address and phone number and amenities, like cable (usually), pool (occasionally), room service (almost never); and drive times (three hours, five hours, eleven hours). So far, the book is only about six weeks long, because that's all that's been officially scheduled. Randy's told me that we'll add more dates as they come in.

When it's finally time to leave, Buck and Laura disappear around the corner. Robby turns away from us and bends over, wrapping his arms around his back so it looks like he's making out with someone. I walk Guy back to his car across the parking lot. I begin to cry as I reach to hug him. He pulls me against his chest and I can hear his heart beating hard and fast.

It's still hot when we get to the club, your run-of-the-mill rock dive. The evening sun is setting on everything—the marquee with my name on it, the door to the club, the sidewalk. We're only about three hours from home, but it will be thousands of hours until we get back. I think of the sun hitting the rotting windows of my apartment, hitting Guy's car in the lot behind his studio. I stick out my hand, look at the sun on my palm.

Backstage before the show, a bunch of people I've never met show up with a case of champagne, all wearing little hats. They're local reps, they tell us. Warners hires them all across the country to "greet the artist" and set up radio interviews and meet-and-greets and "in-stores" (performances in record stores).

I peek out at the floor. With about half an hour till show time, the place is only half full.

"Don't sweat it," says one of the locals. "Next time you come through, there'll be a line around the block."

At 3 A.M., I'm lying in a queen-size bed with my duffel next to me, listening for Buck and Robby even though they're four rooms away. I'm staring at the white-cork ceiling. There's no minibar. No table or chair. Just a low dresser with a TV on top that I've left on with the sound off.

★

Being out on the road is like skiing down a mountain *fast*. We're here! There! EVERYWHERE! We pull into a town and *Cockamamie* posters are in the music store windows, taped up on graffiti-scrawled walls. We open local papers and our faces are splashed across the entertainment listings. We're *The Pick!* We're *What's Hot!* "Better Than Nothing" is on this station, that station, coming through someone's car window.

"Hey," says the girl behind the counter in a coffee shop. "Aren't you that chick? On MTV? From the gas station? 'I'm Feelin' Good,' right? RIGHT?"

The clubs are pretty packed and people are actually showing up for the in-stores, even in the middle of the afternoon. Everyone wants my autograph, an interview, a hug.

"I've been on tours with new artists where you show up at the club and it's like a ghost town," says Burns. "Like the fucking tundra."

All the Warner locals tell us, "If you guys think *this* is fun, just wait till things *really* take off!"

Well, we can't wait.

We can't wait!

WE CAN'T WAIT!

We pull into a city somewhere with dirty streets and clouds. We've only been out a couple of weeks, but it feels like forever. We finally find the motel, a big cement sprawl painted Florida pink. The parking lot has exactly two cars: a black windowless van and a rusting orange two-door. To one side of the motel is an overgrown lot with a chain-link fence, to the other a shabby self-storage facility.

Burns jumps out and heads inside the motel office. We let him take care of everything now, like he's our counselor and we're just on one long trip into town from camp.

"Look at those guys," says SoundBoy, pointing over at the black van. "Does that guy have a gun?"

"What?" I say.

Everyone smashes their faces against the van windows.

"You're crazy," says Buck.

"No," says Robby, "I think I see a gun."

"Let's get the fuck out of here," I say.

Burns comes walking back across the parking lot, opens the side door. "Okay kids."

"Look," I say. "See those guys? The guy in the sweatshirt has a gun."

Burns squints and stares. "You're crazy."

"I saw it too," says SoundBoy.

"Me too," says Robby.

"You're all fucking crazy," says Buck.

Burns looks again. "I'm with Buck," he says. "Everybody inside."

We grab our bags and head into the motel.

The corridors smell strongly of chlorine—chlorine and something else. We don't see another soul.

"What's that smell?" I say.

"Chlorine," says Burns.

"But there's something else."

Someone grabs me from behind, presses an arm across my throat. I scream.

It's Buck.

Everyone laughs.

I push him away. "Thanks," I say.

"Here we are, madam," says Burns, unlocking a door and pushing it open. "Your room."

I stand there for a moment as the rest of them continue down the hall looking for their rooms.

"How come there doesn't seem to be anybody else here?" I say.

"Cuz they're all dead," yells Burns.

I hoist my duffel bag over my shoulder because I don't want it touching the floor. My room is hot, with a double bed covered with a ripped flower-print blanket. On the bathroom sink are four Dixie Cups, and there's no sanitary wrapper on the toilet seat. I count six hairs on the towel hanging on the back of the door. Everything reeks of chlorine and—and—and—old cheese? Spoiled milk? Rancid meat? ROTTING FLESH?

I scamper back out into the hall. Slowly, Robby appears, then Buck, then SoundBoy, and finally Burns. We stand there, looking at each other, until Burns says, "Okay, we're outta here."

We hightail it out of the parking lot, where the two guys are still standing around with their gun. SoundBoy leans out of the window and yells, "Don't shoot!"

Ring!

Where am I where am I where am I? A phone is ringing, right there on that night table beside this bed where I am. Today is today is today is . . . Thursday. I'm being picked up at 7:45 for the photo shoot. FUCK! Did I oversleep?—I grab my teeny-weeny travel clock radio: 6:56 A.M. Okay. I'm okay.

Ring!

I sit up, rubbing my face in my hands, shaking my head. I pick up the phone.

"Hello?"

"Oh my god, I got you."

My mother never says hello.

"You must have a trail of messages from me," she says.

For nights on end, there've been slips of paper clipped to our reservation cards at check-in. *Jen's mom says call her.* I've managed to forget to do this every day for the past four days.

"What is it there, eight?"

"Seven," I say.

"Oh," she says. "It's just that I've been calling and calling and I keep missing you and you never call me back. Are you all right? Did I wake you?"

"It's okay."

"I'm sorry. Do you want to hang up?"

"I have to get up anyway. I have a photo shoot."

"So early?"

"Yeah."

"What for?"

"*Rolling Stone.*"

"Well, that sounds good. You must be happy about that."

As usual, I can tell my mother's not impressed. Never mind that *Cockamamie* is going to be *Rolling Stone*'s summer Hot Issue's "Hot Debut Album." Except for the day she heard me on NPR, her general attitude is *rock star, shmock star.* A few weeks ago she described this "whole music thing" as a "good experience," as if it were nothing more than an elaborate preparation for some other life she pictures me leading, the one where I work at Goldman Sachs or write for *The New York Times* or teach at Harvard—the kind of life where I wear all the silk scarves and gold bracelets and other stuff she's given me over the years, the accessories that she imagines someone who is her daughter ought to wear.

"I can't believe they make you get up so early to do these sorts of things," she says. "Are you going to be on the cover?"

"No, Ma, not the cover."

"Well, if they're not going to put you on the cover, you should tell them to take your picture later in the day."

"That's not the way it works," I say. "If they *were* gonna put me on the cover, then maybe I'd have a prayer of having the shoot later in the day, but as it is, no one really listens to me about much of anything."

"You sound so anxious," says my mom, and I can feel her shaking her head. "Are you sleeping? When did you go to bed last night?"

"Around 3:30."

My mother gives her little whistle—a simple slide down the scale—that indicates she thinks I'm living my life unwisely. "I don't know," she says. And again: "I just don't know." She pauses, but can't seem to resist the urge to Get Into It. "I just wonder what kind of life this must be. You barely sleep, and that message you left me last week sounded frankly—I don't know how to say this, but I'm your mother and I've got responsibilities so here it is. Are you on drugs?"

"What?"

"You can be honest with me."

"Mom—"

"Now Jennifer, I know this makes you uncomfortable and believe me, it's the *last* thing in the world I ever wanted to ask you, but there it is. Are. You. Doing. Drugs." She says it slower this time, articulating each word as if I'm so messed up I can't even understand what she's saying. "Because even right now, you're sounding a little groggy."

"You woke me up," I say.

"I need you to answer me."

Sometimes I get the feeling that she thinks that I've ended up in this "whole music thing" because she was a bad parent, because my father left, because everything went Helter Skelter.

"No. I'm. Not. Doing. Drugs," I tell her, clear as a bell.

She whistles her little tune again. "Because Mona's daughter is going with someone who plays the drums in a band—I think they're called Under The Table. Have you ever heard of them?"

"No."

"No, me either—frankly, I don't think they're doing very well—and Mona was very very impressed when I told her what you were doing—not that I've really been telling people because what do they know about it and you know how *boring* it can be when people go on and on about their children—"

"Mom—"

"So Mona says this boyfriend is a druggie and that he had to go to rehab."

"Mom. You're being ridiculous."

"And I spoke to your father the other day and he said some friends of his went to your show in Detroit and they told him that you looked very tired."

"I *am* very tired."

"Does anyone in your group do drugs?"

"No, Mom."

"You're always just so far away and I call and I call and I can never get you."

It's 7:05 and my teeny-weeny travel clock radio begins to beep.

"I know, Mom. I'm sorry, but I really gotta get going."

"What's that sound?"

"My clock."

"Do you have a concert tonight?"

"Yeah."

"Whew, that sounds like a long day," she says.

It's 7:56 A.M. and Sheila Capuano, my Warner Bros. publicist, is next to me in the rental car she can't believe she had to drive from the *fucking* airport because the *fucking* limo guy was a no-show for, apparently, not the first fucking time.

"What is he, on crack?" she says. "He needs what? My flight number, a limo, a watch." She flicks her perfectly manicured, bright red fingernails into the air, *one, two, three.*

Sheila's wearing a New Yorky black pants suit and big hoop earrings that are shining beneath her big curly black hair. She also seems to have pulled every last hair from each of her eyebrows and then drawn on fake ones, making her look a little like Groucho Marx, a little like she's on her way to a KISS concert.

She looks at me. "What're you staring at?"

"Nothing," I say.

Sheila's here at the behest of Head Honcho, because "You don't fuck around when it's *Rolling Stone.*" So, despite everything she'd planned to do today (what *does* she do all day?), here she is with maps on her lap, cutting people off, eliciting elongated honks from horn after horn as her index finger flags behind the windshield like a wiper. "Oh no no no, my friend," she's saying, "fuck *you!*"

I ask Sheila how my little snowflake of creativity got picked as *Rolling Stone*'s Hot Debut Album.

"We have our ways," says Sheila, with her right hand against her head pantomiming a phone, shaking it as if somewhere far, far away, another hand is ringing, as if she has the ear of all the Important People, as if the magical Say-So is hers. All I can wonder is if any money exchanged hands, and if that'll be recoupable to me too.

I'm trying not to imagine the looks on the faces of all my struggling musician friends back home opening the next issue of *Rolling Stone* and seeing my picture. And I'm really trying not to think about how Buck and Robby might be feeling about not being invited to the shoot at all.

"Why can't they use some picture we already have, and why do we have to do this so early in the morning anyway?" I say. "I mean, look at me." I turn toward Sheila, put my fingers under my eyes, and drag my ever-present bags down toward my mouth.

"Don't be ridiculous. You look great," she says. "Kinda heroiny. You know, kinda shitty, in a good way."

We pull up to a corner where people are milling around, smoking and drinking coffee and unloading lights and tripods and ladders.

"Pleasure pleasure pleasure," says Tristram, the photographer, who's tall, with short bleached blond hair and thickly rimmed black glasses. As we're shaking hands, his eyes travel up and down my body like searchlights, engaging my First Impression Sensors, which help me detect other people's disappointment that I'm me (*So this is the bidding-war chick. Huh.*). By his smile, I'm gauging that I'm rating around a 7, maybe even a 7.25, on his rock-chick-looks-o-meter, and for that, I'm grateful.

Tristram introduces me to his assistant, Bo, who smiles at me, lightly touching a few strands of the hair across my face, mouthing, *Love your hair.* "And that's Michaela," says Tristram, pointing to a heavy woman in a gray sweatshirt who's yawning. "She'll be doing your makeup."

I stand in the alley where Tristram says he wants to "check for light." A little long-haired dude keeps coming at me with a silver contraption, flashing *pop pop pop*. Something smells like piss. Like piss and throw-up. I light a cigarette and watch Tristram who's saying, "*Yeaaaahhhhh*," and rubbing his hands together, pacing back and forth across the entrance to the alley. Bo hovers behind him, camera after camera draped around his neck like Olympic gold medals. Then Tristram motions me a little deeper into the alley, asks if I can get a little closer to the Dumpster, where I throw down my cigarette and stamp it out, right next to a used condom.

Tristram begins taking pictures with a big, noisy, old-style Polaroid. After each flash, he pulls the picture from the bottom of the camera and tosses it at Bo like a Frisbee. Bo manages to catch each one, waving it in the air and checking his watch before adding it to the growing row on the sidewalk. Now Tristram and Bo and Sheila are standing above the Polaroids, inspecting them this way, then that way. They're shading their eyes and looking at the sky, then down the alley. They're squatting, jumping, laughing, joking, as I'm trying to discern if anything that's happening is at my expense.

After a hushed conference, Sheila looks up at me and yells, "Is that what you're wearing?" I ask her what she means. "Didn't you bring any other clothes with you?" I've done enough of these things to know that I'm supposed to bring a choice of outfits. But frankly, there's nothing back in my duffel at the hotel that's all that different from what I'm already wearing, and everything's dirty anyway. Plus, I forgot.

Bo approaches with one of the Polaroids, rolling his eyes in Sheila's direction. "It's *sooooo* frustrating," he says, leaning into me so I can smell his high-pitched cologne. "Don't you listen to her. I mean, she works at a *record* company. Just *look* at you! You're like capital-D a*dor*able. You are completely *so now* with your little tight T-shirt and those 70s corduroys. Where did you find those?"

Michaela waves me over to her makeup area, where I sit on a creaky fold-out stool. She puts her hands on her hips and looks me over. "I'd die to be as thin as you," she says. "I'm not kidding. I'd kill myself." She grabs a puffy pink ball and swabs at my face like she's dusting me off. "I bet you don't even have to work at it."

"No, I do," I say. "I totally have to watch what I eat and everything."

"Uh huh," says Michaela. "You see these?" she says, grabbing both of her large breasts from beneath and presenting them to me like puppies.

"I'd love to have tits like yours," I say, which isn't true.

"You can have them," she says, letting them fall back into her body with a jiggle. "Okay okay okay," she says, hands back on her hips, staring at me. "You got some killer bags under your eyes," she says.

"I can't help it," I say. "I'm a Jew."

Michaela laughs. "Me too," she says.

Many layers of makeup later, I'm standing back in the alley.

"You just relax," says Tristram. "Today, you're the Hot Debut Album, but next year, *next* year, you and me, same Bat time, same Bat channel," and he looks up at the sky, holding his hands out like he's framing a cloud. "Jennifer Trynin on the cover of *Rolling Stone.*" He looks back at me, miming like he's taking my picture, and says, "Click."

After two hours of standing this way, that way, chin up, chin down, look over here, no, over here, close-ups, body shots, makeup touch-ups, let's try squatting, leaning, laughing, scowling—Tristram assures me that "we've got it." But somehow I can't imagine the picture looking any way other than how the world's been looking to me all morning, which is blurry, tired, and out of breath.

Sheila drops me back at the hotel and I'm waiting for the elevator when I hear Buck's voice.

"Yes, my friend!" he's yelling. "Yes yes yes yes yes!"

In the bar, Buck, Robby, Burns, and SoundBoy are watching baseball. Sox against some other team. Everyone turns and gives me a nod except Buck, who's staring at the TV and pounding his hand against his mouth, eating nuts one at a time.

★

We pull into a rest area and Burns clicks off the engine.

"Jen's gotta make a call," he says.

"I do?" I say.

"Yeah," he says. "Randy wants you to call him."

"What's up?" I say.

"Just call him."

Everybody except me piles out and heads for bathrooms and coffee and Egg McMuffins.

I'm standing at the pay phone with the receiver pushed hard against my ear. It's sunny and hot, with a warm wind blowing through the trees and trucks galore roaring by right behind me, which is maybe why it's so hard for me to hear what Randy is saying.

"Danny Goldberg's out," he says, or that's what I'm afraid he's just said as a semi booms by right over my shoulder. I ask him to repeat himself two or three times to make sure I heard him right, and each time it's like a sledgehammer pounding me into the pavement.

"Was he fired or something?" I say.

There've been some "problems of philosophy," Randy explains, and things "not jelling at The Company." In the end, it'd been a "mutual decision."

I stand there, trying to shake off my sudden sense of doom, as Randy tells me everything's still fine, Head Honcho is still totally dedicated to my record; in fact it's really he who's been leading the Jennifer Trynin brigade at The Building, since Danny never even really established an office there.

This is the first time I notice anyone using the word "still" in reference to anything having to do with me.

★

"Better Than Nothing," Jennifer Trynin—Don't be fooled by Trynin's dazed and confused delivery. The singer offers up the most provocative opening line of the year—"Maybe we could

talk in the shower"—and backs it up with lean and crunchy
power chords. A–

—Entertainment Weekly

★

Why is everything sounding like shit? *Fucking B-string.*

"Buck. Check your tuning. Yeah, I know. Check it anyway." What
is it with the tuning attitude from him?

Place is packed—maybe not completely packed, but pretty fucking packed. All the shiny happy faces, singing along. Good good good
good good. City 24 loves me. Danny Goldberg's gonna be sorry. Is
that guy gonna give me those flowers or what? If I were a *real* rock
star, I'd just reach down and snag those suckers right out of his hand.
Maybe I will. I should grab my mic stand and thrash it around and
throw it out into the crowd, and then kick something over and then
just reach down and *grab* those fucking flowers and the guy'll be like
What? and then he'll be like *Wow!* and then everyone'll be like *Wow!*
and they'll all be clapping and hollering and then I'll rip apart the really rather nice flower arrangement and just *fling* those fuckers into
the audience. YEAH! And then I'll whip off my guitar and *pound* it
on the stage– POUND POUND POUND—and then I'll throw it up
in the air like that Nirvana bass-player guy did at that awards show
and it'll come back and hit me in the head and there'll be *hilarity* and
screaming and a general air of *bedlam* and—FUCK! Why can't I really
be like that?

Fucking B-string.

I wish to God I could mount this *fucking* tuner on my mic stand.
Why oh *why* do I have to sweat so much? It's pooling in my eyes and I
can't even see the stupid little tuning lights all the way down there on
the floor.

Are people staring at my mouth? *Relax your mouth, Jen.* You
don't need to curl your lips around your teeth to tune. Fuck Einstein.
Do you think you could stop making so many faces when you play gui-
tar? How come when guys make faces when they play it's cool, but
when a chick does it, it's "unattractive"? Maybe if I could just keep

my hair hanging a little more completely over my face when I'm playing, no one would really be able to make out that —

WHAT THE FUCK AM I DOING?

You're onstage, goddamn it!

Tune!

Focus!

Some drunk guy is yelling at me.

"What?"

Yell.

"What?"

Here comes Burns from the wings. "He's saying, 'King's Foot,'
boss," says Burns.

"King's foot?"

"Sure. You know," says Burns, making a silly, I'm-drunk face.
"Like, You guys are fucking great! You're like King's Foot!"

Ha ha. "You're a weirdo, Burns."

Burns salutes me. Walks back offstage.

"PLAY FREEBIRD!"

Tell me someone did not just yell "Play 'Freebird'!"

"Who just yelled that? You? You know, nobody's *ever* yelled that
before. Let's give this guy a hand."

Clap clap clap.

Only four songs to go. Am I getting a headache? Hey Jen, maybe
if you didn't get so loaded every night you'd be in a tad better humor
during the day. Note to self: STOP GETTING SHIT-HOUSED!

Fucking B-string.

Maybe my machine head is loose.

People are getting restless.

I detect some definite milling.

Get it together, Jen.

Focus.

Has this club ever heard of AIR-CONDITIONING?

Do I have sweat stains on my ass? Because that's also really at-
tractive.

I should say something.

SAY SOMETHING FOR FUCK'S SAKE.

Finally. B. Just E to go.

This feels like the perfect moment to pull out a bit of nonsensical drivel in my Steven Wright persona:

"This little piggy went to market."

Am I talking slow and spacey enough?

"This little piggy stayed home."

Almost E. Almost E.

"This little piggy ate roast beef."

Yes! E. Okay.

"And this little piggy —"

"I'LL SHOW YOU HOW TO EAT ROAST BEEF—FUCKIN' PLAY SOMETHING ALREADY!"

Sudden quiet, as people check out the dickhead heckler.

"You wanna show me how to eat roast beef? Yeah? Fantastic. How about you ask your little girlfriend there if it's okay if you come up here and show *everybody* how to eat roast beef. Oh, she's not? Yeah, I didn't think so. She's waaaaay outta your league, buddy." Laughter. "This next song's for you."

"Too Bad You're Such a Loser."

Then just three more songs.

I'm almost home.

Backstage is a free-for-all, everyone angling for beers, peering over everyone else's shoulder, with plenty of drunken name exchanging (*Eddie? Oh, Betty? That's cool. So, like, you're a chick?*).

Burns comes over. "Don't forget we're driving tonight," he says. "We're outta here in forty-five."

"Fantastico," I say.

"King's Foot," says Burns.

Buck and Robby are holding court by the cooler, checking out the chicks, which is making me feel quite squirrel-like, perched atop this stool, worriedly collecting and stashing memories of moments when I've felt as bold and happening as that cute little number right there who's reaching out and grazing the back of Buck's hand just once, just right, just enough.

I catch a glimpse of myself in a mirror. My sweat-drenched "No Nukes!" concert T is hanging off me like a wet towel on the back of a chair. From this angle, I have no tits at all. Sweat has also plastered my stringy hair against my skull, making my nose pointier, my chin longer, my ears even bigger. *The chicks wanna be you and the guys wanna fuck you.* Right. Most of the time it's feeling more like the chicks wanna fuck the guys in my band, and all the guys just wanna fuck the chicks at my show.

Finally. Some guy is staring at me.

I sit up a little, push my hair out of my face.

He smiles. (Nice smile.)

I smile, nod.

He walks over. (Nice walk.)

"Hi," he says, sticking out his hand. (Nice hands. The kind I like. I feel them on me.)

"Hi," I say, as he's shaking my hand, holding on for too long.

"Do you always talk in the shower?" he says, as I imagine what I always imagine when some guy quotes this line back to me, which is that he's picturing me naked, if even for an instant.

"Not always," I say, feeling what I always feel, which is slightly thrilled. "Sometimes I do other stuff in the shower." I'm always saying these kinds of things as if any of this might lead to something. But, as always, as soon as the words are out of my mouth, my mind begins fast-forwarding through my own rock-and-roll fantasy, which always ends in the same way—with me in the passenger seat of some dirty car that smells like gasoline and cigarettes as some guy is speeding me back to his apartment with one finger on the wheel where the lights will flicker and the fridge'll be empty and we'll stay up all night doing coke and downing shots and having sex until I wake up in a field with cigarette burns on my arm.

"Could you sign these for me?" asks the guy, holding out two copies of *Cockamamie* and a pen.

"Sure," I say. "What's your name?"

"Ben," he says.

"Ben," I say. *To Ben,* I write. Then I draw a little heart because I don't know what else to do. As I'm signing my name, I can hear Buck.

"That chick?" he's saying. "The one with the hair?"

"Yeah?" says Robby.

"She just showed me her tits."

Robby laughs. "I thought you were saving yourself for Kava*ll*ah," he says.

I hand Ben his signed CD.

"Would you sign that other one too?" says Ben, pointing. "To 'Mandie'? With an *i-e.* My girlfriend's really into you. Especially that 'Feelin' Good' song."

"Oh," I say. "Okay. Mandie. With an *i-e.*" Big heart. My name.

In the van, I end up sitting next to SoundBoy. Buck's in the back with Robby. I'm leaning my head against the window, staring at the black night, with something in me crawling back to wherever it came from. I feel myself growing smaller and smaller and farther and farther away, disintegrating, dissolving to a hum, buzzing down the wire along the highway, untouchable, skittering, flashing by *you* and *you* and *you.*

We're in the studios at MTV and there's the usual table full of donuts and bagels and cream cheese and bags of Doritos and potato chips that always seems to be everywhere anywhere around video-type people. It's 10 A.M., which isn't really that early but it feels early because I didn't get to sleep until four. I've had no coffee, no cigarettes, no food, and my eyes are puffy.

My noneating buildup for my first-ever TV appearances has been stupendous. My tan cord cutoffs are slipping right off my butt. My red sports jersey is billowing around my stomach. The only problem is that my brain feels like it's in a brown-out.

We're introduced to Matt, the fat bald guy who hosts *120 Minutes.* He's wearing the same knee-length shorts we're all wearing and a gray T-shirt that says WALLOW. He shakes my hand. "'Feelin' Good,'" he says, nodding, smiling. "Cool song."

Okay, I admit it. I should've called the damn song "I'm Feelin' Good" instead of "Better Than Nothing." It's been confusing people from the get-go and has already caused a myriad of marketing snafus. And I can only imagine that when people are calling up radio stations and requesting "the 'Feelin' Good' song" instead of "Better Than Nothing," the DJs are playing the song "Good" by the band Better Than Ezra.

Regardless, things are going great and "Better Than Nothing" is high up on the Alternative and Modern Rock charts, and climbing. At least that's what My Team has been telling me. Since I've been out on the road, I've not allowed myself to look at so much as a single music magazine or playlist. I don't want to know the specifics. As long as my song's still climbing, I've got nothing to worry about. That's what everybody keeps telling me. *But what happens if it stops climbing?* I ask them. *We'll cross that bridge when we get to it,* they say. Then they laugh. But I don't know if it's a *Don't-be-ridiculous, that-day-ain't-never-gonna-come* laugh or if it's a *Don't-be-ridiculous, we-don't-even-talk-about-such-things* laugh. Lately I can't seem to decide what's more frightening: that it'll stop climbing or keep climbing.

I've never been in a TV studio before and all I want to do is run around—*What's this? What's that? Who're you? Can I press this button? Where does that door go?* But I just stand there, trying to act nonchalant, which I'm afraid is coming off snooty. Head Honcho has told me to watch out for the glaring.

"I'm not glaring. I'm looking around."

"People think you're glaring."

"Well, what am I supposed to do? Shut my eyes?"

"How about smiling?"

"Smiling at what?"

"Smiling in general."

"I need to smile specifically."

"Why are you so difficult?"

"I'm not difficult."

Now I feel like everyone's staring at me and I don't know if it's because they love my music or because they hate my guts (*Isn't that the
big bidding-war chick?*) or maybe they're just wondering who the fuck
I am and why I'm glaring at everything.

The actual *120 Minutes* studio surprises me. On TV it looks like this
little cozy room with a nice cozy Oriental rug in it. But in reality, it's
this cavernous space with lots of baffles and dark corners and people
in the shadows behind cameras who don't say anything. Oh. And
there's an Oriental rug on the floor. And it's about 2 degrees.

Burns and SoundBoy have already set up our gear. First, we're
going to play through three songs three times each. Then, we interview. That's what I've been told. Buck slings on his bass. I put on my
guitar. Robby sits behind his drums up on the riser. We're waiting,
I'm not sure for what. No one's talking. Now all I can feel is nervous-
ness. *Nervous. Nervosa. Necrophilia. Philadelphia.* My mind is racing
and my mouth is tight. *Blight. Fight.* SHUT UP!

A voice comes over a speaker. "Go ahead," it says.

Buck and Robby and I look at each other. I count us in.

We play through "One Year Down," and my face feels so tight it's
like my lips could crack.

When we come to the end, silence. Shuffling of cameramen's feet.

The voice comes over the speaker again. "Take two."

The interview. The three of us sit on a big trunk in what I can only
imagine are unflattering positions, hunched over, our legs dangling. A
woman is sitting behind a camera with a huge light above it shining in
our eyes. I can't really see her. She says something I can't really hear.

"What?" I say.

"When did you start playing guitar?" she says.

Dear God: Please don't let this be one of those interviews.

"Around eleven," I say, mouth tight, hair in my face.

"When did you decide to pursue music seriously?"

God? I asked nicely.

"It was like the day after Halloween when I'd just moved to

Boston," I say, as Buck inspects his cuticles and Robby softly kicks the tip of his cane over and over with his sneaker.

"Did you move to Boston for the music scene?"

"I didn't even know there was a music scene."

I'm afraid. Afraid that this whole interview is going to focus on me me me, which is going to stick in Buck's craw and he's going to freak out. On camera. On MTV.

"Didn't you used to be a jazz artist?"

Okay, now this chick is blowing my cover. I fumble over my answer, trying to be funny or cute or smile or something, anything.

"So tell me, Jen," says Buck, suddenly turning to me, hand on his chin, crossing his legs. "Weren't you born a small black child?"

I laugh. Robby laughs. I punch Buck on the arm. He winks at me. We carry on.

The *Conan O'Brien* studio is even colder than the MTV studios, and I'm terrified that my nipples are pinging through my T-shirt. Everything is much smaller than it looks on TV—the desk where Conan O'Brien sits and the couch next to it, the stage to the right of that, and still farther to the right, the little area for the Max Weinberg Seven. There's only about twenty feet between the stage and the steeply inclined rows of seats for the studio audience, which right now are empty.

"What happens if I blank out?" I ask Doogey the stage manager, who has a whistle dangling from his neck. I wonder if he ever uses it, and if so, when?

Doogey drums his fingers on the underside of his clipboard. "You get one shot," he says.

"What if there's some kind of, like, technical difficulty?"

"Listen. If a bomb goes off then maybe, *maybe,* we'll give you another take. But basically, you just play your song and that's it. Warts and all."

"Oh," I say, unable to shake the memory of that time in a summer camp talent show when all I could remember of "Needle and the Damage Done" was the first words to the first verse and the last words

to the last verse, which I sang over and over, to an ever-swelling tittering in the audience, so that by the fourth time I sang, "But every
junkie's like a setting sun," I swore to myself that I'd never get on a
stage again. Not to mention: junkies. What did I know about junkies?

When we get back to the "green room," where we're supposed to
relax, Buck tells me to stop worrying.

"If you screw up, I'll kick you to the side and sing the bugger myself," he says.

"Even I know the words to this one," says Robby.

"Jen," says Burns, "at this point, I think *I* could sing that song."

This is when Kavallah walks in, her blond perm twirled into glo-
rious tendrils, her tight blue jeans cupping her tight heart-shaped ass,
her breasts all bounce and curvaciousness, her snug baby-T revealing
a navel so small and oddly modest as to invite a fingertip.

"Welcome," says Buck, standing up. "Welcome to our lair." He
bows.

"How was MTV?" she says.

"Great!" says Robby.

"Great!" says Buck.

"Where's Randy?" I say.

"Randy says he is soooooo sorry, but he's up to here," says Kavallah, putting her hand like a salute to her forehead. "He says he'll be
here by the taping."

She pulls from her bag a bunch of papers for us to sign, "union
stuff" she says, handing out pens.

Buck says he's not going to sign.

"Buck," I say.

"You gotta sign it or else you can't do the show," says Kavallah.

"I'm not signing something if I don't know what it is," says Buck.

"Come on," says Robby. "I'm sure it's nothing. Just the usual stuff."

Buck stands up, stretches. "I'm not signing it," he says.

My throat begins to swell with emotion, though I'm not sure exactly which emotion it is. Anger? Fear? Irritation? Did I already say
fear? I stand up.

"Buck! Why can't you just—"

"Just what?" says Buck. "Lie down and play dead?"

I can feel the tears in my eyes as I lurch over the coffee table, past Kavallah (who smells lovely—lemony, yellowy, like a fresh spring morn) and out into the hallway, where I cry unreasonably hard, especially considering the world is my own personal rock-star oyster.

The steeply inclined seats are filled with people. The lights over our half of the stage are dimmed. Conan is behind his desk, laughing it up with Crystal Bernard, the chick from the TV show *Wings*. When he says, "We'll be right back with singer Jennifer Trynin" and holds up my CD for the closeup, my heart gives me one curvilinear THUD, bringing my hand to my chest in an I-knew-I-was-going-to-die-of-a-heart-attack-today sort of way. I figure I have three or four minutes to calm myself down before we're back from commercial break—but then Doogey gives me the high sign, twirling his hand in the air as if lassoing, because we're not really broadcasting live, we're just pretending.

Holding the CD up to the camera again, Conan says, "Here with us tonight is Jennifer Trynin, hailing from Boston, Massachusetts, with her new record, *Cockamamie,* out now on Warner Brothers Records. Please help me welcome Jennifer Trynin!"

Clap clap clap.

Robby starts playing the opening beat, which I can barely hear over my pounding heart and my spinning brain which is reeling through the first words to the song again and again: *Maybe we could talk in the shower—Maybe we could talk in the shower*—I know the words. I swear I do. And what's the real likelihood of my having a heart attack within the next three minutes and twenty-six seconds anyway? And even if I do have a heart attack, I'm young, it won't be fatal. They'll just stop the tape and pick me up, call an ambulance, administer fluids. They won't just, like, leave me here to die.

Right?

I hear my guitar come in as if by magic (my fingers are here, here, here, now they're there) and then I start to sing. *"Maybe we could talk in the shower"* (here here here there) *"I bet we'd be gone in an hour"* (here here here there) *"Maybe we could leave all this behind"* (here

here here there) *"Or we could just stay home"* (here here here here) *"It's better than nothing"* (there there there here) *"It's better than nothing"* (there there there there!) *"I'm feelin' go-od, I'm feelin' go-od, I'm feelin' go-od for now!"*

I'm trying to calm my beating heart, stop it from pumping blood through my veins at unfathomable liters per cubic inch, constricting my throat and making my voice bear an unfortunate resemblance to Kermit the Frog's.

AND DON'T FORGET:

1) Let air completely out of lungs before taking next breath.

2) Relax your mouth.

3) Don't make those silly faces when playing guitar.

4) SMILE!

5) Make sure you get the wah off after the bridge and *DON'T FORGET THE BRIDGE!*

Suddenly, the studio audience erupts with applause and Conan O'Brien is at my side, throwing a substantial shadow over me since he's about a hundred feet tall.

"Hey, that was great!" he says, shaking my hand, turning back to the audience. "We'll be right back!" he says. Then he turns to Buck and Robby. "That was great!" he says, and then he just stands there, running his fingers through his hair.

"You know," I say to Conan O'Brien, because he's standing right next to me and how many times in my whole life is Conan O'Brien going to be standing right next to me? "I sat at the table next to yours in a restaurant in Connecticut." This sounded far more interesting in my head than it sounds coming out of my mouth.

"You did?" says Conan O'Brien.

"Yeah," I say. "You were with a woman."

"I was?"

"Yeah."

"What did she look like?"

"She was lanky. And blond."

"Oh," he says. "That's possible." He smiles.

I smile.

"Okay!" yells Doogey, and suddenly Conan's gone and people's hands are all over me, lifting my guitar over my head, snaking a wire up the back of my shirt, clipping one of those little black microphones to my collar, and leading me over to The Couch next to Conan's desk, which Conan is again behind.

AM I GOING TO TALK?

Crystal Bernard is sitting to my right, just a little farther down the couch, and she reaches out and touches my arm. "I think you are *so* cool!" She doesn't look real. She looks bloodless and Lilliputian, like a small wax replica of the perfect female specimen. Next to her, I feel like a giant, a different species altogether.

Doogey is twirling his arms in the air and an APPLAUSE sign lights up. Everyone begins clapping. Conan is thanking the guests and when he says my name I can feel myself smiling, nodding my head in a very aw-shucks sort of way. Great. Real rock star. I should be FLIRT-ING or CAVORTING or at the very least wearing some kind of tummy-revealing little T-shirt to ENTICE THE FOLKS WATCH-ING AT HOME! Then Conan says good night. People keep clapping. Now I'm feeling stupid. What am I doing up here? I didn't even really get to talk, not that I have any idea what we really would've talked about being that I already mentioned the Connecticut dinner thing. But I can't bear to be one of those people who just sits on the couch while everyone's applauding, so I look at Conan and say, "I like your haircut," and I can see my stupid hands making my stupid Jersey gesticulations at him and it's like they're someone else's hands, because I keep thinking, *Stop making stupid Jersey gesticulations at Conan O'Brien!* but I can't, and he says, "My haircut? Does it look different?" and I'm like, "Yeah," and he's like, "How?" and I'm like, "You know, up there" (GESTICULATE GESTICULATE GESTICU-LATE) and the audience is clapping and the Max Weinberg Seven is playing up a storm.

We're back in the green room and it's done. Everyone's there: Randy, Lola, Kavallah, Neil, Mr. Boyg, Erika my business manager, and some Warner locals and a bunch of people from the Warner New York offices.

"You were great on the couch," says Lola. "A natural."

"But I didn't even get to talk," I say.

"But you looked good, relaxed."

"I did?"

Max Weinberg pops his head in the door. "You guys were great," he says, and we're all smiling like crazy. "That's a great song," he says to me. "I'm gonna keep my eye out for you."

My heart is pounding like mad but in a good way. Wow. Max Weinberg, who plays with Springsteen, likes my song.

Down in the lobby, some skinny old man approaches me with a handful of white index cards.

"Hi," he's saying, again and again. "Hi, hi, hi," shoving the cards and a pen into my hands. "Please sign for me, I love you, please sign these."

For a moment, I feel as though I'm being bum-rushed by hundreds of adoring fans and I'm already feeling faint with the attention—but really, it's just this one skinny old man.

I sign one of the cards.

"Another," he says.

I sign another.

"Another," he says.

"One more and that's all," says Randy, suddenly at my side, and although it's a minor rescue, I have a surge of lovey-dovey feelings for him. I sign one more card and Randy gives it to the skinny old man and tells him to be on his way.

"What was that all about?" I say.

"Autograph monger," says Randy. "Gotta look out for them."

"I don't get it."

"They stand outside places and get as many autographs as they can and then sell them."

"Who wants my autograph?"

"You'll see," says Randy. "Just a matter of time."

———

We follow Neil to some fancy restaurant with forty-dollar entrées and ten-dollar drinks. Buck, Robby, Burns, and SoundBoy are looking at the menus and raising their eyebrows, patting their wallets, and I can read Burns's lips from across the table when he mutters to Buck, *I'll have a glass of water and two pieces of bread, please.*

I stand up, raise my glass, thank everybody for their help and support and for coming down to the show. Then I say, "Dinner's on me." Everyone smiles, says no no no, I say yes yes yes, and it's done.

It's not that I really want to treat all these people to dinner, especially not people like Neil and Randy who I know are loaded. It's just that my guys can't afford to eat here (because I don't pay them enough . . .) and I don't want to embarrass them (or myself?) by saying I'll pay just for them, so I say I'll pay for everyone.

I excuse myself from the table because I need some air. Or the bathroom. Or a cigarette. I see a pay phone and dial Tim's number but there's no answer, and by the time his machine tells me to leave a message, I'm crying. "It went really great," I'm telling him. "At least, people are telling me it did. It's just that, I mean, it wasn't fun. I'm not having fun and I don't know why. I mean, here I am. I'm here. This is it. I mean, if not now, when, right? I know it sounds like I'm crying, but I'm not. Or, I am, but it's just that I'm feeling a lot. Do you know what I mean? Like when you feel so much it's like you're burning?" I keep going on in this way, hoping he's not sitting in his living room in the dark with Plus One, making out, laughing at me.

★

The van night is humming along flat and windless. It's late and there's nothing left to say. I vow to stay awake so I can leap over the seats and grab the wheel when Burns nods off, which in my state of almost-sleep I'm sure he's going to do. I can't shake the theme song from *Deliverance.* The tittering guitar line. The toothless grin of the Mongoloid on the porch.

The van bumps to a stop and I wake. The engine goes off and the lights click on. Everyone's coughing and yawning as we stumble out the side doors into a parking lot. We stand beneath a streetlamp as Burns tosses the duffels to the ground. One by one, we grab our stuff and head into the hotel, our third Days Inn in a row.

I sit up in bed in the dark, smoking and drinking vodka and orange Hi-C. I pick up the phone to call Guy, but halfway through the number, I realize it's getting on 4 A.M. (if we're still in the same time zone), which makes it 6 A.M. back home, and that's really too late to call. Guy's probably already asleep under the big red blanket with Ranger curled on my pillow next to him.

It's hot. Really fucking hot. We have the night off and Paula, this city's Warner local, is taking us to a baseball game. I don't really want to go. I'd rather stay in my room and eat pizza and watch TV.

I'm washing my face when there's a knock at my door.

"Well, helloooo," says Buck, leaning in the doorway, smiling, looking at me the way he looks at me sometimes. "Ready to go?"

"Where's everybody else?"

"Down in the lobby, I guess."

"Wanna come in for a second?"

Buck and I have been being good, keeping things uncomplicated. Pretty uncomplicated. Mostly, we've just been trying to steer clear of one another.

Buck sits on my bed, bounces a little. "Your bed's bouncier than mine," he says.

"Bounce away," I say.

"I think I will," he says, grabbing me by the arm and throwing me down on the bed, straddling me, putting a pillow over my face, then taking it away, leaning into me, closer and closer, sending a rush through me like hot water.

I look at him.

He looks at me.

"We gotta get out of here," I say.

"Check," says Buck.

———

We're sitting in the bleachers at the baseball field in a line: Burns, SoundBoy, Robby, Buck, me. Sweat is dripping down my neck, along the bone in my back. It's 10 p.m. and still hot as living hell. In a corner of the scoreboard, the temperature is displayed in bubble lights: 104 degrees.

Paula, the local, is sitting behind us next to Jamie, her husband. They both have short black hair and are wearing black pressed clothes. Paula is very nice and a little nervous, but mostly she's incredibly pregnant. I turn around and ask her how she's feeling. She says she's feeling okay, smiles. Jamie gives her a kiss on the cheek. I tell her to take it easy. She says she will and thanks for my concern.

But I'm not concerned.

I turn back around and reach under my seat for my beer. I grab Buck's knee and dig my fingers into the bone just to make him laugh. Then he puts his hand on my knee, gives a light squeeze, leaves it there for a moment. I wonder if he's thinking what I'm thinking—there's a knock at my door and it's Buck, so I take his hand, trying not to think about how different it feels in mine from Guy's, trying not to be frightened by his different smell, the stubble on his different jaw, the firmness of his different lips, until I'm nowhere and no one besides whoever I am at that very moment, with that very man, whoever he is, and I'll exist nowhere but in his hands, wherever he's touching, falling into what I fear I need, even as it erodes the only thing I truly have. Later, when the door clicks shut and the room shudders with its bigness, I'll know I've never been so alone in my whole life.

There's a loud crack from the field as a white ball goes shooting into the sky, but I'm staring at the moths flying in circles around the lights.

EIGHT

The windows at Wally's Records are covered with *Cockamamie* posters that have JENNIFER TRYNIN LIVE AT 3 P.M.! scrawled in black Sharpie along the bottom. In front of them is a guy in a black beret with a big gut and a tiny goatee that's hanging off his chin like a little black tail. We get out of the van and he tosses his cigarette on the sidewalk and walks over.

"Jennifer?" He's smiling, pulling on his goatee. "I'm Mr. Mac."

"Warner local?" I say.

"At your service," he says. "So, if the rain can just hold off, I think we're gonna get a lotta people out to hear you today. We've done a bunch of radio spots about the in-store, and we've placed a few ads and I got this team of kids putting up flyers and just generally talking you up. Should be packed."

My stomach begins to ache.

There's no winning with me. If there's no promo, I'm pissed that no one will know to show up. If there's tons of promo, I worry that not enough people will show up to justify it and I'll feel like a fool. Not to mention that, whatever the level of promo, lately not all the shows have been selling out, and if the shows aren't selling out, how many people are really going to drag their asses into some smelly record store in the middle of the day to hear me eke out a few songs through some shitty PA?

Burns and Mr. Mac are up at the counter talking to the record store guy, who has a shaved head and very black sideburns zigzagging across his cheeks like lightning bolts. Burns is motioning to a small PA wedged into a tight space by the window and a lone mic stand, explaining how I prefer to do these things as a trio, or at least as a duo. The record store guy shakes his head and shrugs—no more mics, no more stands, no more room. Burns waves us over and tells us that maybe it's best if I just do this one solo, which is when Buck and Robby decide to go roam around town.

"Thanks for coming in," the record store guy says to me. "My brother's like a mondo fan."

"Thanks," I say, wondering what I always wonder when people say this kind of thing: *Are you a mondo fan too?*

"He's totally bummed he couldn't get off to come see you today. But you're playing at the Rox tonight, right?"

"They're playing at the Annex," says Burns.

"I thought you got bumped up to the Rox," says the record store guy, smoothing one of his sideburns. "Oh, that's right, that's Alanis Morissette. Hey, so let's get you checked," he says, and walks toward the PA.

"Who's Janice Mori-whatever?" I say to Burns.

"Some singer," says Burns.

I do a simple line check (*tap tap* "Is this thing on?") and then stand around, nervously waiting to see if anyone's really going to show up.

Mr. Mac comes over. "So how was the drive?"

"Fine," I say.

"You feelin' okay?"

"I'm feelin' good," I say. "For now."

"Ha ha," says Mr. Mac. "I love that song. It hit the Hot 100 this week."

"It did?" I don't tell Mr. Mac that I'm not completely sure what the "Hot 100" is.

"Yeah. And it's really goin' through the roof around here. You're number two in phones, four in call-out."

"Phones" is short for how many people call the station and request your song. "Call-out" is short for "call-out research," which is when radio stations call random people on the phone and play them a snippet of your song, then ask them if they liked it.

"Great," I say.

I've asked Randy to tell the locals not to give me these daily reports, but some of them can't stop themselves. I've begun to hate hearing how great my song is doing. Or I should say, I've begun to hate hearing the silence when it isn't doing so great.

Finally, a bunch of people show up, enough to make me feel good, so I play my set with as much feeling as I can muster at three in the afternoon. During the last song, Buck and Robby appear in the store window, laughing and waving. They hold up a piece of paper that says KING'S FOOT!!!

After soundcheck at the Annex, Mr. Mac takes us all over to some bar where we play pool with a bunch of people who've won a contest to "Have Dinner With The Band!" Buck and Robby and I are drinking beers and laughing, exchanging can-you-believe-this smirks as the contest winners just stand around staring at us. But then we have to sit down for an actual dinner with these people in a big round booth:

How long have you been on tour?

How long have you been playing the guitar?

If you were on a desert island and you could only take one record/movie/book/sandwich, what would it be?

I'm not saying that part of me isn't tickled by this kind of attention, or that down deep I don't appreciate what seems to be these people's genuine curiosity about me and my music. But I am saying that in reality, in real time, when people ask me these kinds of questions, I begin to feel sad and lonely and a little confused. It's never my intention to lay my head down on a table and then bolt upright and roar into the faces of my unsuspecting fans, "TULIPS! CHOCO-LATE! FRIDAY! *TO KILL A MOCKINGBIRD!*" I never mean this anytime I do it, which is, from Head Honcho's perspective, every time.

"Do you have a problem?" he keeps asking.

"I don't think it's a secret that I guess I have some issues," I tell him.

"Well, lose 'em," he says. "This isn't the time. Explore your inner sanctums after the record's over."

"Check," I say, but it isn't check. It's more like, *Go fuck yourself.*

When I open the door to the band room back at the Annex, Buck is sitting alone, drinking a beer and reading a book with the cover torn off. One bare bulb hangs from the ceiling and the walls are completely covered with band stickers and flyers and graffiti (STACEY = A+ PUSSY, FUCK THE BEATLES, TURN LEFT AT MY DICK, ARKANSAS KICKS ASS!).

Buck looks up, closes the book, and tosses it on a table.

"Hello, beautiful," he says.

I put my backpack down and fall into a chair next to him. "I'm so fucking glad that's over with," I say.

"Oh, I know how much you hate it when everyone loves you," says Buck.

"Why are you such an asshole sometimes?"

Buck looks at me, takes another swig of beer. "Oh, c'mere," he says, reaching over, grabbing the bottom of my folding chair and pulling me next to him, so our thighs are touching.

"Where is everybody?" I ask.

"I don't know," says Buck. "Out front or something." He knocks his leg against mine. "Some weather we're having," he says.

I smile. "Yeah," I say. "Nice weather."

"Incredibly nice," he says, leaning into me.

"Very nice," I say.

"Very very nice," he says, bringing his hand up and touching the center of my bottom lip with the tip of his finger. "You got something on your lip," he says, "right here," lightly tapping all around my mouth, leaning in closer until I can hear him breathing, then feel his breath against my skin, warm and slow, until our lips meet, which is when the doorknob clicks, the door swings open, and in pops Mr. Mac's head.

I push Buck away, punching him on the arm. "Stop fucking around," I say.

"Ow!" laughs Buck.

"Knock knock," says Mr. Mac.

"Who's there?" says Buck.

"Sorry to interrupt," says Mr. Mac.

"Orange," I say.

"Orange who?" says Buck.

"What?" says Mr. Mac.

"Orange you glad I didn't say banana?" I say.

"Do you know you can't rhyme anything with orange?" says Buck.

Mr. Mac furrows his brow. "Is that true?" he says. "Listen. Jennifer. Do you think you could come out front for a minute? Talk to a few people?"

Buck reaches to the floor and picks up a bottle cap, begins rolling it across his knuckles.

"People like what kind of people?" I say.

"You know," says Mr. Mac. "People. They want an autograph and, you know, to meet you."

Buck snaps his fingers, sending the bottle cap across the room and against the wall, where it plinks to the floor. "Stardom calls," he says.

I stand. "Come with me," I say to Buck, as Mr. Mac takes my arm.

"No way," says Buck. "I stay with the beer. You don't need me anyway. Have fun." He waves at me as Mr. Mac pulls me out the door, down the hall, and into the club, where tons of people are milling and chatting. When I close my eyes, it all sounds as distant and hollow as a seashell.

"Remember me? Huh? Do ya? Slacka-Wacka? The Blue Team?"

I'm sitting on the edge of the stage after the show, signing autographs and selling T-shirts, when suddenly some guy is all over me.

This time it's sixth-grade summer camp, and how could I forget that backpacking trip? I'm not sure what he remembers or what he's intimating I should remember as he grins at me, his thumb and index fingers making circles around his eyes. "I got contacts way back," he's saying, "and I'm a little taller. Maybe about two feet." He thinks this is really funny.

But he is coming back to me, fuzzily, in a rather forced and fill-in-the-blanks sort of way. I remember blisters on my heels and a lot of Spam, and I'm beginning to conjure a loose rendition of Spin the Bottle in which a bunch of us campers were sprawled in sleeping bags on the floor of a lean-to, taking turns sliding our hot hands down each other's pants. Could it really have been through this guy's underwear that I felt the outline of my first dick? That's the likely allusion his constantly moving eyebrows are making. Well my my my. How inappropriate and downright creepy. When he asks if he can take me out for a drink, show me around town—he's lived here eleven years now and is an optometrist, can I believe it?—I do my usual duck and cover. "I can't," I say, pointing over my shoulder at the stage. "Load out."

This keeps happening. I'm a sitting duck for random "old friends" who catch wind that I'm coming to town through ads and interviews and my song on the radio and feel compelled to "come on down to the show." Like the construction worker–biker–songwriter from the restaurant back home who showed up backstage in City 21, reeking of cologne, with a what-me-worry smile on his face. Although we hadn't parted on the best of terms, he seemed fully committed to letting bygones be bygones. Of course, he'd dumped me, so that wasn't such a big stretch on his part. He brought me flowers, something he'd certainly never done when we were going out. I was pleased that he wasn't nearly as cute as he'd been when I'd known him. He told me how proud of me he was, how knocked out he was when he heard me on the radio. Oh, yeah, he was still doing music too, and was kind of wondering, did I have any advice/connections/shortcuts?

I smiled. "Yeah," I said. "Write some really good music and try to get someone interested in you."

He pursed his lips. "That's it?"

"Yeah," I said. "That's it."

I have to admit, it was a very good moment.

Then there was this kid I'd known when we were little. He'd had a lisp back then, which I could still just make out, and that—coupled with the fact that he'd grown into a very cute guy—made me kind of want to kiss him. He graciously told me from the get-go who he was and how he'd had a crush on me way back when. He was so happy I remembered him, which I was finding utterly charming. In fact I was finding him, in toto, pretty utterly charming. So much so that when I saw his head bopping around during the show, I got sort of flustered and turned too fast, losing my balance and landing my boot on my guitar cord, unplugging myself during the encore. As we were finishing up the last tune, I was watching him again and I saw that he was beginning to go completely crazy—slamming himself all over the place, bumping into people, knocking their beers out of their hands. When he came stumbling toward me after the show, I had one of the bouncers keep him back. I could still see him yelling after me from my seat in the van as we drove away. He just got smaller and smaller until we turned onto the highway.

My old Slacka-Wacka pal from summer camp is satisfied with a free T-shirt and a hug.

Next up is some guy in a white button-down, blue sweats, and sneakers. He hands me a piece of paper. "You with glasses," he says. I look down at the paper, where there's a cartoon drawing of me with a huge head and a teeny body with gigantic round glasses on my face. The guy hands me another piece of paper with a drawing just like the first but without glasses. "No glasses," he says.

"Thanks," I say.

"I like to draw," he says, and he walks away.

Some guy pushes a thick stack of paper at me, held together with a big black clip, and says, "I know you're gonna think this is like really fucking weird and everything, but, but, this is my movie, my script, and I want you to star in it." He takes a deep breath.

I laugh. "What?" I take the stack of paper. Look at the front page. It says "Lucy's Night."

"I want you to be Lucy," says the guy.

"No no no," I say, still laughing, shaking my head. "You have no idea what an incredibly bad actress I am," I tell him. "You put me on a stage and if I'm anything but me, all I do is laugh. Really." I try to hand the stack back to him. "You have no idea."

"Will you just read it?" he says. "It won't even be like acting for you, I swear. You're like, you *are* Lucy. Just take a look, okay? My contact info's on the inside. I'm not going to bug you or anything, just, you know, read it, enjoy it, and call me, okay? Please. Would you? Please." The guy pushes the script back into my hands, makes a peace sign at me, and leaves.

I toss the script into our box of *Cockamamie* T-shirts.

"Hi," says another guy, smiling like crazy, wearing a backwards baseball cap and a blue blazer. "You must hear this all the time, but I swear, I'm like your biggest fan. And I'm, well, I'm Ira's brother-in-law. Will you sign this for me?" The guy hands me a *Cockamamie* CD and a pen.

"Sure," I say, taking the CD, still looking at the guy. Ira's brother-in-law. Ira's brother-in-law.

"Ira Brooks," says the guy. "Your dentist."

"Right," I say. "Of course. How is Ira?"

"He's good," says the guy. "He says you have awesome teeth."

I sign the guy's CD and draw a big smiley face with lots of teeth.

Next in line is this girl holding a ratty old rose that has about four petals left. She's wearing a red short-sleeved sweatshirt that has *Leave It To My Beaver* scrawled in big bubbly script across her chest. Both her eyebrows are pierced with safety pins and she has one of those studded dog collars around her neck. "Guess what?" she says, like we're old friends. She lifts the bottom of her sweatshirt, revealing the word *SLUT* in capital letters across her admittedly beautiful belly. "I just got it done," she says. "Cool, right?"

"Totally," I say.

She lets the sweatshirt fall back down and runs her hand across her stomach underneath it. "This is for you," she says, holding out the ratty rose, and I can't tell if it signifies "You're the sister I've always wanted" or an invitation back to her dorm. She's beginning to remind me of that girl in City 9 who somehow maneuvered me into a doorway just outside the club, pushing me against a store window and coming at me with her big open mouth. Her dark hair was perfectly slicked back above her ears. She had on jeans with a black belt and a white T-shirt with a pack of cigarettes actually rolled into the sleeve. She basically looked like The Fonz, which made the encounter a whole lot funnier than I'm sure she was intending. I broke out laughing, freezing her mid-accost, and ducked under her arm saying, "I know you're just kidding," which I knew she wasn't.

Mr. Mac comes out to the van just before we take off. He's fingering the little tail on his chin, telling me how great today was, how great I did, how great my record is, how great his job is. He's drunk. And then he says, "Wait! I got it!" and puts his finger up in the air. "Lozenge," he says.

"Lozenge?" I say.

"Yeah, lozenge," he says again. "Rhymes with orange."

I laugh. "No it doesn't," I say, as Mr. Mac hugs me good-bye, kissing me on the mouth before I know what's happening.

★

Everything is blaring. Something's in my mouth. I spit it out and discover it's my own hair, so it just swings to the side of my head. Apparently, my alarm is going off, the phone is ringing, and my arm is flailing around like it's someone else's. I knock my teeny-weeny travel clock radio to the floor but manage to pick up the phone.

"Huuhhh?" I say. I clear my throat and reach to the floor, my fingers stabbing at the buttons on my teeny-weeny travel clock radio until the thing finally shuts the fuck up. "Hullo?"

"Good mornin'," says a deep, gravelly voice, deeper and more gravelly than my own, which is impressive. I figure it's the downstairs desk guy. "This would be your wake-up call," he says.

"Thanks," I say, my arm already heading back toward the cradle when "It's 6:30" drifts from the earpiece like a little puff of smoke. I put the phone back to my head. "Right. I know it's 6:30. Thanks," I say, but I can tell the guy isn't going anywhere.

"You still with me?" he says.

"Yeah," I say, squeezing my eyes shut tight while my head pounds. Have I managed two hours of sleep? Three? Am I still drunk?

"Sure you're awake?" he asks, and it dawns on me that he's just being nice, that the desk guy is keeping me on the phone to make sure I'm really awake, and something about this completely chokes me up. I tell myself that he doesn't do this all the time, that he saw me dragging my sorry ass through the lobby at 3 A.M. and decided to take me under his wing. I want to bring him with me all day, make him my personal bouncer.

"I can hear you breathing," he says.

"Oh, yeah, I'm awake. Thanks. I'm up. You up?"

He laughs. "I'm always up, sweetheart," he says, making me fall completely in love with him, leaving me extra bereft when we finally hang up.

My only shot at coffee is from one of those mini Mr. Coffees in the bathroom, complete with packets of nondairy creamer, which I just can't take. I light a cigarette and sit naked on the toilet while I smoke it, staring at a little pink message slip—another Call-me from Head Honcho—which has somehow ended up on the side of the sink. Am I going to throw up? I realize, post-shower, that I've washed my hair with hand cream. Yes, definitely still drunk.

Noncaffeinated, I make my way down to the lobby. I'm resigned to the fact that my hair is going to be plastered against my skull all day, and I'm wearing the same smelly, smoky clothes from the night before because all my clothes are smelly and smoky and these were handily strewn on the floor. I scan the lobby for Peg, this city's Warner local.

Not seeing anyone who looks like a Peg, I slump down in one of the overly stuffed lobby chairs and close my eyes. Suddenly there's a frighteningly bright-eyed, blond-haired, chipper woman in front of me.

"Jennifer?"

"Peg?"

"Hi! I wasn't really sure it was you, I mean, I've seen your pictures but your hair is longer or you look different sitting down but I'm new, I mean, I just started three weeks ago and I've had the flu and I wasn't sure but now I am—so, hey! How are you? Jeez, it's early! Isn't it early? I don't know how anyone could sing this early! When'd you get in? Have you slept? How're you feeling? Are you ready to go? Do you need coffee? Is this your guitar?" She's staring at me, grinning broadly, panting lightly, probably because this is the first time she's drawn breath.

A wave of hangover nausea sweeps through me and I stupidly say "yes," which seems to answer for Peg every question but the one I'm focusing on, which is: *Can I jump over hill and dale to bring you a cup of coffee with actual cream, the kind that comes from an actual cow?*

"Great," she says, grabbing my guitar and walking out of the lobby, her hair bobbing about like Happiness itself. I assemble my soggy body parts and hoist myself up, following her out into the morning like she's a carrot dangling at the end of a long stick, thinking *coffee coffee coffee*.

Peg drives like a maniac, albeit a slow-witted maniac—not terribly fast but very, very incautiously. No blinkers. Active lane wandering. She's telling me about Andrew, the guy she left back in Tampa because he was a "friggin' control freak."

"I mean it," she's saying, abandoning the steering wheel to gesticulate with both hands. "Complete. Everything. What sweater I should wear." I get the blow-by-blow of the last twenty minutes of their relationship. "Then he throws the newspaper across the room . . . So I go, Laundry? I'll give you laundry! . . . But you know how some guys are sexy when they're mad? . . . I mean, it *was* his apartment . . ." Peg runs a second red light and we narrowly miss being sideswiped by a Ryder truck.

"Friggin' moron!" says Peg.

"You just ran a red light," I say.

"What?"

"You just ran a red light."

"What light?"

————

The lobby of KRCK (pronounced "kay-rock") is freezing. There are no windows anywhere and all the surfaces are either black or white, which on top of the milky, post-alcohol film encasing my body is making me feel like I'm in a space pod. The reception area has all the telltale signs of a recent format shift from Rock to the more hip-and-happening Alternative Rock. There are tons of framed and carefully hung posters of old-school bands (Aerosmith, Def Leopard, Joan Jett and the Blackhearts), signed and inscribed—*KRCK rules!* or *KRCK fucking rules!* or *KRCK can kiss my ass!* or just *Kiss my ass!*—but there are also unframed posters of much more trendy bands tacked and taped all over the place, sometimes right on top of the framed posters of the old-school bands. The whole scene reminds me of that book *Alive!,* where the survivors of a plane crash eat their dead friends.

As usual, I end up looking everywhere for any sign of me and my band, hoping and anxiously praying that we're seen as accessories to the station's determined pursuit of Cool. But as usual of late, I don't see a thing. No huge poster of me splayed and staring at a big red chair, no smaller cardboard replicas of my huge poster, no head shots or band photos, not even a fucking sticker.

Nothing.

In fact, I haven't seen hide nor hair of anything remotely to do with me up anywhere since that lowly *Cockamamie* sticker on the back of a folding chair leaning against a wall in the hallway of that station where the AC was down.

I do, however, spy with my little eye a poster of a band from back home, a band I'd opened for and later let open for me, a band composed of people I loosely labeled Friends—a gigantic poster of their grinning unsigned-to-a-major mugs hanging from two black thumbtacks above the water cooler. I'm breathing deep, trying not to fall down my personal hole of hell. I think about my really old grandmother and how great it is that she's still alive and smoking and drinking and kicking all the other old ladies' asses at gin rummy. I think about how lucky I am that I'm young and healthy and living in one of the most advanced countries in the world—that I'm not one of those half-limbed, barely clad victims of land mines hobbling around on one crutch through the muddy streets of Bosnia or Lebanon or some other place I imagine is chock-full of land mines—

Fuck it. How about I sweep all the *Rolling Stone*s and *Spin*s and *Details* off the shiny black coffee table, climb on top of it, stamp my feet, and raise my fists to the cruel, cruel gods—WHERE THE HELL IS ALL THE PROMO SHIT I KNOW IS UNDER SOME PILE OF CRAP IN SOME MORON'S OFFICE AND WHO THE FUCK PUT UP MY FRIENDS' BAND'S POSTER INSTEAD OF MINE? Then I'll whip out my semi-automatic gun-of-some-kind and point it at the girl behind the reception desk (*Was it you?*), at the little backwards-cap-wearing, goatee-donning intern dude (*Or you?*). Then I'll let a few bullets rip into the cooler and water will spray every-where—all over the wall-to-wall, all over the framed posters of old-school bands, all over Desk Girl and Intern Dude, and last but not least, all over my friends' band's gigantic poster, bleeding their red scribbly script down the paper, down the wall, and puddling like a murder on the stain-resistant off-white carpeting.

I slump myself down into the black leather love seat behind the coffee table and take another deep breath. I want to be happy that my friends' band's poster is up, but I'm not. What I am is (in no particular order): jealous, angry, insecure, petty. Note to self: *Grow the fuck up.*

Desk Girl, who looks like she's twelve, is busily trying to jam a furry pink ornament onto the end of her pen. Her hair is purple and her eyeglasses are purple and her lips are purple. And her fingernails. Peg explains that we're from Warner Bros. and when she says my ac-tual name, Desk Girl suddenly perks up and screams at me in a rather accusatory and scary fashion: "'I'm Feelin' Good!' You're the 'Feelin' Good' chick! I LOVE that song!" She darts around from behind her desk, clutching a Sharpie in her fist as if she's going to stab me, asking me to sign something cool on her coffee cup (of which I'm very jeal-ous because it has coffee in it). I write "K-RoCK lives!" and immedi-ately feel like an idiot, but Desk Girl screams, "That's *per*fect!"

Peg's beaming at me like I'm her baby, like she's been with me every step of the way for the past seven years and this moment is her triumph too. She leans over and pinches me lightly on the shoulder. "See? You're gonna be a friggin' star."

A white guy with dreads suddenly materializes via skateboard, stopping right in front of Peg. "Ciao," he says, one foot still on the board.

"Oh," says Peg, startled, like someone just whacked her on the ass. "You must be Dirk!"

"Derek," he says, glaring at me like I'm the idiot who just screwed up his name, like if only I were more talented, better-looking, fuller-figured, I'd have better people working for me, people who didn't screw up his name.

"*Derek.* Of course," says Peg, smiling. "Do you think you could take Jennifer back to the studio?"

Derek flips his skateboard up under his arm with one deft flick of his foot. "I guess," he says, still glaring at me. *That's right. I don't like you or the little pop song you rode in on.*

I've been getting this kind of vibe a lot from the young interns and assistants at the big stations. They're generally white, upper-middle-class college-educated kids whose daddies subsidize the free time they have to sit around discussing the nuances of the guitar tones on the latest Guided by Voices disc. In the current Po-Mo (Post Modern) climate, there are legions of these high-heeled boys (and girls) who are into bands called Fuk Er Raw or Hill O Beans—bands who can't play or write or sing worth shit but by indier-than-thou consensus are more *real* than "sellout" bands who dare to practice or promote themselves or simply *try* a teensy bit. Never mind that the high-heeled boys and girls who work at stations like KRCK get paid with the money advertisers pony up for airtime, the biggest bucks going to the stations that attract the largest demographic, which are generally those that play the purest pablum.

I'm suddenly feeling rather chummy toward Peg and thinking about keeping her between me and Derek as much as possible, but she's already walking down the hall with her arm around the shoulder of some guy who I think is the program director, having neglected to introduce me. Very auspicious start.

A roly-poly woman walks in holding a clipboard. "Hey babe," she says. "Can I get you anything?" She's late thirties, early forties, and is stuffed into black jeans and a very tight David Bowie *Glass Spider* concert T. It's clear that, having consolidated her musical identity in the previous decade, she couldn't give a flying fuck about me or my music. She's simply doing her job. After Derek and his attitude, she's a huge relief. "Are you into Bowie?" she asks, because I'm staring at what she thinks is her shirt. But in fact, I'm staring at the nipples standing mightily erect beneath it, thanks to the full-blast AC. "I'm like a die-hard," she says. "You know he's being positioned for a major comeback and I don't want to jinx it or anything but I got the advance and it's am*aaaa*zing. It's going to be massive. Huge. Isn't this the coolest shirt you've ever seen?"

"Yeah," I say. "Is there any coffee around here?"

"Anything you want, babe. All the trimmings. Cream? Sugar?"

"Is it real cream?" I say, and now I feel like a total dweeb, as if I just asked her whether the bean sprouts were organic.

"Oh, sure," she says, "whatever. It's that Carnation stuff? Flavored I think—vanilla?"

I know it's stupid—so what if I can't get a good cup of coffee? But suddenly all I can think of is what time it is back home and my bed and Guy and Ranger asleep under the big red blanket.

The Bowie woman leaves me standing in the hallway with Derek and I'm wondering if I look as shitty in the fluorescent light at 8 A.M. as he does. He's wearing army fatigue shorts that come down to his shins, black combat boots, and a dirty muscle shirt. His skin is white white white. He has a complicated tattoo that begins on his neck, just below his right ear, and travels down to his shoulder, exploding into something I can't quite make out and continuing down his arm, all the way to the tip of his middle finger.

"Nice tattoo," I say.

Derek cranks his head to look at his shoulder, as if the tattoo erupted on his skin spontaneously, like a spectacular rash. "It's getting there," he says.

"Did it hurt?" I say, which is the only question I ever ask about tattoos, because I think the pain is intrinsic to the machismo of the whole ridiculous thing.

"Yeah," he says, and he grins.

Then he wants to know if he can carry my guitar but he's asking like he has to, not like he wants to. I conjure the nicest smile I can manage sans café and say, "Oh, no thanks, you don't have to carry my guitar. I mean, that's not your job." Maybe I'll get him to think I'm okay, a good kid, a team player, not some major-label pop-song princess he's supposed to wait on hand and foot.

Derek actually looks me in the eye. "That song you did, all the *ooh*s and everything, 'I'm Feelin' Good' or something. That's your song, right?"

"Yeah," I say. "'Better Than Nothing.'"

"I guess," says Derek. "It's pretty rad, you know, for a pop song and everything."

"Thanks," I say, trying to smile.

He gives me something back that I tell myself is a very small smile. Then he reaches out and takes my guitar. "I got it," he says.

I never know what's going to happen at these radio gigs. A couple of days ago, at a college station with a signal strong enough to reach maybe the campus cafeteria, the DJ greeted me by telling me how he'd been up all night writing a paper on the similarities between *Henry IV, Part I* and *Reservoir Dogs*—a topic he proceeded to veer from not once throughout the entire interview.

Another time I was interviewed by a little guy dressed like a clown—the big floppy shoes, the red nose, the whole shebang. He referred to himself as Mack Bozo and squirted water at me from a trick pen.

Last week, at a commercial station not unlike KRCK, the DJ, Svenlotta, was convinced there was a fruit fly in the studio. She kept waving her hands and swatting at imaginary insects while she fired basically the same question at me, over and over: "How long have you been on the road? When do you get off the road? Do you like being on the road? What's your favorite thing about being on the road?" I answered, "Uh, well, you see, um—" while she stared right through me, rubbing her nose over and over. Then she said, "Well, okay then. Let's have a song!"

So I played my song, rather deftly for me in that I remembered all the words and hit basically the right notes over the right chords at more or less the right time. There were even a few moments when I was actually having fun. Then it was over.

Silence.

I looked up.

No Svenlotta.

I looked through the studio-door window.

Nobody.

So I clapped. I gave myself a few *woohoo*s.

Still no sign of Svenlotta, or anyone else for that matter. So I decided to fill the dead air by asking myself a few questions.

"Tell me, Jen," I said. "May I call you Jen?"

"Only if I can call you Jen," I said.

"Sure you can!"

"Great!"

"Knock yourself out!"

"I will!"

"Okay then. So, Jen. What's the name of that little jewel you just played for us?"

"It's called 'Better Than Nothing,' Jen."

"Hey, terrific! Catchy number. You know, I thought that song was called 'I'm Feelin' Good.'"

"Yeah, well I'll tell you, Jen, that's been a point of some confusion for people. Sometimes I think I should've called that song 'I'm Feelin' Good,' since that seems to be what everybody thinks it's called."

"Well, you know, Jen, I hate to say this, but I think that would have been a top-notch idea. Tell me, who's the moron who called it 'Better Than Nothing,' anyway?"

"Well, that's the funny thing, Jen, because that moron would be me."

I laughed a little—*heh heh*—but I knew I was flailing.

"So Jen, about how long do you think we're supposed to be doing this solo interview thing?"

"That's a mighty good question, Jen. Tell me, how often do you find yourself interviewing yourself?"

"Not very often," I said, craning my head around, hoping that someone, somewhere in the station, might actually be listening to the broadcast and come help me out. "In fact, it's getting a little spooky in here."

"Is it?" I said. "How so?"

"Well," I said, "I'm feeling a little like I'm in the end of that movie *Westworld,* like this station is run by machines who just look like human beings and they're all short-circuiting somewhere out in the back, and any minute now Yul Brynner is going to come crashing through that plate-glass window and kill me."

"Wow," I said. "That *is* spooky."

And this is when my little gremlin of desperation took over.

"You know, Jen, I'm beginning to wonder whether Svenlotta's general jumpiness and then her sudden disappearance might suggest that she's in the ladies' room having, perhaps, a *Coke.*"

"Really, Jen? You think she's jammed into one of those little stalls having a Coke?"

"Yeah, I do. A Coke."

"What kind of Coke? A Diet Coke?"

"Maybe."

"A Classic Coke?"

"Perhaps. You know, Coke!"

"Coke?"

"Coke!"

"*Coke* coke?"

"Yeah, *coke* coke!"

I was growing frantic and confused, chirping and spitting *coke coke coke* like some spastic bird, until *finally* Svenlotta burst through the door, rubbing her face in her hands and slamming her headphones back on her head.

"Well," she said, out of breath. "That was awesome! What was the name of that tune?"

"'Better Than Nothing,'" I said.

"Great! Well, it was great having you here. And tonight, you're playing at . . . at . . ." She shuffled through a stack of papers. "Where're you playing tonight?"

"The Ballroom," I said.

"Right! The Ballroom! And, so, um, what time?"

"Doors are at eight," I said, not finding Svenlotta's presence particularly different from her absence.

"Okay, okay. Eight o'clock. Tonight. Make sure you all get out to the Ballroom to see—" And then Svenlotta's face went blank. She went so white, I actually felt a little scared.

"Jennifer Trynin," I said.

"*Jennifer Trynin!*" screamed Svenlotta. "Well, thanks, Jennifer Trynin, for stopping by! Have a great rest of your tour! And, yeah, good luck!" And with that, she popped in a cartridge, her headphones clunked back onto the console, and she was gone.

When Derek and I enter the studio it's dark and cold, with one bright spotlight shining down on the DJ, who's wearing headphones and humming with his eyes shut. He's maybe forty-five and nearly bald, with wisps of long gray hair hanging off the edges of his skull like tinsel. He has silly-looking muttonchops, a thick neck, and purple fingernails, making me wonder if he's doing Desk Girl.

Derek is situating me in a chair behind a big, fat microphone on the other side of a console that takes up most of the space in the room, like a brain in a skull. It's hard to move without bumping into something. The room is very quiet and stuffy, as if it's been ziplocked. It feels even more like a space pod than the lobby—like a smaller, night-trip space pod.

I take out my guitar and begin tuning, but the DJ snaps his fingers at me, like *Who the hell are you and why aren't you shutting the fuck up?*

The Bowie woman finally comes in with a cup of coffee—nondairy creamer, whatever, it tastes fabulous.

The DJ is playing air-drums to whatever he's hearing in his phones. Then he settles back down, rapping his fingers on the console until his face scrunches up and he takes a huge breath. Then he raises his right arm, index finger fully extended, freezing in this position for three, two, one—his finger darts down, hitting a button as he bolts into the air with "Hey hey HEY! It's 95.5 and you're listening to the Boneman back at ya with tickets tickets TICKETS! You be the tenth caller to 555-9555 and guess where you and a buddy are going?" He clangs a cowbell. "You be over eighteen and you're going to Soul Asylum this Saturday at the way-out Way Out! I'm talking *two* free tickets. I'm talking *two* backstage passes. I'm talking kick-ass rock and roll from some of rock and roll's newest and best! And next up, we got ourselves a treat. But first, something I know you can't live without because I know I sure can't. We got a little band we like to call NIR-VA-NA!" He hits a button, flips a switch, twirls a knob, and bounces back in his chair, whipping off his headphones and looking right at me: "And you are?"

"Jennifer Trynin?" I say, like it's a question, because even though I'm pissed that he doesn't seem to know who I am, I'm mostly confused. Is this guy for real? He talks like those old DJs on WPLJ from the 70s.

"Of *course* you're Jennifer Trynin!" Big smile. "Who else would you be?"

"Vanna White?" I have no idea where this comes from.

"Vanna White?" Bigger smile. "Vanna White? Hey baby, if you're Vanna White, you're gonna have to show me your letters." He waggles his eyebrows as if this is a remarkably clever and lewd suggestion.

"I can't. I forgot them at the hotel," I say, making the Boneman laaaaaugh and laaaaaugh. He actually slaps his knee.

"I see we've got a live one here!" he says, giving me a wink and sliding the headphones back over his ears, reimmersing himself in the console, sucking any frivolity we'd managed to muster right out of the room.

I lean down until my ear is almost touching my guitar strings and continue trying to tune, as quietly as possible. Suddenly the big, fat microphone clunks me on the head. It's holding me down like a yoke and I'm afraid to move until Derek comes over, tilts it back in place, and screws it tight.

I smile at him. "Hey, thanks, Dirk," I say.

Derek whips around and glares at me, igniting the tiny *ping* of a headache somewhere above my right ear. *Tell me I did not just call him Dirk.* I barely control the urge to jump up and grab him as he's leaving the room, force him to turn and face me. "Let me make it up to you," I'd plead, caressing his dreads, looking deep into his eyes. "I could know you. Let me know you."

The door suctions open and closed with a *shwump* and Desk Girl is standing there, smiling and waving at me. Peg is next to her, also waving. Then I see two teenage girls sitting in the corner, giggling and waving my CDs in the air like shiny plastic flags. I figure they must be contest winners. I wave back.

"Do you know Alanis Morissette?" says one of the girls.

"Who?" I say.

"Hey, you got ten seconds," says the Boneman, and he winks at me.

This is when my heart begins racing and my palms begin sweating. I tell myself for the millionth time that I've *done* this a million times, that I *won't* black out and fall to the floor, requiring ambulances and tracheotomies, that I *won't* die in a third-rate hospital in this lousy city with bugs in the bed and no one to comfort me but Peg, who'll pat my hand over and over, whimpering, "But you were s'posed to be a friggin' star. . . ."

The face scrunch, the big breath, the extended index finger, three, two, one—"Hey hey HEY! We *are* 95.5 and you're back with the Boneman and we're here *live* with Jennifer Trynin. Tell me, Jennifer, how's the world of rock and roll been treating you?"

"It's treating me pretty well, Boneman," I say.

"Hey, that's great. I bet you been havin' a blast out there on the road, goin' crazy. You're goin' crazy, right?"

"Completely bonkers," I say. The Boneman keeps looking down, reading from what I can only assume is my Warner Bros. bio. I'm afraid he's going to zoom straight to The Bidding War Question, which I've come to dread.

"Great, great. So, I hear there was a pretty major bidding war for you. Tell me, Jennifer, what was that like?"

"I don't know," I say.

I realize that, as a DJ, if you don't know anything about the artist you're interviewing, the easiest thing to talk about is the most obvious point of interest in the artist's bio—which for me is, admittedly, the bidding war. I mean, I wasn't married to Kurt Cobain, there's been no naked dancing or extreme drug-taking in my past, and so far the release of my record hasn't caused the deafening KABOOM in the marketplace that everyone seemed so sure it would. This is becoming very embarrassing. I wish I could scribble out the whole bidding-war section of the bio and write, *Let's talk about my music.* But that would presume he's actually listened to my music.

"Aww, come on, Jennifer. I've heard you had every label known to man trying to sign you!"

I remind myself that not everyone knows things aren't going quite as well as expected. In fact, so far, it's like no one seems to know it. No one but me, and I don't even know it for sure. It's just something I feel—in the air, in the pit of my stomach.

"Actually, Boneman," I say, "it was pretty amazing. I mean, label after label flying me from coast to coast and boy are my arms tired."

"What?" says the Boneman.

I take it up a notch.

"My wife is so fat that when she sits around the house, she really sits *around the house,*" I say, in my best Steven Wright deadpan.

"Your wife?" says the Boneman. "Your wife? Is there something you're not telling us, sweetheart?"

"Boneman, there's a lot I'm not telling you," I say, finally realizing that this interview is heading south. I go for the cheap thrill. "Like for instance, the other day we found a dead body outside our hotel."

It's true a dead body was found outside our hotel, although I never

saw it, as I always claim. It's also true that the lyrics to the new song
I'm working on, "Washington Hotel," are about me imagining that I
come to a hotel and hang myself. But it's not true that it happened in
Washington, though it was an honest mistake—I thought we were in
Washington. SoundBoy got up early and went out to check on the van.
There was a field on the other side of the parking lot, and he decided
to go on a little hike. But when he hoisted himself over the fence, he
discovered it was quite a drop to the other side, and when he landed
he found himself face to face with the body of a large black man wearing a red Nike running suit.

Lately I've been using the dead-body-outside-the-hotel story to
distract people from The Bidding War Question, and it's been working like gangbusters. It's certainly working on the Boneman, leading
to some lengthy and witty repartee about all kinds of gruesome matters including the Boneman's appendix, which he keeps in a jar on his
kitchen table.

I manage to play through "Happier" and "Better Than Nothing"
without passing out. I even remember to slur the word "fuck" in the
choruses of "Happier," which is a major achievement.

As I'm walking back down the hallway, Derek glides by on his
skateboard.

"Thanks a lot, Derek," I say, but he doesn't even turn around.

When I get to the reception area, Peg is laughing it up with the
Boneman and Desk Girl. She jingles her keys in the air. "Ready to go?"

Desk Girl gives me a thumbs-up and the Boneman turns around,
smiling and telling me he wishes he'd realized I was the "Feelin'
Good" chick, because he loves that song.

Back in my hotel room, I click on the TV and put the volume on about
3, paranoid that someone in my band will walk by my room, hear the
TV on in the middle of this gloriously sunny morning, and think,
*Jesus, doesn't she have anything better to do with her time? How about
working on some new material so we don't have to play the same songs
every fucking night?* I consider walking somewhere, anywhere, making

some kind of effort to slow the full-body paralysis brought on by the endless driving, sitting, sleeping, drinking—could I even just read a book, for fuck's sake? What's the matter with me?

I lower the volume to 2.

I'm weighing how much better the cigarettes I'm surely going to smoke will taste with coffee rather than soda, and wondering whether that difference will finally be enough to send me out into the street. I distinctly remember seeing a Dunkin' Donuts sign in some kind of strip mall on our way back from the radio station, but I wasn't paying attention so I don't have a real feel for how far it is.

It's my first personal decision of the day and I'm paralyzed. I reach into my duffel bag and pull out an Elmer Fudd–style hunting cap I bought for 99¢ at a Goodwill next to some club where we were playing. I'd finally reached the point when I couldn't bear to sit around anymore in the stenchy dark in the middle of the afternoon, fingers in my ears because SoundBoy was "flushing out the system" by finding each and every frequency that could possibly feed back during the show, causing the room to screech and wail like some demented cat.

I put on the hat and stare at myself in the mirror, wondering whether I have it in me to venture out into the regular world, walk alone down a regular street, talk to a regular person—because I don't want to be reminded how strange I look, how *other* I've become, how too much living Outside The Box has swiveled my fashion sense into some hurly-burly kaleidoscopic thirteenth dimension. The fact is, I'm a grown woman wearing a teenager's too-tight corduroys and a raspberry-red velour top that zips to my chin under a stained white leather jacket. My secondhand buckled boots are so many sizes too big that I have to layer the bottoms with three or four shoe pads so I'm not constantly falling down. My hair hangs all over my face.

Just two years ago, I would've laughed at someone who looked like me. But now, it's like I'm proud of it. It's not easy to wield such a confounding combination of fashion faux pas with the all-important rock-and-roll attitude of "Yeah, I know I look stupid." Because When In Rock, the stupider the better. But when I find myself at a truck stop in Alabama ordering a bowl of soup from some old broad with a beehive do and squeaky shoes who's generous enough to call me "Hon," even though I *know* damn well she's dismissing me with a silent, curt, monotone "Hollywood"—my carefully constructed sense of cool implodes like a sinkhole.

I throw my silly hat back into my duffel, realizing that I don't have it in me to deal with another human being of any kind, friend or foe. Should I just sink to the depths of Mr. Coffee? My eyes land on my teeny-weeny travel clock radio that a chambermaid must have returned to the night table. *Thanks, chambermaid.* It says 1:39 P.M., and I can feel something tugging at me.

Déjà vu?

Or a feeling of something being amiss?

And then I remember with a thud.

1:39 P.M.?

1:39 P.M.!

Silent beat, then slow-motion intake of breath accompanied by arm-raising, forming full-blown, hands-on-head "oh-my-God" stance, followed by silent AAAAHHHHHH!

I'M LATE! My eyes dart to the phone, my heart freezing at the sight of the little blinking message button—I'VE ALREADY MISSED LIKE HALF OF THE ZILLION ARDUOUSLY SCHEDULED AUSTRALIAN PHONE INTERVIEWS!

FUCK! (fuck fuck fuck)

Now everything's going to be all screwed up. I can just hear Mushroom Records' Australian organizer lady: *Ms. Trynin, we rang your room at twelve P.M. your time, as scheduled, but you didn't answer— SSSOOOoooo, I suppose our only choice is to move directly into the next interview and I'll reschedule the missed ones, hopefully for some time later today—you spoiled little piece of Alt-Rock shit.*

I always feel like everyone thinks I'm doing heroin.

I hit the message button.

"This is Room 246. I have a message?"

"Yes, let's see . . . Head Honcho called. Please call."

Oh yeah. Head Honcho.

"Janice called. She says, Where are you? Can you put her on The List plus two?"

Oh yeah. My cousins.

I forgot they lived here.

I never called them.

My mother's going to kill me.

"And?" I ask with my eyes closed.

"That's all I got for you this lovely mornin'."

I hang up, more confused than ever. Is today Tuesday? I shuffle around the room in a tizzy, finding the info sheet Burns jammed into my back pocket late last night, grabbing the phone, dialing my crew.

No one answers.

I hit the message button again.

"Yeaaahhhh," I say, very nonchalant, like if I ask all smooth and calm no one will send a guy up here with a net. "Umm, I was wondering—" I consider warming up with a question or two about room service or extra towels, but fuck it. "What day is this?"

Silence. Then, "Excuse me?"

"I'm just kind of wondering, basically, what day this is."

"Oh. Umm . . ."

"Like, is today Tuesday the fourteenth or what?"

"Yes," says the message lady, sounding relieved. "Yes, it is. It's Tuesday the fourteenth, 11:48 in the A.M. on this beautiful mornin'."

"It's 11:48?" I say. "Are you sure?"

"Do you need some help?" asks the message lady.

"No, no," I say. "I'm good. Thanks." And just as I hang up I spot the big hotel clock on the night table, which says—guess what?—11:48.

Oh. I must've screwed up the time on my teeny-weeny travel clock radio this morning in my still-drunk phone-grabbing scramble.

Of course.

No one's called because the interviews haven't begun yet.

So I have exactly twelve minutes until the phoners begin, six twenty-five-minute interviews, back-to-back, with five minutes in between to cleanse my interview palate. Who knew there was so much talking in the World of Rock?

It's all very confusing. You forget what you've covered during the interview at hand but you don't want to ask if you're repeating yourself, because then the interviewer will know you're just saying the same old shit to everyone. You want each interviewer to feel very *special* and to think that everything you're saying is very *news-flash.* And then there's always the scintillating conversation about The Bidding War and the ever-popular Wondering Whether All the Hype Is Going To Be Worth It (i.e., *Are you ever gonna turn into a raging rock star, or what?*). Maybe I'll tell the dead-body story.

The phone rings.

It's only 11:53, so I don't officially have to be here. And if it's Head Honcho or my cousin, why stop avoiding them now? So, whoever it is, I'm not here.

I stand very still.

The phone keeps ringing.

Doesn't everyone know I'm not here?

The phone finally stops ringing and I'm still just standing there, staring at my big green backpack, considering digging around for some pretzels, when my teeny-weeny travel clock radio clicks on. It's playing an old song, from when I was nine, maybe ten, back when my family got turned on its head. It's one of those sweet, slow, sad songs that can still make me cry.

Hey, did you happen to see the most beautiful girl in the world?

It's one of those songs that made me stop listening to music.

Tell her I love her. Tell her I need my baby.

And still, whenever I hear it, all I can think of is crying at the top of the stairs, until Tim was at my side, shaking me, hugging me, with my father just behind him, one hand on the banister, one leg on the landing.

I go over to my teeny-weeny travel clock radio and shut it off.

Ring!

It's 11:59.

Ah, yes.

The arduously scheduled Australian phoners.

I'm a rock star.

I'm not even to the van when I hear it. Buck's in a mood.

"There sure as hell *is* a difference," he's saying as I cram myself onto the edge of the seat in front of him and sling the door shut. "Welcome back," he says to me.

I know Buck's pissed at me because I'd told him we'd hang out this afternoon, forgetting about the arduously scheduled Australian phoners. Like I had a choice.

"What I'm saying is, he's not a *murderer,*" says Buck, looking at SoundBoy. "He's a *serial killer.*"

"There's no difference," laughs SoundBoy.

"Oh, right," says Buck. "How about the difference between words like 'one' and 'many'? Or do you really think there's no difference between the situations of, Gee, I lost my head, and, Oh, let's say I plan this out and do it over and over again. See what I'm saying or do you want me to, like, slow down?"

"Killing is killing," says SoundBoy, "and anyway, I thought we were talking about suicide." SoundBoy gives a quick scan around the van for a little help—me, then Robby, then Burns—but each of us is suddenly engaged in a vital moment of eye-rubbing or shoelace-checking. "Whatever," he says.

"No, not whatever," says Buck. "And killing isn't just killing. Did you know someone who's killed once is *seven times more likely* to kill again than someone who's never killed anybody is likely to commit murder *ever*?"

I shoot a smile at Robby, who mouths, *Factoid Man,* at me.

"Whoa," says Burns, starting the engine. "Watch out for low-flying statistics."

"And there's other stuff to consider too," says Buck, "like intent, malice of forethought, like force of habit." He ticks them off on his fingers.

"Does that have any relation to force majeure?" I say.

"What?" says Buck.

"Uh oh," say Robby and SoundBoy in unison.

"Nothing," I say.

"No. What did you say?" says Buck.

"Here we go," says Burns.

"I didn't say anything," I say.

"Yes you *did*," he says.

"No I *didn't*," I say.

"What am I, hearing things?"

"Maybe."

"*Jesus Christ!* Just *say* it."

"I'm sorry I said *any*thing."

"Oh, so now you *did* say something."

I turn around in my seat to face him. "You're so fucked," I say.

"*I'm* fucked? And what're you? Miss I-Have-It-All-Together? Miss I'm-In-Fucking-Charge?"

"Can't you just shut up?" I say.

"Why don't you both shut up," says Burns.

"You started it," says Buck

"What are we, five?"

"Oh, I know, Jen, because you're so mat*uuuuure*. May I touch you?" he says, reaching out and cupping his hand over my mouth.

We look at each other.

I pinch the flesh of his palm in my teeth.

"*Fuck!*" screams Buck, yanking his hand away from my mouth.

"*Jesus! H! Christ!*" yells Burns. "Would you guys cut it the fuck out? Get a room or something!"

"What?" I say.

"What?" says Buck.

Robby and SoundBoy look at each other.

"What what what?" says Burns in a silly voice as he peels out of the parking lot.

On the sidewalk outside of Rosco's, there's a chalkboard that says, TONIGHT! WARNER BROS. ARTIST JENNIFER TRYON!

I smack Burns on the arm. "Nice," I say, pointing to the sign.

"Relax," says Burns. "I'll kill someone for ya later."

Inside it's the usual: a big room with a bar along one wall and a stage at the end. There are booths along the other wall and a few scattered tables and chairs. Rosco's is one of those places that everybody plays, and I'm checking out the posters on the wall above the booths—posters of all kinds of bands except mine. I fast-forward through my where-the-hell-is-all-my-promo-shit feelings because I'm just too tired to get into it.

A jukebox in the corner is playing some song I've been hearing everywhere lately, and it's making me nervous. I remember first hearing it back at home, on MTV, just before I left for the tour. It was this video of some chick with long dark hair and white clothes singing in the desert. I didn't catch who the chick was, but I remember thinking the song was pretty cool. But the more I'm hearing it, the more I'm realizing it isn't pretty cool. It's fucking amazing.

The bartender is cutting limes on the bar and chatting with some guy sitting across from him. "I love this song," I hear him say. "What's her name again? Alice Morrison or something? I think that's her name."

"It's Alanis Morissette, you idiot," says the other guy. "Don't you know anything?"

Fuck.

So *this* is Alanis Morissette.

Suddenly, I need some air. Some cigarettes. Something.

SoundBoy's at the door, peering out onto the street from behind a curtain.

"What're you doing?" I say.

"You don't wanna know," he says.

"Okay," I say, reaching for the door.

SoundBoy grabs me. "Don't go out there," he says.

"What's the matter with you?" I say.

"There's this guy out there," he says. "I swear, he's the same fucking weirdo from last night. Remember that guy? He was hanging around outside when we were loading out?"

"Umm, no."

"I think he's following you."

"You're crazy."

"I don't know," says SoundBoy. "Burns!" he yells.

Burns comes over.

"Check it out," says SoundBoy. "Psycho at twelve o'clock."

Burns peers out at the guy from behind the curtain.

"Weirdo from last night, right?" says SoundBoy.

"Could be," says Burns. "Where's a gun when you need one? Just stay inside," he says to me. "SoundBoy, hup to. They're ready for you."

SoundBoy heads to the stage and I go over to Buck, who's sitting at the bar reading the sports section of some paper and eating nuts from a bowl.

"Hey," I say. "There's some psycho outside that's like following me or something."

Buck keeps eating nuts.

"Did you hear me?"

"Your public calls," says Buck.

"Fuck you," I say.

"Gladly," says Buck, putting the paper down and throwing a nut at me, a big one.

"Where'd you get all those nuts?" I say.

"Over there," says Buck, pointing to a table with the usual pre-show foodstuff for the band. No one ever gives us nuts.

"Can I have some?" I say.

Buck holds out the bowl. I reach in and take a cashew, my favorite. I take another. Buck reaches in, takes a cashew. I fish around with my finger and unearth another from the bottom. Buck snatches it from the bowl and shoves it into his mouth.

"That was mine," I say.

"How can you tell?" says Buck.

I fish around again, but I don't see any more cashews. "Have you just been, like, sitting here eating all the cashews?"

"No."

"Then how come there aren't any more?"

Buck shrugs.

"I can't believe you just went ahead and ate all the cashews before—"

"Before you got to the bowl and ate 'em all yourself? Like you were about to do? Before that, you mean?"

"I wasn't gonna eat 'em all."

Buck smiles. Nods his head. "Sure you weren't."

"It's not even the point whether or not I *would* have. The point is you *did* and I can't believe you."

"Is this one of those call-the-kettle-black sort of moments?" says Buck.

I stare at him.

"Want me to throw 'em back up?" he says. He holds out the bowl to me. "Try an almond," he says, which is when I smack the bowl out of his hand, spilling the rest of the nuts all over Buck and all over the floor.

Burns walks up. "Nice move," he says.

"First of all," I say to Burns.

"She ate all the cashews," says Buck.

"Both of you, shut up," says Burns. "C'mere, Jen." He's pulling me away by the arm when something small, say the size of an almond, hits the back of my neck. I whip around, "Buck!" I yell.

"Jen," says Burns. "Cut the shit. Listen, someone just gave me a message that your father called."

"What?" I say, turning to face him. "My father never calls me."

"I don't know what to tell ya."

A sound like the gonging of a very low bell begins to swell in my head. "How does he even know where I am?"

"Maybe he called Randy or something. I don't know."

"That's the whole message? Just call him?"

"Yeah. You can use the phone in the office back here."

Some guy who's maybe the manager of the club puts his arm around me and tells me to make myself comfortable at his desk, to use his phone, to take my time. I look him in the eye, trying to see if he knows something that I don't. He walks back out into the hallway and closes the door behind him.

I sit down at the desk, which is cluttered with sheets of paper and stinking ashtrays and cold coffee in dirty cups. Above the desk is a chalkboard with this week's lineup. My name's there for tonight: Jennifer Tryon Band.

As I reach for the phone, my heart is pounding and my fingers are tingling and then I feel something sliding down my back like a bug. I twist around, trying to kill it, and then I see a lone almond fall to the floor. I pick it up and whip it across the room, hitting a lampshade.

FUCK! What the fuck has happened that made my fucking father call me?

I dial his number.

Okay. My father isn't dead because he's the one who called.

Ring.

If my mother died, my brother would've called.

Ring.

If my brother died, my mother would've called.

Ring.

Maybe my mother and brother were together and and and—

"Hello?" It's BB.

"It's Jen," I say.

"Oh, Jen! Jen! Where are you? How are you?"

How am I?

"I'm fine," I say. "What's the matter?"

"Why?" says BB. "Do I sound funny?"

"*No,*" I yell. "I just got this message that Dad called and I'm supposed to call him like right away and—"

"What?" says BB. "Your father's playing golf. He's been out all day. He's not even home yet."

I start to cry.

"Honey. Oh you poor thing. He didn't call you."

I cry harder.

After soundcheck, we head downstairs for a meet-and-greet in The Wreck Room, which is just a cinderblock basement with the walls painted black. *Cockamamie* is blaring out of some two-bit ghetto blaster and there's a disco ball spinning fast in the middle of the ceiling, shooting specks of light around the room like swarming bugs. There are *Cockamamie* posters all over the walls and streamers hanging every which way and beer and Doritos and tons of pizza and a trillion people. Okay, maybe thirty people—DJs and reporters and people from KRCK and plenty of Warner reps, including Peg, who's arranged the whole thing and is flitting about as if this were her Sweet Sixteen.

She comes whipping toward me, squealing, "Jennifer, Jennifer!" She kisses me.

Then she hugs me.

Then she stands there, staring at me, smiling, panting, her nostrils flared. "Isn't this great? Aren't you just psyched? I mean, this is only my second meet-and-greet and not nearly this many people came out to the first one! Don't you feel special? Don't you just love it?" She pinches my skin at the elbow. Then she leans into me. "I told you you're gonna be a friggin' star," she says, her breath reeking of Doritos.

May I say that I hate few things more than these kissy-face, suck-up meet-and-greets, chock-full of names? I'm Tom Dick Harry, and my wife Pauline Sandra Mary Lou and her friend Francesca (*she's a big, big fan and I mean BEGGED to come meet you . . .*), and questions questions questions: *Do you like to be called Jen or Jennifer? Where're you from? Did you cut your hair? Grow your hair? Can I get you another beer? Bean dip? Sweater? Are you cold? Hot? Happy? Is this everything you've ever dreamed of? Imagined? Wanted? What's your sign? Favorite color? Favorite record?*

The whole thing is like one big, fat blind date. I try to be good, give real answers: *It doesn't matter. New Jersey. No. Apparently. Yes. No. No. Just my fingers. Kinda. Only when drunk. Only when asleep. No. I've come to realize I don't know what I want. Capricorn. I like all the colors. I don't really listen to music.*

I spot Derek, stuffing his face with pizza. I smile at him and give him the international rock-and-roll hand signal—fist raised, pinky and index finger extended. He gives me a half-assed wink and looks away.

My mind begins to swirl. It's like any hint of unadoringness of me I see as a sign—a sign that the jig is beginning to be up, that someone, anyone, everyone knows that it's only a matter of time till my ship goes down. The hotter the fever-pitch of the party, the more suspicious I'm becoming, as people touch me and breathe on me and grab my arms, offer me pizza, napkins, beers, advice (*You shoulda STARTED the record with that song*), and then there's some guy, kinda cute, just looking at me and saying, "You know, I mean, fuck *Spin*, what do they know, right?" And I'm like, "What're you talking about?" And he's like, "The five, you know, the review." And I'm like, "What? What review?" And he goes, "You know. The review." And I go, "*Spin* gave me a five?" And he says, "Yeah, but I mean don't worry about it cuz everybody knows that that writer hates chicks"—but all I can think is:

5?

FIVE?

FIIIVVVE?

—and then this little dude with yellow hair is coming at me with crazy eyes and a big black Sharpie, which he pushes into my hand. "Do you know Juliana Hatfield?" he says, as Burns is at my back. "Let's go," he says, pulling me away—*5? FIVE?*—but the little yellow-haired dude has gotten ahold of my other arm. "Hey!" he says, "Wait! You gotta sign something for me—" which is when I begin yanking my arms out of everyone's hands and grabbing the big black Sharpie from the yellow-haired dude's fist, ripping off the cap and raising it above him, pointing it down at his ever-loving nose, saying, "You want me to sign something for you? You sure you want me to sign something?"

★

It's 4 A.M. and raining. My hotel room reeks of Fantastik, 409, Lysol. I crack the window and look out. I'm just smoking, listening to the rain, and thinking about home. Any home I've ever had. Seaverns Ave. Groveland Street. Chapel Hill. I want to be somewhere that smells familiar.

The sky is beige and feels like a cup I'm in, captured like a fly. And that's all right with me. More than all right. I want to feel contained. I want there to be boundaries. The rain is giving way to a fine mist blowing in the wind. There are trees at the edges of the hotel parking lot and I can see the specks of rain whipping around the lamplight like snow. The moon is barely there.

When I was little, I didn't understand why I couldn't reach the moon by just jumping a little farther each time. And I wondered why trees only grew so high. I could never understand why they didn't just keep going. The laws that governed these things seemed as mysterious as the unison motion of birds, banking to the right, banking to the left, diving down, then shooting straight up, as if there were some kind of natural agenda that was clear to everything but me. I remember watching the sea, big as the sky, rolling up against the sand, closer and slower, until it paused, hanging between just far enough and too far, keeping safe my world as I knew it, with parking lots and houses and roads intact on dry land. For no longer than a heartbeat, the surf would stare up, winking with bubbles, and just as I'd begun to believe it might keep going, the ticking foam would begin its retreat, back and back and back into itself.

I know if the moon ever dislodged, the sea wouldn't know what to do. Then it really would just keep going, or it wouldn't go anywhere at all. I can't help but wonder if there's some moon inside me, spinning and shifting without my consent, making here over there and over there here, and I'm afraid I'll end up rolling out, beyond the lifeguard stand, up and over the dunes and into the parking lot, sprawling into the roads, unearthing houses and lampposts, drowning children I've knocked from their bikes. I stare at the farthest reaches of the tallest trees, jutting up like the tips of an explosion, and I imagine touching them but it feels all wrong, like fingering the corners of my heart—somewhere that shouldn't be touchable, a place that shouldn't be reached. And wherever that is, I know that's where I am.

★

I sleep for a few hours and then throw on my jeans and walk down a curving stretch of highway until I reach a small town center and find myself a copy of fucking *Spin*.

There it is. Five out of a possible ten stars. The accompanying re-

view describes me and my music with the following words in the following order:

arm's-length

deadpan

sparing with her passion

slapdash

workmanlike

paralyzed

emotionally exhausted

grovel

laconic

bitter

sarcastic

smart

perfectly captures

catchily

without resorting to clichés or sappiness

deluge of hate and love

It ends: *In theory, Trynin's chilly personality is alluring, but in reality, the record can leave you cold.* Cockamamie *veers between Boston
new wave, generic advertising-jingle rock, and watered-down PJ
Harvey.*

I toss the *fucking* magazine across my *fucking* hotel room.

I want to call Guy and cry or something, but I'm too embarrassed.
I call Tim.

"Did you see that *Spin* review?" I say.

"Uh, yeah," he says. "When'd you see it?"

"Just now," I say. "When'd *you* see it?"

"About a month ago."

"A month ago? A *month* ago? Why didn't you tell me about it?
Has everyone seen it? Like, Guy and Randy and everyone?"

"Yeah," says Tim.

"Why didn't anybody tell me?"

"Nobody wanted to weird you out."

"That is so fucking embarrassing," I say. "I bet everyone in my whole crew knows. *Fuck!*"

"Aw come on," says Tim. "*Spin* is just a bunch of pretentious ass-holes anyway. The *Rolling Stone* thing is good, right? It's awesome! My friends are all like, Wow, your sister's hot shit."

"Yeah," I say. "I'm hot shit."

"Must be tough being a star," says Tim.

"I bet it's not so tough being a *real* star," I say. "It's this fucking *fake* star stuff that's wearing me out."

"You can't worry about it," says Tim. "Nobody reads that magazine anyway."

"Don't tell Mom, okay?" I say. "Or Dad."

We hang up.

Fucking *Spin*.

They'll see. When my next record's huge, like hell I'm ever gonna give 'em that must-read interview, so they won't be able to put me on their stupid cover *EVEN WHEN THEY BEG*!

And that record?

I'm gonna call it 5.

Yeah.

And the T-shirts?

Pure black with big red fives.

Yeah!

And my swag?

Big red candles in the shape of a five.

Decks of cards with nothing but fives.

And we'll have buttons and stickers like eightballs, but they won't be eightballs—they'll be *five*balls.

And then I'll get a fucking five tattooed on my stomach.

No, my forehead!

No, wait! How about my ass!

YEAH!

NINE

The phone rings, rousing me from a deep dream in which I'm rolling around in the backseat of Tim's old white Mustang, making out with someone I keep telling myself is Guy, but I know it's not really Guy. I groggily reach for the receiver.

"Hello?" On the muted TV, there's a low-level riot going on in a city somewhere.

"How's my favorite rock star?" It's Head Honcho, bolting me upright and flurrying my synapses. "Did I wake you?"

"No, no. I was just watching TV," I say. "You know, the news."

"It sounds like I woke you."

"Maybe a little."

"How's the weather out there?"

My curtains are closed and I can't remember. "Raining," I say, because it'd been raining in big, sloppy drops against the car where me and the guy who wasn't really Guy were making out.

"Raining? I got the weather channel on here and over you it looks clear as a bell."

"Oh, well, then, I guess it's sunny." Unfortunately for both of us, Head Honcho is like my dad in that he's a bit of a tripper-upper.

"Don't you know if it's raining or sunny?"

I realize that these are reasonable expectations: for me to be up on the weather, to know what day it is, to remember where my cousins live. But lately, my connections have begun to fissure, shredding my already thinly tethered awareness of the outer world.

I could, at this point, simply break down, come clean—tell Head Honcho that I think I'm losing it. Confess my looming dread of dying somewhere far from home. Trust him with my big, ungainly secret— that I'm not A Star—and with my bigger, unfurling fear that my big secret is getting out. But what I say instead is: "What am I, a weatherman?"

I'm from Jersey. This is how we act.

Head Honcho exhales and asks whether I really think he deserved that.

"Deserved what?"

"The weatherman comment."

There's no doubt that Head Honcho is sporting a major agenda. Usually, he really appreciates my snappy-answers-to-stupid-questions demeanor, but I'm getting the feeling that this isn't going to be one of those times.

"Do you mean you're wondering if you deserve to know that, in fact, I'm not a weatherman?"

"See? This is exactly what I wanted to talk to you about," he says.

All I want is a cigarette, but I can't chance Head Honcho detecting that I'm smoking. Ever since the dear departing of Danny Goldberg, Head Honcho and I have been developing a very *Charlie's Angels/Kung Fu* kind of relationship. He keeps materializing, telling me what to do, how I'm being perceived, how I should be being perceived. Lately he's begun lecturing me about my bad habits, as if my smoking, drinking, and all the rest are things I do simply because I don't know any better, not things I do the way some people can't help but pick at their scabs. It's beginning to irritate me. I mean, we've only known each other about six months. And even if he's right, well, who the hell does he think he is? Who died and left him boss? Who is he, God?

"I don't know why you're having so much trouble accepting I'm not a weatherman," I say, trying to cute my way out of whatever dreadful conversation is surely Mack-trucking its way toward my already shaky sense of well-being.

Head Honcho begins clicking his tongue against the roof of his mouth. "How do you think everything's going?" he says, with the unmistakable air of asking a trick question. (*Ah, small grasshopper, conjure answer and you will be free . . .*)

"I don't know," I say. "How do *you* think things are going?"

"No. I want to know how *you* think things are going"—pause—"then I'll tell you how *I* think things are going."

Oy.

"How do I think things are going? Things like in general?"

"Things like yesterday's meet-and-greet," he says.

I figure I'll make a last-ditch attempt at an alternate self, a spacey, waifishly alluring persona that I attempt by pitching my voice unnaturally high. "Yesterday's meet-and-greet? When was that, like, yesterday?"

"Come on, Jen."

For a little while, we just breathe at each other through the phone. Finally, "Right," I say. "The meet-and-greet."

"How'd it go?" says Head Honcho, and it's like I can hear doomful music in the background, something a little like the *Jaws* theme.

"Fine," I say.

"Fine?" he says. "Really. Well, I gotta tell you, Jen. I've been getting reports. There've been some complaints."

My heart begins to pound. "Complaints?" I say.

"I heard you were a little difficult at the meet-and-greet."

"Difficult?"

"I heard you had a little run-in with the DJ from XYZ.

Fuck.

I didn't know the little yellow-haired dude was a fucking DJ. And who told Head Honcho anyway?

Peg.

Peg told him.

But wait. Maybe she didn't tell him. Maybe Head Honcho's talking about some other terribly rude thing I did altogether.

"Someone said you wrote on his face with a Sharpie," says Head Honcho.

Fuck.

I guess Peg did tell him.

"He said he wanted my autograph—" I say.

"Jen—"

"But isn't that what rock stars are supposed to do?"

"Jen! Seriously. What the hell are you *thinking*?"

Three P.M. with a hot purple sky. Buck and I are lying on my bed, half asleep, with the TV murmuring in the corner. It's the *Twilight Zone* episode where this old lady in a shack is being terrorized by a robot who's no bigger than a brick. The robot just keeps appearing—on her window sill, down her chimney, inside her only cooking pot.

The phone rings. Everyone knows I'm here. I have to answer it. But I'm afraid if I do that Buck will get angry at me for not allowing us this time together, away from it all. And I'm afraid if I don't that Burns or Robby or someone will decide it's an emergency and come pounding on my door and there Buck will be, in my room, on my bed.

Ring!

I reach over to the night table.

"Hello?"

It's Randy. He mumbles on about ticket sales (*going good over here, a little sluggish toward the west . . .*), radio (*growing steady in these parts, and they were thinkin' you could come by for a drive-time on-air . . .*), in-stores (*you'd have just enough time between soundcheck and the meet-and-greet . . .*), future touring opportunities (*maybe come fall do an opening slot and then we're lookin' toward Europe, Australia—you ever been to Australia . . . ?*).

I should be sitting up and taking notes. But all I'm doing is staring at Buck in the shimmering blue light of the TV, as his face dissolves to an x-ray, just a skull and teeth and his eyeballs like eggs in a cup.

★

We're heading east on the Mass Pike toward Boston, passing familiar truck stops, familiar foliage, road signs, town names, toll booths—and as much as I want to enjoy it, to allow myself to feel something that feels like home, the whole thing seems more like we're in one long skid.

We're out in front of TT the Bear's, unloading our gear, when SoundBoy says, "Holy shit," and rips a flyer from a wall. "Oh boy," he says.

"What?" I say.

"Nothing," he says.

"Oh, come on," I say.

SoundBoy hands me the paper and goes back to unloading. It's a black-and-white blown-up xerox of the cover of *Cockamamie* with the "amamie" scratched out and a crude drawing of a big cock going straight for my head.

We play two shows at TT's, which sell out both nights, and I'm relieved as hell though I'm determined not to show it. Everyone's touching me, staring at me, saying things I don't quite catch. The club's so packed that when I need to go to the bathroom it's easier for me to go down the street to the Frontload, which is where I run into this old musician friend from college, the guy whose band were the skinniest guys in the world with guitars hung to their knees that they played loud and angry and fast. He says, "So I hear you're rich now."

Friends who never felt that much like friends to begin with now seem like strangers. I can't remember people's names or what bands they're in or who they're going out with or where they work or where we are or who I am anymore.

At home it's worse. Ranger keeps sniffing me. I lose my keys and my car won't start. Even with Guy, it's like I'm talking to him through a spacesuit, where all you can really hear is your own breathing.

★

The blue of the sky is flat as the road and extends in every direction, like a TV screen. I'm sprawled on the van seat, hands behind my head on a pillow on the arm rest, legs crossed at the ankles, and all I can see is blue blue blue. Road sign. Puff of cloud. Glinting truck we leave in the dust.

We've already been driving for hours, through throat-clearing, coffee-drinking, stretching and coughing, more sleeping, and it's getting to feel like lunch. My bladder is beginning to glow. I count rest-stop signs as we pass them, seeing how many I can go before I ask Burns to pull off. And then when we do, when there's time, and depending on the stop, sometimes we take a break. We shop. I already have T-shirts from five states: New Jersey, Illinois, Texas, Wyoming, Arizona. And a black penknife that has one of those mumblety-peg things in it. I've even been playing a little mumblety-peg out on the grass when there's a picnic area. I bought a black plastic wallet. A crappily duped copy of *Plains, Trains and Automobiles.* Old-style metal buttons with things on them like chickens or pigs. A fancy cheese bread at this place called the Czech Stop.

Our only tape of *Simpsons* episodes is in the VCR, which is wedged in a cubby on the ceiling of the van. Homer is eating donuts at his desk again, screwing something up again.

"Jen," says Burns from the front. "Next stop, call Head Honcho."

"Again, Mr. Burns?" I say.

"Again, wiseass," says Burns, just before Homer let's out a "D'oh!" which begins a series of *D'oh! D'oh! D'oh!* around the van until it comes to me, the only one yet to *D'oh!,* but I'm just not feeling it. Then there's a hand on my head, grabbing my skull and shaking it as Buck says, "D'oh!" and begins another round.

We pull off at the next rest stop and everybody except me piles out and heads for bathrooms and coffee and Egg McMuffins. I'm standing at the pay phone with the receiver pushed hard against my ear.

"Well," says Head Honcho with one of his now-familiar exhales. "You've really done it this time."

"What?" I say.

"The no-girl-opener thing. People, well, there are some girls who are very angry. They think you're reverse-discriminating."

"I am reverse-discriminating."

"Well, right. People don't appreciate it."

"Well, that's tough. I mean, you know where I'm coming from. I just don't wanna be left to rot in the all-girls-night ghetto, you know? And besides, we still have chicks opening for us all the time."

"It's a perception thing," says Head Honcho. "You might as well know you're heading toward a bunch of interviews about this."

"I am?"

"People are calling. You know. It's a story."

"Oh, is this like the Big Scoop?"

"Could you cool it with the attitude for a second? This is serious. You gotta explain yourself. You don't want to be alienating your female audience."

Robby and I are in the airport, waiting to get picked up. Buck and Robby drew straws and Robby won, so he got to go with me to the radio convention. We drank champagne, had our asses kissed every which way, and got to stay in the kind of swanky hotel we stayed in during the bidding war, with millions of towels and minibars. I stayed up late watching *Pulp Fiction* and *Dumb and Dumber* on pay-per-view and ate a jumbo Hershey's bar. When I finally turned off my light, I fell into the deepest sleep I've had since we went out on tour, the kind of sleep that's just black. When I finally woke up, I decided once and for all that I have to stop playing footsie with Buck. That's it. The end.

There. Done. Easy. No more Buck.

There are no seats anywhere, so Robby and I are sitting on the floor, our backs against the wall, bags at our feet, people bustling all around us. I'm staring at Robby who's reading a copy of *Details,* when suddenly, an overwhelming feeling comes over me, some sensation I can't quite put my finger on.

And then I do.

I'm bored.

This is a first. Before I was no longer me, I'd never been bored in an airport in my whole life. No matter how long the delay or the layover, I'd just perch somewhere and watch people, because airports are one of the few places where you're allowed to sit and stare and nobody minds. I can't decide if I'm bored with other people or if I'm simply bored with myself when there's no one staring at me, telling me who I am, telling me that I'm going to be a rock star.

"Holy shit!" says Robby, thrusting the magazine in my face. "You're in here!"

Suddenly, I'm no longer bored.

However.

The title of the piece is "Whiny White Chicks."

This is the subtitle: "Welcome to the Prozac-free nation, populated by women generally small of stature, whispery of voice, and broken of heart, whose motto is Don't Be Happy, Be Worried."

Underneath is a chart of five "whiny white chicks," and I'm the fifth.

I can barely breathe as I whip through the other chicks' descriptions:

Mary Lou Lord: Grunge munchkin.
Jill Sobule: The weird girl in third grade who had cooties.
Lori Carson: (Who cares, because I've never heard of her.)
Alanis Morissette (with a really bad picture of her—ha!):
A little girl with a pit bull stuck in her throat.

Damn, these guys are harsh!

Worry worry worry. What if it says I'm a weird girl with Helen Reddy stuck down my pants?

ARTIST: Jennifer Trynin
ALBUM: Cockamamie
DISTINGUISHING MARK: Alterna-rock girl-next-door.
IMAGE: High in indie credibility; low-fat attitude.
MUSIC: Mid-80s-influenced rock you'd hear on your local alternative-radio station.

*WHINE VINTAGE: Sounds like she substituted bourbon for
milk in her Spider-Man thermos.*
*WHAT SHE'S WHINING ABOUT: Taking it on the chin,
turning the other cheek, and the guy who robbed the Store 24.*
OVERALL: Kinda cool, in an Urban Outfitters sort of way.

I look at Robby and smile. "I've emerged unscathed."

Robby laughs. "It must be tough being you," he says, shaking
his head.

When we get to the hotel, the rest of the crew hasn't arrived and our
rooms aren't ready.

"What happened to your leg?" says the guy behind the desk,
who's wearing flip-flops, an earring, and a Hawaiian shirt.

"Surfing accident," says Robby.

"Cool," says the guy. He looks down at a piece of paper. "Oh, hey,"
he says, "you got a fax or something."

It's from Head Honcho. It's an article called "Everything But the
Girls" that says, among other things, "Jennifer Trynin may be garnering
rave reviews for her debut album *Cockamamie,* but when she performs
at the 7th St. Entry on Thursday, the Boston rocker may be in for less
than a warm reception. In fact, Cindy L., the former Clams leader and
current Whoops, Kitty! frontwoman, is considering organizing a protest
of the concert." The article continues, explaining how I have an "un-
written rule" that no "female-fronted bands" can open for me, and how
this Whoops, Kitty! chick is going to call up all her "rock-chick sisters"
and cause me problems for my "reverse sexism." Then the article
quotes Sheila Capuano as saying, "There's no conspiracy theory. Jennifer has had female performers open for her before, but she wanted to
have male artists on this tour, just because it's less monotonous. She's
been doing it more for the diversity of the bills than anything else."

I call Head Honcho. "'Less monotonous'?" I say.

"I told you this was gonna happen," says Head Honcho.

"But I never said that. And there's no way I ever said no chick openers had anything to do with diversity. I don't want Sheila talking for me."

"That's Sheila's job."

"You just tell people to call me directly."

"Fine."

"FINE!"

By the time my room's ready, there have already been two calls from journalists, and over the following days there are a bunch more. I handle the No Chick Openers Debacle the best I can, telling everyone what I hope are charming little anecdotes about my early days in the Sunday-through-Wednesday-night-folk/acoustic-chick-band waste-land and my determination never to wind up there again. I explain that my problem has nothing to do with chicks and everything to do with narrow-minded booking agents who put chicks on the same bill just because they're chicks, not because their music is compatible. "You wouldn't want clubs having all-Jew night, now, would ya?" I ask, which usually leads to a lengthy silence on the other end of the phone, which is when I say, "I'm a Jew, so I can say that." This is around the time the interview usually ends.

The whole thing amounts to little more than a headache but leaves me stunned that so many people are taking me and what I think so seriously. Part of me wants to run for president and the other part of me wants to crawl into a hole and shut the fuck up.

On stage during soundcheck, Buck smacks me on the ass and I don't react. Then he spits a piece of ice at me and I tell him to cut it out. Later, when I'm in front of him climbing a steep stairwell, Buck grabs my back pocket and gives it a yank, so I whip around and yell at him to cut the shit.

"What's your problem?" he yells back.

When I look at him, I get that bad feeling, the one where it's like a hole's been blown in my chest. "It's just," I say, looking around, every-where, anywhere.

"You can't even look at me?" he yells. "What the fuck?"

I look at him. "I just, I can't do our thing, you know, anymore. I just can't."

"*Fine,*" says Buck. "Whatever. Just don't treat me like a piece of fucking shit." He turns, taking the steps two at a time, up the stairs, and he's gone.

I sit down on the steps and light a cigarette.

Buck and I do nothing but bicker for days, until we're drunk and laughing out behind a club and it starts to rain.

We're all gathered in Buck and Robby's room, eating pizza and drinking beer on the beds and channel surfing, because this hotel has premium cable. We leave it on MTV, because *Beavis & Butt-Head* is on. I can actually eat the pizza, because we don't have a show tonight and I don't have to worry about cheese clogging my throat.

Suddenly we go silent.

Then we realize—THAT'S US!

ON *BEAVIS & BUTT-HEAD*!

"Whoa," says Butt-Head, as the TV screen fills with a fish-eye lens's view of the clerk's mouth chewing gum at the convenience store where we shot the video. "Now that's a big face."

I almost drop my pizza. My hands are shaking and my heart is pounding HARD HARD HARD!

"Fuck," I say.

"This is awesome!" says Robby.

"Well, wowee zowee," says Burns. "You've really hit the big time now."

"And here comes another big face," says Beavis, as a fish-eye lens's view of my mouth comes in singing, "*What could make me happier than sitting right here?*"

"They're gonna rip me to shreds," I say, my eyes beginning to sting because I can't seem to get myself to blink.

"Relax, Madonna," says Buck.

But they don't rip me to shreds. They don't say I'm ugly or wonder if I'm a guy or say I suck. They just talk about big faces and convenience stores. And then it's over.

"You made it," says SoundBoy. "You can still show your face in your home town."

"King's Foot!" yells Burns, and everybody drinks.

Guy comes to visit me and we spend two days alone in a city with a lot of coffee shops and diners. We walk around and look at things, have a lot of sex. I cry now and then for reasons neither of us wants to analyze. Nature of the beast, Guy keeps saying. Touring. The pressure. He says he's sure everything will get better once I'm back home.

It's 5:30 A.M. and even though it's still dark outside, I'm somehow showered and dressed and sitting on the bed with my guitar in my lap. Somewhere around 2 A.M. I'd decided I should get my ass up really early and actually warm up before this morning's earlier-than-fuck radio show. But now my head feels stuffed and my throat's scratchy. My eyes are blurry. And my fingers are swollen. And I feel fat.

I begin strumming, humming, but all I want to do is sleep. I fall back onto the bed with my guitar on my stomach. A cool breeze is flowing through the room, very cool, cold really, as it becomes more like a wind until the window bursts open and water rushes in, pushing my guitar off my stomach, lifting my feet up over my head—

I sit up, nearly knocking my guitar to the ground.

I reach into my case and pull out a strap. I put it on my guitar and stand up. I begin playing "Better Than Nothing" as softly as I can, singing as lightly as I can. Then I play it again, a little louder, stretching out my throat, slowly and carefully, as if pulling on an old rubber band. It doesn't feel too bad. So I begin playing "Happier" almost at full volume and voice, and it's feeling surprisingly good, considering. Then I hear this sound, like someone stomping, so I play a little louder, until I realize that the sound is someone knocking somewhere, so I stop. And then I hear a voice.

"Hey," it's saying. *Knock knock knock.* "Hey you—" *Knock knock.* "What you think you doing?" says the voice, which sounds like an old Japanese woman who must be in the next room.

I sit back down on the bed.

"You wake me up," says the voice. "You think you alone?"

By 6:30 A.M., the sky is gray and damp, not raining, just misting.

I'm actually looking forward to seeing the Magic Man, this city's Warner local. I think his name is Dennis, but I've never heard anyone call him that. He took me around the last time we came through here and he never bothered with the usual inane questions (*How's the tour going? Getting any sleep? How long you guys been out?*). He just smiled a lot and pulled things out of my ear or told me to pick a card.

I leave my duffel bag at the front desk for Burns to take with him later today when everyone moves across town to one of the swanky hotels we get to stay in once in a while, because Burns has wangled some deal through his travel agent. I check out a vending machine that offers an impressive array of miniature items, including tiny tubes of toothpaste, individual condoms, and single-serving bottles of mouthwash and NyQuil. I slip a few bucks into the machine and buy three bottles of NyQuil, sticking two into my backpack and opening one.

I take a swig. *Ahhhh.*

Outside, the Magic Man honks and waves at me from behind the wheel of his old blue Chevy.

When I get in, he comes in for a hug, which actually feels pretty good. "Gotta love this cool weather, right?" he says, smiling at me with what feels like genuine affection, and even though I know he smiles this way at everyone, I decide to take it personally. I smile back.

"This is the most clothing I've had on in like months," I say.

"You sound a little sick," he says. "I got just the thing for that." He reaches into the cuff of his sleeve and pulls out a long string of handkerchiefs. "Presto."

———

When we get to the radio station, the Magic Man tells me to hang on a sec before I get out of the car. There's something he needs to tell me.

"The thing is, it seems as though there are some, well, women," he says, looking up in the air on the word *women,* "who appear ill at ease concerning your booking policies."

I rub my eyes. "Are these chicks gonna hold a sit-in before my show tonight or something?"

"'Fraid so," says the Magic Man.

"Great," I say.

"Just wanted to give you the heads-up," and the Magic Man pulls a bouquet of paper flowers from the inside of his jacket. "For you," he says.

Inside the studio, the DJ's on overdrive.

"So," he yells, clapping his hands together. "Sit," he says, pointing to a chair.

I sit.

"Guitar?" he says, pointing at my guitar case.

"Machine gun," I say.

He smiles. "Okay," he says. "So we thought we'd have you on drive time *this* morning, but it ends up something got screwy and now we're gonna put you on drive time *tomorrow* morning." He moves his finger in an arc toward the floor. "So we record now, but you gotta act like it's live."

I pull out my bottle of NyQuil. "NyQuil?" I say, holding it up to him. He looks at me. I take a swig and put it back in my pocket.

"What I'm saying is, you have to *act* like tonight's show already happened and so it's like you're talking about it in the past tense. Comprende?"

"Mucho comprende," I say.

"Great," says the DJ. He sits behind the console and we put on our headphones. He holds three fingers up in the air—*three two one*—and says, "And we're back in the studios of VRM"—flicking a switch that lets out a deafening engine *vvvvrrrroooom*—"with Jennifer Trynin. Welcome, Jennifer."

"Hi," I say.

"So," says the DJ. "That was some fiasco."

"What?" I say.

"Last night," says the DJ, pointing, again, in an arc toward the floor, silently mouthing, *Tomorrow* and nodding his head at me really fast.

"Oh, right, last night," I say, and the DJ gives me a thumbs-up. "I don't know if I'd call it a fiasco," I say, shrugging my shoulders, looking at him like *What fiasco?*

"Man oh man, those chicks were bustin' for a fight, right?" The DJ is waving his hands at me like I'm a jet he's flagging in for a landing.

"Uh" is what I say.

"Let's fill everybody in here, shall we?" says the DJ, and he explains the No Chick Openers Debacle and how that chick from Whoops, Kitty! led some kind of sit-in out in front of the club in protest of my "reverse sexism booking policy."

"Right," I say.

"But that didn't stop you guys from bringing down the house, right?"

"Uh, no, we had like a really good time. Last night."

The interview goes on like this for a while, and then I play a couple of songs. My voice keeps giving out, and I keep downing NyQuil.

On my way out of the studio, I ask the DJ what happens if there's no protest at my show tonight.

He shrugs. "Ehh, it's only rock and roll, right?"

"But you like it," I say.

"Right on," he says.

Back in the blue Chevy, the Magic Man is smoking with the windows shut. Through the windshield, the sky is purple-green, with thick clouds slowly tumbling in the wind. Three bobble heads affixed to the dashboard (two trolls and a Miami Dolphin) stare at me with jiggly eyes. The smoke swirls around the dolls like mist, as if they're waiting for me on the shore of some murky sea I didn't even know I was in.

Maybe it's all the NyQuil I've downed that's exacerbating the whole *The Shining* vibe to the Grand Hotel. Or maybe it was the Magic Man pulling that cigarette out of his nose. But what with the queer purple tinge to the sky, the hot prickliness of my neck, the squeaking of the revolving doors as I'm sucked into the lobby, I have a sudden urge to lay my hot cheek down against what I imagine is the coolness of the faux marble floor.

The lobby is bustling—big guys in blue uniforms with tasseled shoulders blowing whistles and hustling families over here, over there, get in this line, that line, piling bags onto rolling carts and wheeling them away. Confused tourists. Chirping and fretting. Old guys in shorts, their wives in velour track suits. Cameras: FLASH! Little kids racing around.

Burns is standing with his hands on his hips at the end of one of the many lines snaking through the lobby to a concierge's desk that's about twenty feet long, with five or six people behind it, like the post office from *Green Acres*.

SoundBoy is clicking his little black penlight into his eyes and squinting as Buck stands with one hand in his pocket, the other holding an open book, which he seems to be reading. Robby is smiling at me.

"Hey," he says. "How was it?"

"It was okay," I say. "I got shit for the no-chicks-opener thing."

"Ouch."

"I told you you shouldn't have done that," says Buck, not looking up.

A little boy runs right into me like I'm a wall he didn't see. He comes to just above my bellybutton. He looks up at me. He has a crew cut and a dirty mouth. In my haze he seems to be floating like heat above the road.

"Whaddaya say?" I ask him.

He narrows his eyes at me.

"You say 'excuse me,'" I tell him, and he begins backing up, very slowly, like I'm a wild animal.

"Bobby!" yells a plump woman in acid-washed jeans that pinch her off at the waist like sausage casing. Her sneakers are as white as a baby's teeth. "Bobby! Get over here!" The kid isn't budging. He's still just looking at me.

"Boo," I say, and he takes off, the lights in the heels of his sneakers flashing.

Burns is next in line at the check-in desk when suddenly he turns toward us and starts jumping up and down without letting his feet leave the floor, very ants-in-his-pants. He's pointing his right index finger into his left palm and mouthing something in our direction, but when we say *What? What?* he makes shushing motions, until finally we see what he's so worked up about. Up at the adjacent check-in area is a middle-aged man in calf-length pants and a short-sleeved linen shirt, revealing doughy white shins and forearms. He's slumped against the check-in desk as if he's been shot, as if, were the desk to disappear, he'd fall limp and boneless to the ground.

"Oh my God," says Robby. "It's Brian Wilson."

"That's Brian Wilson?" says Buck.

"From the Beach Boys?" I say.

Robby looks at me. "What planet do you live on?" he says. "Yeah, from the Beach Boys."

"You've heard of them, right?" says Buck.

SoundBoy is rummaging around in his millions of pockets. "Where's my fucking pen?"

"What in the hell is Brian Wilson doing here?" asks Robby. "He doesn't tour anymore, does he?"

"Maybe he's on a loony retreat," says Buck.

Standing next to Brian Wilson is a fat guy in black jeans and a blue windbreaker, who's talking to the desk clerk. I figure he's Brian Wilson's tour manager, or maybe he's his AA sponsor, or maybe he's his only friend left in the world. I want to go over and give Brian Wilson a hug, feed him a steak and ten cups of coffee, ask him what happened, how it's all come to this.

Then Burns is snapping his fingers and waving us over to get our keys, as Brian Wilson meanders away with his pasty white arm hung across his buddy's shoulder and walking as if he's made of rubber.

Burns is giving me my room key when something smacks into my leg. It's the little boy with the dirty mouth, staring up at me.

"Boo!" he yells. "Boo! Boo! Boo!" and he runs away.

I make a pit stop at the gift shop for a pack of smokes while every-one else goes on up to their rooms. Burns is always getting me non-smoking rooms in which I'm always smoking and I'm sure that one of these days, I'm gonna get nabbed. *You've been smoking in our non-smoking rooms!* they're going to yell. *I know!* I'm going to yell back. *What the hell's the matter with me?*

"A pack of Camel Lights," I say to the woman at the cash register. By my feet is a pile of *Rolling Stone, The Hot Issue*s—right next to *Spin* (fuck *Spin*).

There are eight elevators, four to a side. The shiny gold "up" button is as big as my hand.

The elevator sways like the tongue of a gigantic bell. *Four . . . five . . . six . . .* , until the big golden doors wheeze open on the seventh floor. I drag my stuff down the very long and totally empty REDRUM hallway to room 742.

Inside, the room is as still and stuffed as the air in my head, and all I want to do is clump off my shoes and peel off my jacket and fall into the cushy bed with the boomfy pillows and eat both mints I can al-ready see from here. I won't even bother turning off the lamps on ei-ther side of the bed, which are shaped like stylized naked women sans genitalia, nipples, or bellybuttons. I'll just flick on a comforting episode of *I Love Lucy* on the oversized TV that's wedged into the hulking faux-teak armoire, lie back, and pass out.

I dump all my stuff at the foot of the bed, sit down, and take off my shoes. The curtains drawn shut across the window are so thick, I can't see the outside at all. Like there might as well not be an outside. Like I could be anywhere. Or nowhere. I stand up and am looking for the TV remote when I realize there's another open door I hadn't seen before. I walk through and find myself in another room exactly like the first. Two naked-lady lamps, two mints on boomfy pillows, a big bed, and an oversized TV wedged into another hulking faux-teak armoire. I fall back onto the bed and reach above my head, grabbing both mints from the pillows, eating one and sticking the other into my jacket pocket, where I find the bottle of NyQuil and take the last swig. I can see myself reflected in the blank TV screen, lying on the big bed between the two night tables underneath the two naked-lady lamps, and to the right . . .

I sit up and turn to see another open doorway, which I can't help but stand and walk through, entering another room just like the first two, grabbing the mints and turning on the TV, searching for the weather channel but getting only static. Channel 2 4 5 7 39 41. And then, of course, I look to my left at the next open door, which leads this time into a large room with a faux-teak desk and two matching brown sofas facing each other over a faux-teak coffee table.

I toss the empty NyQuil bottle into a wastebasket but what I'm really looking for is Kleenex, so I just keep walking. And before you can say *What the fuck is going on here* I'm through another door and into another room with another big bed and more naked-lady lamps and another open door, which this time leads into a kitchenette with a little stove and a microwave and drawers with forks, knives, spoons, and another doorway through which there's another room with another bed and another door and I just keep going, through room after room after room, like it's me who's standing still and all the furniture that's moving by—more beds, more lamps, more doorways—as if everything's blooming into view just for me, like my childhood fantasy that I made things appear and disappear just by looking at them, and maybe, if I were to turn around really fast, super fast, faster-than-the-speed-of-light fast, I myself would disappear.

Six, seven rooms later, I can feel my heart pounding in that peculiar way it pounds when I feel I've slid off the spinning wheel of the space-time continuum. All of a sudden I turn around, then around again, and I can't remember what room I'm in or which way I was going. I strain to see back through an open doorway—*Is that where I came from?*—but it's telescoping its way away from me, skittering backwards like a crab, getting smaller and smaller and sinking into I don't know where—

Ring!

I look up.

Ring!

A phone. Beside the bed. I walk over to it.

Ring!

On the phone, it says Room 756.

I scurry through the next door, into the next room, and find the next phone. Room 758.

I turn around, hightailing it in a tiptoe sort of way, back through room after room, retracing my steps as if moving along shifting slabs of ice, in search of the only thing I know for sure, which is My Stuff.

When I see my duffel bag and guitar and backpack at the foot of my original bed in my original room, my body goes slack with relief.

I sit on the bed.

Then I laugh.

I mean, come on. There must be some kind of explanation for this.

I call downstairs.

Ring.

Ring.

Ring.

Ring.

Ring.

Just as I'm about to fall into another panic—*no one's answering at the front desk because there is no front desk because there is no hotel because I've obviously entered the fucking Twilight Zone*—"Operator."

"Hi. I'm in room 742 and it's, well, it's just that—"

"What's the problem?"

I don't know how to explain that I've been nearly sucked into a gaping vortex.

"It's just that my room, it's, it's too big."

"Too big?"

"Yeah."

"Is it a Master Suite?"

"I don't know."

"Did you ask for a Master Suite?"

"I don't think so," I say. "But this room has a kitchen and an office and like a million beds."

Silence.

Then the operator tells me somebody'll be right up.

I'm lying across the foot of my bed with one arm draping down so I can keep a finger on My Stuff, sucking on the fifth or sixth of what seem to be about twenty mints in my pocket, when there's a knock at the door. I get up, my head spinning from sleeplessness, NyQuil, and sugar.

A very short woman in a blue uniform is at the door, carrying a clipboard and wearing a walkie-talkie holstered to her hip.

"Hello young man," she says. She looks at her clipboard and taps it with a pen. "Nobody's supposed to be up here yet," she says. "You're not with the convention, are you?"

"Not that I know of," I say.

"Didn't think so," she says, walking past me and into the next room.

I follow her as she begins shaking her head, sucking her teeth.

"No no no," she's saying, peering into a wastebasket, reaching down and pulling out a mint wrapper. She holds it up to me. "You?" she says.

I try to smile.

Then she points to the bed where the covers are a little mussed and the mints are missing. "You lie on this bed?"

"I guess," I say. "I didn't mean to. I mean, I thought this was my room."

"Uh huh," she says.

We go into the next room, where the TV is still on.

"You turn this on?"

"Evidently," I say.

And then the next room.

"This your NyQuil bottle?"

"I'm pretty sick," I tell her.

A half hour later, I'm reassigned to a room on floor six, a regular room, one bed, two lamps, one TV, no extra doors.

I double-lock the door and bounce back onto the bed, eating more mints and clicking on the TV, searching for *I Love Lucy*. As I'm surfing through channels, I come to one that's scrambled and flickering. But I can just make things out. A shoulder. A breast. A knee. So I lie back, squinting, blurring my vision, straining to hear the low-volume groaning, convincing myself I know what's going on. He's on her. No, she's on him. There're two guys, two guys and two chicks, one chick, no chicks. Doesn't matter. All I need is the rhythm of the bodies and the sounds. I can fill in the rest.

And as the blue TV light flops against me like a fish, I can't help but wonder if Brian Wilson is lying listless and alone in his own big bed, staring at his TV, thinking about his life, about all the things he's afraid he'll never feel again.

The phone wakes me. It's Burns, telling me how I'm going to be picked up in ten minutes for a last-minute on-air, but I don't have to play or anything. The naked bodies are still flickering on the TV.

Ten minutes later, I'm sitting next to Ned, a local who has a cool old white car with black bucket seats and a pair of swimming goggles hanging from his rearview. He says he's "so pumped" he was able to swing this show for me. He's got a mustache and an earring, and I can't stop myself from picturing him flopping around on my TV screen.

I take a swig from my last bottle of NyQuil even though I'm not really feeling sick anymore. "So, Ned," I say. "You like to swim?"

Ned touches the goggles with his fingertips. "Not just swimming, my li'l lady," he says, putting his hand on my knee, giving it a squeeze. "Scuba diving."

"Hmm," I say. "Ever see a shark?"

Ned looks at me. "Not just sharks. Hammerheads. Tiger sharks. Great Whites." He pulls his sleeve up over his shoulder. "See this?" he says, revealing a scar about the size of a Chapstick. "Close encounter," he says, continuing on about all things scuba while I relax back into my black bucket seat and stare out the window.

A half hour later, I'm sitting in the radio station studio fooling with a rubber band, chatting away on air with a DJ who for once seems to know who the hell I am.

"Boston, aye?" he says. "I love those Sugar guys. You ever run into Bob Mould up there?"

"Umm," I say.

"Hüsker Dü," he says. "The best, right?"

"Totally," I say.

Everything's going fine until the DJ is suddenly talking about Alanis Morissette, how she was in town last night and gave a *rocking* good show, and do I know her, do we *par-tay* together. Then he wants to know if I'd ever fight her. I don't know what he's getting at, but I know he wants some kind of action answer so I tell him that, clearly, I could kick her ass. The DJ claps his hands, bounces in his seat. That's what he wanted to hear. 'Atta girl. He knew I was The Real Deal. Had The Goods. He picks up the phone.

"Let's call her right now," he says, "tell her you're gonna kick her ass."

He starts to dial.

I consider my options. There aren't many, and I pick the simplest one. I let loose the rubber band in my hands, which flies straight into the DJ's forehead.

"Hey! Ouch!" he says, hanging up, grabbing the rubber band and shooting it back at me.

This is mostly what goes on for the rest of the interview, and he forgets all about Alanis Morissette.

Ned drops me off at tonight's club for soundcheck, and the second I walk in, Burns comes at me. "Call Head Honcho," he says.

"And how are *you*?" I say to Burns.

"Here's the deal," says Head Honcho. "How 'bout you give that Whoops, Kitty! person a call. Make it right."

Head Honcho has already tracked down the chick's number, so I dial it. When she answers, there's a screaming baby in the background. At the beginning of our conversation, she is, as they say, cold as ice. But I explain my position to her, tell her I'm all over women's rights and stuff like that, tell her I'm a big fan of her band, tell her I'm just plain sorry. Really.

She calls off her rock-chick sisters. I leave a few tickets for her at the door. She ends up coming down to the show and we have a few laughs.

Ha. Ha. Ha.

★

We're at an outdoor stadium, a 10,000-seater, playing the KROQ show. There are four Warner bands on the bill and we're first. Then it's the Goo Goo Dolls, Filter, and Candlebox.

We're in the middle of soundcheck when my amp goes dead. I stand there in the middle of the gargantuan stage, like a little car that's run out of gas. A bunch of crew guys rush at me, unplugging this, checking that, yelling PLAY. Nothing. Flick a switch. PLAY. Nothing. Unplug, plug back in. PLAY!

Nothing.

"I think one of your speakers is blown," says one of the crew guys.

Oh.

So now we're all just standing there, hands on hips, in pockets, on chins, saying "Oh," one after the other. *Oh. Oh. Oh. Oh.*

"Hey!" yells one of the crew guys. "Think we can borrow an amp from the Candlebox guys?"

My little Fender Super Reverb is suddenly swooped off to the side and I'm plugged into some huge Marshall stack and told to PLAY, so I let my hand come down on the strings and a sound comes ripping out of the amp like a million shiny metal arrows straight through my skull.

"Whoa!" yells Robby. "Heavy Metal O'Trynihan!"

There's an area behind the stage where all the bands and various hangers-on can hang out. It's like someone's idea of a mirage in the desert, with tents and incense and candles and, thank God, a shitload of beer. We meet the Goo Goo Dolls, another rock trio, but way more punk and thrashy than we are. They're telling us how they've been around ten years now and had started to think about packing it in, especially since their latest record wasn't doing dick. But now they're reconsidering because they have this one really sappy song called

"Name," a total album cut, a song never meant to be a single, and suddenly all the cool stations are playing it like crazy.

There's another Warner Bros. band skulking around called Super Big or Super Colossal or Super Something who aren't on the bill tonight but are in town shooting a video. They have a girl singer everyone calls Roach, who has long black hair like oil and skinny white legs.

"So, you guys have a bus?" says Roach, not looking at me.

"Naah," I say. "Just a van."

"Oh," she says. "I figured you'd have a bus or something. Because, like, we're in a van, but we're not you guys."

"Why would we have a bus?" I say.

"You know," she says, looking at me. "Cuz you're *the* Warner Brothers new band," she says, air-quoting *the, Warner Brothers, new,* and *band.*

"What do you mean?" I say.

"Who's playing this show?" she says. "You or us?"

Ricky the video guy is here. "Hey, Jennifer," he says. "How's the tour going?"

"Pretty well," I say.

"This is Roach," he says to me. "This is Jennifer Trynin," he says to her.

"We met," I say.

"Yeah," says Roach.

"Everybody having fun?" he says.

Roach shrugs.

"Yeah," I say. "How about you?"

"Ah, man," he says, rubbing his cheeks in his hands, then slapping his face a few times. "Can you say jet-lagged?"

"Jet-lagged," says Roach.

"Traveling a lot?" I say.

"Let's see," says Ricky. "New York, L.A., back to New York, back to L.A., Denver, Chicago, England, back to New York, and now here, and all I can think about is heading back to the Four Seasons, putting up my feet, and ordering a steak and a bottle of gin, and watching like a million pay-per-views. And then I'm gonna raid that minibar all night long."

Roach rolls her eyes and makes a *pfft* sound with her lips. "We're staying at the Motel 6," she says.

"You gotta admit, that's kinda fucked up," I say.

"What?" says Ricky.

"You know, that like me and Roach are staying at the Motel 6—"

"You guys are at the 6 too?" says Roach.

"Yeah," I say. "So we're staying at crappy places like that while you're at the Four Seasons drinking gin and watching movies all night and ultimately, at the end of the day, it's us who end up paying for it. I mean, like, no offense, but it's people like you who're basically ruining the music business."

"*What?*" says Ricky.

Roach lets out a small laugh.

"I mean, you're here making a video with Roach's band with all your expenses going onto their account which is ultimately recoupable to them. So before they ever make any money, not only do they have to recoup all the usual bullshit, but they also have to pay for your fifty-five Toblerone bars. All I'm saying is that if people like you didn't do things like that, then bands would start seeing more money sooner and maybe they could even afford to have, like, you know, a bus."

As I've been talking—or as I've been unable to shut the fuck up—Roach has skulked her way behind Ricky, where she's silently laughing, miming slow-motion clapping at me. Then she sticks two fingers up behind Ricky's head.

"Jesus *Christ*," says Ricky.

"Excuse us," says Burns, who's suddenly at my side. "Photo op," he says, as he pulls me away for a picture with all the musicians on the bill gathered together like a baseball team.

Four hours later, we finally take the gigantic stage and it's fantastic and strange. The stadium is almost filled, thousands of people all sitting, waiting, breathing, smoking. The stage is dark as Robby gets behind his drums and Buck and I sling on our guitars, and it seems like there are a million miles between us. I stare down into the empty space between the stage and the barricade in front of the first row of seats. A loud clank sounds as the lights blare on, blinding me, and the crowd explodes into applause that's everywhere and deafening, like a hurricane we're caught in.

★

We're back in New York at Brownie's, one of about a hundred bands playing all over the city as part of the MAC Festival, which I think has something to do with Mac computers but might actually be an acronym for something else about which I never ask. Inside, the club is stifling and water is dripping from the ceiling as people fan themselves with their hands.

I'm standing out on the sidewalk with Tim when he says he has "something kinda important" to tell me.

"That sounds awfully ominous," I say.

"I'm thinking about taking that job in Brazil," he says.

"*What?*" I say.

"Yeah," he says.

A searing pain shoots through my stomach. "But, but, I mean, it's so far away. I mean, when would you start?"

"I'm not sure yet. I'm gonna be heading down there next week. Just to check things out. You know."

"Oh," I say, staring at him as my heart pounds, trying not to feel as desperate as I do, trying to stop myself from seeing him as the little boy with the cape. Finally, "Oh," I say again. "All right. I mean, congratulations."

Tim looks at me. Makes a face. "You suck at faking it."

"Well, I mean, what the *fuck*? What about being my manager and looking out for me and every other fucking thing we talked about? Was that all bullshit or what?" A tear goes down my cheek.

"Jen," says Tim, taking me by the arms. "Look at me. I'm still here," he says.

I look at him.

"Hi," says Tim, and he waves at me. "See? Still here."

I swipe the tear away. "So, how long would you be gone?"

"Like five years," says Tim.

"Five years?"

"Come on, Kiki. Settle down. There are phones, right? And I'll be back all the time. I'll have plenty of business to do here in the States. I mean, how can I pass this up? You think you're the only one who can be a rock star? I'll be like the fucking CEO of a multimillion-dollar company."

I try to smile. "You'll be like Mr. International Dude," I say.

"Mr. *Rich* International Dude," says Tim.

Suddenly, someone's hand is on my elbow.

"Jennifer?" says this bald guy with a beret.

"Yeah?" I say.

"George," he says.

"Hi, George," I say.

Tim looks at me like *Do you know this guy?*

I shrug.

George pulls from his pocket a folded piece of paper that he unfolds and hands to me. It's a full-page article ripped from some magazine, with phrases highlighted here and there in yellow marker—*Jennifer Trynin's the real thing, Alanis Morissette is a flash in the pan,* and *Liz Phair who?*

I smile and hand the article back to George. "Thanks, George," I say.

George folds the paper and puts it back in his pocket. "Just wanted you to know that there are some of us out here who're getting it," says George. "You just hang in there." He waves at us and walks into the club.

"I feel sick," I say.

"Why?" says Tim. "Whoever wrote that article fucking loves you."

"Not the article," I say. "The fact that some guy feels like he has to show me that article, like he's feeling sorry for me or something."

"You really gotta stop thinking that way," says Tim.

I look at him. "Okay," I say. "So I guess this means you're never really gonna be my manager."

Tim smiles. "I'll cover the Brazilian tour," he says.

"Right," I say, trying to feel happy for him. "Good luck. I mean it."

We hug.

I tell him I love him.

We're the third of six bands and each band gets only six songs, so by the time I'm getting into it, we're already done and dragging our gear back out onto the street. Everyone's milling around out front as Burns and SoundBoy are packing our stuff into the back of the van. Tim's still inside with Buck and Robby, who're gathering people to come drinking with us.

Neil comes bounding out of the club, wiping his forehead with the back of his hand. "Jesus H. Christ!" he yells. He pulls out a handkerchief and wipes his face. "Hot," he says. "But you guys were great, really, it's just, Jesus." He folds the hanky back into his pocket.

"I thought you said Lola was coming down," I say.

"Yeah, well she said she was gonna but I hear she hasn't been feeling well."

"Oh," I say. "I was looking forward to seeing her."

"So, how goes the road?"

"All right," I say.

"Just all right?"

"Yeah. I don't know, sometimes . . ."

"What?"

"I don't know. I'm just feeling sort of funny a lot of the time. Hard to explain."

"Ah," says Neil. He puts his arm around me. Hugs me. "There's nothing wrong with you that a hit song wouldn't cure."

Neil takes off and I walk a little ways down the street to smoke a cigarette.

"Hello, Princess."

I turn. "Well, look what the rat dragged in," I say.

"I've missed you too," says Johnny. "How's my little rock star?"

When we hug, Johnny kisses me on the mouth and it feels good.

"Saw you on *Conan*," he says.

"Yeah?" I say. "How were we?"

"You were aaaaaaaall right," he says, with his head tilted down, eyes glimmering up at me. "I've seen you better."

"Thanks a lot," I say.

"I'm just being honest, Princess. Someone has to be."

"And that's your job?"

"That's my job."

"Why do you even care what I'm doing?"

"Why do you even care what I think?"

"You know what? I'm just too tired for this shit, okay? Just be nice to me."

"Are you writing?"

"What, like songs?"

"No. Like your life story. Of course, songs."

"Not really. A little. Here and there. It's hard writing on the road."

"You're gonna have another record coming up before you know it, Princess. Better start focusing. Don't let your little rock-star soul go and eat itself."

"What's that supposed to mean?"

"Just don't go forgetting what got you here."

"Wherever that is."

"Well put," says Johnny.

"I gotta go, Johnny," I say. "I got family here and everything."

"Don't let me hold you up," says Johnny. "I'm really here to check out the last band. Big buzz with these guys. Next big thing, you know?" Johnny smiles, mimes tipping a hat to me, and disappears into the club.

I'm lying in bed, drinking the last of the room-service coffee, staring at my duffel bag, smoking.

Fuck.

I can't put it off any longer.

I've got to do my laundry.

I don't want to do my laundry.

I call Guy.

We talk.

At least it seems like we're talking.

He tells me about this band he's doing a record with. Some new band. Some band with a bunch of guys I've never met. And a girl. The bass player.

"How alt-rock of them to have a chick bass player," I say.

Guy tells me to stop being testy. He asks how things are going.

I tell him they're going okay.

He says he misses me.

I say I miss him too.

We hang up, and I start to get my laundry together. The phone rings. I'm hoping it's Guy calling me back, that he'll say something that'll break through to me so I'll be able to remember him so I can really miss him.

"Hello?" I say.

"My ever-elusive rock star." It's Head Honcho.

"What'd I do this time?"

"Are you smoking?" he says.

"No," I say, dropping my cigarette into the empty beer bottle on the floor next to my bed.

"Okay. Well, this time, I know I must be hearing things wrong, so I just want you to enlighten me about something."

"Shoot," I say.

"For what possible reason would you have told Ricky that he's ruining your life?"

"What?"

"Sheila heard from Ricky that you said that he was ruining your life and I just need to know what the hell that's all about."

"What're we, *twelve*?" I say. "Are we playing, like, Telephone or something?"

"Jen—"

"I never said he was ruining my life. I said he was ruining the *music* business."

"*Jesus,*" says Head Honcho. "Are you *trying* to sabotage yourself?"

———

An hour later, I'm sitting on a hard plastic chair in the Laundromat, watching my dirty clothes slop around in circles.

Sabotage.

Sabotage shmabotage.

What matters is that I'm out of cigarettes. I look around. No cigarette machine. Chances are if I go out for some, no one's going to steal my clothes, right? I mean, this seems like a friendly little town.

I walk out into the beautiful day, dry and clear and warm. I stare at the sun on the street, the sidewalk, my hand—and now I'm eleven, walking the long way home, back when life was new and everything was still possible.

I wander into an outdoor pavilion with all kinds of booths selling incense and leather wallets, fresh fruit, candy, coffee, ice cream. I buy a handful of Bazooka, unwrap a piece, stick it in my mouth, shove the rest in my pocket. My fortune: *Your success is only limited by your desire.* I smile and stick it in my wallet. I watch a bunch of scruffy-looking guys slapping fish onto a long tilting table, laughing, smoking.

One of them smiles at me.

I smile back.

Then I blow a bubble at him until it pops.

A little farther down the hill, a trolley car creaks to a stop and four guys come tumbling off with screwy hair and chains dangling from their back pockets—scratching a needle straight across my dreaminess.

I know those guys.

They're that band Filter from the stadium show. I'd ended up talking to them out in that field. They were all cute, which was making me nervous. I was trying to feel like they were flirting with me but I knew they weren't. They were just wasting time, waiting for soundcheck, shooting the shit with some singer from some band. I'd felt about as sexy as a stick.

Now they're crossing the street and heading in my direction, but I don't want them to see me. I just want to be whoever I am with no one looking at me.

I duck into the nearest doorway, which ends up being a pawnshop where there are these three guys: a skinny guy, a fat guy, and a big guy with a patch over his eye. They're all greasy in their sweatshirts and dirty hair. A bell tings as the door clicks shut behind me.

I walk quickly to one of the glass counters and look down, trying to appear as though I'm looking for something in particular, but all I see is guns. Up on the walls are rows of shelves with stuff just stuck up there: a few guitars, a bow-and-arrow set, dusty answering machines and cameras. I can feel the three guys eyeballing me to death as I'm skulking my way around the store, trying to look like I'm inspecting the guns with some clear idea in my head other than *Get me the fuck out of here.*

"Hey," I finally grunt.

"Looking for something?" asks Fatso.

"A gun," I say.

"A gun?" he says. Skinny and the Pirate grin at each other. "What for?"

"Oh, you know," I say. "To shoot."

"For self-defense or hunting?" asks Fatso.

"I guess a bit of both," I say, nodding. "You know, a little hunting, personal safety. The usual."

"You don't seem like the gun type," says Skinny.

"Oh yeah?" I say, feeling suddenly very mysterious, very incognito. "What type do you think I am then?"

"A musician," says the Pirate.

"Oh really," I say. "Why do you think that?"

They all laugh.

"Your jacket," says Skinny.

"And your shoes," says Fatso.

"And you have a big sticker that says The Strand on your ass," says the Pirate.

"Yeah, well, I guess you figured me out," I say.

"What do you play?" asks the Pirate.

"Guitar," I say.

"We have a few guitars over there," says Fatso, pointing to some shitty Japanese reissue of a remake of some guitar that sucked to begin with.

"You from here?" says the Pirate.

"Boston," I say.

"You on a tour or something?" he says.

"Yeah," I say.

"You on a label?"

"Warner Brothers," I say.

"Wow," says Skinny. "Are you famous?"

"Evidently not," I say.

"Do you have a song on the radio or something?" says Fatso.

"Yeah," I say.

"What's it called?"

"'Better Than Nothing,'" I say. "Or, 'I'm Feelin' Good.' I mean, that's what everyone thinks it's called."

"Is it like a hit?" says the Pirate.

"Kinda," I say.

"Have we heard it?"

"Probably," I say, and after a little more of this, Fatso finally says, "Could you maybe sing it for us? I mean, just so we could tell for sure?"

"I feel a little silly," I say.

"Aw, c'mon," says the Pirate.

So I sing. "*Maybe we could talk in the shower—*" I look up, sheepish, then back down. "*I bet we'd be gone in an hour—*"

Skinny looks at Fatso who looks at the Pirate who looks back at me.

So I jump to the chorus. "*I'm feelin' good, I'm feelin' good—*"

"Wait a minute," says Fatso.

"I know that song!" says the Pirate.

"You do?" I say.

"That's you?" says Skinny.

"Yeah," I say. "That's me. That's my song."

"Holy shit!" says Fatso. "Famous? You're *fuckin'* famous!"

"I am? Well," I say, looking down, modest.

"*Shit* yeah!" says the Pirate. "You're that Alanis Morissette broad, right?"

Back out on the street.

I look to the left.

I look to the right.

No Filter guys in sight.

Okay. Enough of this. I've got to get back to the Laundromat to put my clothes in the dryer in time to get back to the hotel and down to the van. But—cigarettes.

I cross the street and go into the little shop on the corner, where there's a guy standing behind the counter, staring at MTV.

Then I hear it. The opening drumbeat to "Better Than Nothing."

Ack!

I skitter my way to the back of the store and crouch behind a long magazine rack: *Good Housekeeping, People, Vogue, Monster Cars, Billboard, Rolling Stone, Details, Spin* (fuck *Spin*).

I fan through *The New Yorker,* blowing bubbles and looking at the cartoons, waiting for my song to be over.

I put *The New Yorker* back on the shelf.

Then I stare at the music magazines. *Billboard* specifically.

I unwrap another piece of Bazooka and stick it in my mouth. My fortune: *You're on top of everybody's list.*

Fuck it.

I pick up the top copy of *Billboard.*

I flip to the back, my heart beginning to pound. *As long as your song's still climbing, you've got nothing to worry about.*

I finally find the Modern Rock chart and my eyes go immediately to the songs in bold, outlined in gray, songs marked AIRPOWER with asterisks, of which my song is usually one (so says Randy, Head Honcho, Tim who's been tracking my song like a deer), and while I don't know exactly what it all means, I know it's good. The last time I got an update, "Better Than Nothing" was number 15. Or was it number 10? Or was it 5?

My heart pounds harder as I find slot number 5 and don't see my song. Number 15, not there either. 14? 13? My eyes begin bing-bonging around the page, unable to focus on anything in particular, searching for my song—wondering, hoping, praying—because who knows? Maybe I'm number 4 or 3—hell! Maybe I'm number 1, RIGHT?

Until finally, I see it. "Better Than Nothing." Just sitting there in the middle of the page. It's not circled or grayed or boxed or aster-isked. Just my name and the name of my song, which is currently sit-ting in slot number 17.

And what's at number 1, complete with highlighting box and asterisks galore?

"You Oughta Know."

Alanis Morissette.

I stumble out of the store with air piffing from my chest as if from a slit in an enormous balloon.

After soundcheck, I'm sitting on the sidewalk in a black metal chair outside the club because I had to get out of there. Away from it all. The stench. The dark. My clueless, careless, happy-go-lucky band and crew. Fuck them and their ill-informed optimism. *Doesn't every-one know this ship is going down?*

The sun is still blaring and I have on my Peter Fonda/*Easy Rider* sunglasses. I'm sitting back, arms around my aching stomach, legs crossed at the ankles, hoping to appear as if I'm merely contemplating my outrageous rock-and-roll existence, trying to stop the tears from pooling in my eyes. I take a few of those deep, measured breaths every-one always says you should take to calm down. I smack my cheeks a couple of times and then bend over and back up.

But it's no good.

I figure that if I can just let it out for like three seconds, maybe it'll go away.

I take off my sunglasses and rest my head against my arms, which are folded against my knees, and watch my tears making small dark circles on the sidewalk—until I see two black high-top sneakers.

"Excuse me?" says someone.

I play-act a couple of sneezes, like I'm having an attack of some kind. Then I look up, rubbing my eyes, at some guy, a boy really, maybe eighteen, a Nirvana T-shirt, smiling, a *Cockamamie* CD in one hand, a pen in the other.

★

The following morning, a smudgy fax is slipped under my door. It's a blurry xerox from some newspaper with Burns's name scribbled at the top, but I read it anyway—a review of last night's show: "Trynin's aggressive guitar rock has made her a darling of the day among the buzzmakers. But the club was barely half full by the time she took to the stage. The general public is often slow to catch up with the so-called trendsetters, but the turnout was still disappointing, considering that Trynin's major-label debut *Cockamamie* is a record worthy of the adulation being heaped upon it . . . She and the band raced through material from her CD . . . By the time they loosened up, she had lost much of the crowd . . . Everyone's entitled to an off night . . . With as much talent as Trynin has, there may come a time when she can look back on this show and laugh."

I go into the bathroom. Stare at myself in the mirror. Light a cigarette. Light the fucking fax on fire.

★

The Powers That Be (Head Honcho, Randy, Lola, etc. etc. etc.) assure me that even though it's becoming clear that "Better Than Nothing" isn't destined to be an actual hit, they're all *still* committed to my record, to me, to my future career.

They decide that at this point it might be better for me to be opening for someone else, a bigger band, playing bigger venues, getting me in front of more people while also removing the pressure of headlining myself. This is how we end up doing a bunch of weeks opening for this really cool band called Buffalo Tom, during which nothing much happens for me except that "Better Than Nothing" manages to slip its way off both the Active and Modern Rock charts, and lose what little grip it had at Top 40. In the meantime, there's much discussion over what should be the third single, but no action. The phrase "European tour" keeps being bandied about, but it seems as though there's some kind of "hold-up" with Randy's securing me a European booking agent. I find this out during an interview with this woman who by sheer coincidence happens to be married to some big-time European booking agent. She tells me "off the record" how her booking-agent husband has been trying to "secure my representation" for weeks, but how he's been finding Randy impossible to get in touch with.

This prompts a call from me to Randy, who says, "Well, Jen, you know, things are moving along, you know how things are, how they can be, and I know that's not what you want to hear, but we're working on it and everything's coming together and things are developing for you overseas, let's see, Germany, France, things are happening—"

I finally come to learn that the phrase "things are happening" really means "things aren't happening."

★

It's a cold night and we're finally heading home on the Mass Pike, passing familiar truck stops, familiar foliage, road signs, town names, toll booths. I feel like crying, but I don't know if it's because I can't wait to get home or because I don't want to go home at all. Or maybe it's because I can't remember what home is, or if whatever it is will still be there.

As we pull up to our old rehearsal space to dump all the gear, I reach over and squeeze Buck's hand, and when he squeezes back I look at him.

Buck.

There's Buck.

I smile.

But by the time he smiles back, his face has receded, baring his skull and his teeth and his eyeballs like eggs in a cup.

I yank my hand away.

He looks at me.

I look at him.

Then I hug him, trying to put him back together so I can remember him, because I have the strange feeling I'm never going to see him again.

"Better watch out," says SoundBoy. "Jen's gettin' sappy on us."

I'm the last to be dropped off, so it's just me and Burns in the van. As we pull up in front of my house, I see my little red Honda parked on the street and covered in dust and dirt with bunches of leaves stuck beneath its wheels. I hop out and go around back, opening the rear door and pulling my duffel out onto the street.

"Need a hand?" asks Burns.

"I got it," I say, slamming the door, leaving my bag on the sidewalk and walking around to Burns's window. "So," I say. "It's been, you know, I don't know, *real*, I guess."

"Real it has been," he says, smiling, sticking his hand out the window and patting me on top of the head, messing up my hair. "Enjoy being off, you know? We'll be back out before you know it."

"Don't count your chickens," I say.

"Oh, I'm countin' those chickens," he says.

"Yeah, well, I hope."

"You okay? You got your keys and everything?"

"Yeah, I got 'em somewhere. But, like, do you feel weird?"

"Yeah," says Burns. "It can be a little fucked up at first, but you get used to it."

"I guess," I say.

"So we'll see you at the Kendall later on, right?" says Burns. "Can't be mainlining the home life. Not good for ya."

"Maybe. I gotta see what's going on," I say.

"Well, don't be a stranger," says Burns, revving the engine. "Don't take any wooden nickels. Don't speak unless spoken to."

"Right boss," I say.

"No, right *you* boss," he says. He smiles. "I guess I'll see ya."

"Not if I see you first."

"King's Foot!" yells Burns.

"King's Foot," I say.

I stand on the street next to my bag, watching Burns drive away. He beeps the horn just as he's rounding the bend and I lose him.

Climbing the stairs, I can hear *Seinfeld* coming from the 'tards' apartment, where the door is slightly ajar. I look up the stairwell toward my apartment and see some guy standing on the landing. He's kind of cute and smiling.

"Hi," he says. "I'm Don. Who're you?"

"I live here, up there," I say, pointing, "on the second floor."

"I haven't seen you before," he says.

"Well, I'm not part of the house. You know, I just live here. And I've been gone for a while."

"Oh," he says. "I'm new."

"How you doin'," I say, as I continue slowly climbing the steps, dragging my duffel behind me.

"Need a hand?" he says.

"Yeah." I smile. "That'd be great."

"Sure thing," says Don. He comes down and grabs my bag, and I follow him up the rest of the stairs. He drops the duffel by my door, right next to a completely bare Mr. Potato Head with a sponge balanced on top.

"Vincent," I say.

"You know Vincent?" says Don.

"Yeah," I say.

"Okay, well, it was nice to meet you," says Don. He turns and walks back down the stairs.

"Thanks," I say. "You too."

I'm rummaging through my backpack for my keys when suddenly Don's back.

"Hi," he says. "I'm Don. Who're you?"

I look at him. "What?"

"I'm Don," he says again, sticking out his hand, which I just now notice is curved and stiff. "Who're you?" He's smiling.

I reach out and shake his hand. "You don't work here, do you, Don?"

Inside, my apartment is dark. I put my bags down and stand in the middle of the kitchen, which is cold and perfectly quiet except for the soft creak of wind through the cracks in the windows. I can just make out the kitchen table, and a vase with flowers on it, and out across the street, the tree. There's a note on the fridge. *Welcome home! Had to work—emergency—sorry. I MISS YOU!!!! XXOO*

Something bumps against my leg and I look down and see a little orange cat. Ranger. I remember Ranger. I pick him up and he's purring and warm. I clink some food into his bowl and listen to him eat while I stare at the shadows spreading across the kitchen from the street lamp outside. It still smells like an attic in here. I go into the bathroom and pull the chain and the light blares on. I look at myself in the mirror. I shut the light off. I head to the bedroom and lie down in the dark with the street lamps shining through the windows and across my legs. Ranger leaps onto the bed and begins walking around and around, smelling me, sitting down, then getting back up and walking around again.

I think about heading out to the Kendall. I know everyone's going to be there. It's our moment to be like all those other Major Label Bands, returning home like conquerors after our adventures on the high seas. I could whip out all those pictures I know I took of all the great times I know we had backstage after all the sold-out shows in Chicago, Dallas, Cincinnati . . . Or that time in Denver when all those people were hanging off the balcony dangling that gigantic JENNIFER RULES! banner in the air.

I jump off the bed and head back to the kitchen, suddenly desperate to see what's on all those rolls of film in my duffel, to remember everything that's happened, to remember how great it was when it was great—that it was ever great—because all that seems to be going through my head is that shitty show in Philadelphia when my stomach was tied in knots so fierce that I could barely sing.

I'm putting on my coat when I see the light on my answering machine.

Blink.

Blink blink blink blink blink.

Outside it's cold and windy. I walk around the corner and drop my film at the CVS. On the way back, I stop at the Videosmith to rent a movie but as I'm looking through the aisles, I suddenly remember that the guy behind the counter is from some band I used to play shows with and the thought of having to rent a movie from him makes me weak.

Back home I rush up the stairs to avoid running into Don again. Inside, I grab a beer and lie down on the couch, turn on the TV, and fall asleep. I dream that Brian Wilson is sitting on the couch with me, looking through pictures of my family. He points to person after person, and says, *That's Don, That's Don,* until he takes my hand and leans into me. *Jen's dead,* he whispers, grabbing my arms, kissing me hard and then pushing me away, but not before his tongue comes off in my mouth.

I wake still dressed and on the couch. On the table next to me is a cold cup of coffee with a Post-it note on it. *Call me if you're not dead. xxoo.* I fall back to sleep.

When I wake again, it's late afternoon. I head back over to the CVS. I feel like shit and I look like shit and I'm paranoid as hell that someone's going to recognize me. *Aren't you that singer chick? God, you look like shit.*

The girl behind the counter raises her pierced eyebrow as she hands me package after package. "What're you, some kind of photographer?" she asks.

"I was on a trip," I say.

"Long trip," she says.

When I get back to my apartment, I don't even take my coat off before I begin ripping open the packages, very haphazard and reckless, very little-kid-at-Christmas. I can't wait to see the pictures from *Conan*

O'Brien and MTV, or from that huge KROQ show in L.A. But all I'm seeing is pictures of dark, empty stages after soundcheck. Fields out the van window. Burns with a backstage pass stuck to his forehead. All of us standing around a souped-up hot-dog cart at 4 A.M., laughing and pointing to a sign that says *Open 24-7*. In a few of the pictures I can almost make myself out behind the flash of the camera, my blotted-out silhouette in a mirror backstage, in a bathroom, in the reflection of the van window. There I am, not really there in Dallas, Phoenix, St. Louis, L.A. But mostly I'm seeing pictures of empty hotel rooms, one after another. Unmade beds. Night tables with Styrofoam cups and half-empty beers. My big green backpack slumped in the middle of the floor like a sick bear. A ray of light against one of those low dressers I never put my stuff in.

I remember being in those rooms and how different each one felt and how I took pictures of them all so I could remember where I'd been. It never dawned on me that later on, they'd all look exactly the same.

TEN

We all retreat to our corners—Buck, Robby, SoundBoy, Burns, me.

I do laundry, fall into a full-blown bout of CouchPizzaReruns minus the pizza (*can't get fat cuz ANY SECOND someone's gonna call and I'll be out on the road again—right?*).

Buck calls, asks if I want some company, you know, running errands or something. But I tell him I don't have any errands to run.

Guy tells me he's leaving. He says he figures I'm gone all the time anyway and much as he hates my crappy apartment when I'm there, he hates it even more when I'm not. He says he's also giving up his share of the old place he's kept all this time and is going to find himself a "real" apartment. He says I can come with him or stay here, but either way he's moving.

    I sit at the kitchen table with my guitar in my lap, drinking and smoking, staring at that tree across the street. *Writing notes about being sorry, driving out of town too drunk to see, believing in the day I would be happy, I miss who I used to be.* I watch Guy crouching over the real estate section with a pen, making *X*s, making circles. *I miss the* *time when life was so brand new to me, I could barely keep anything inside. I miss the time that I could never lie to you, I'd never have anything to hide.* I do more laundry, watch more reruns. *If I were me, way back when, I'd pray to God to get you back again, and I'd take it real slow with my favorite pen, I'd write: I'd never do anything to hurt you.*

A few days later, Guy wakes me up. It's cloudy and warm. He's dressed.

"Come on," he says. "I just saw a place. You're gonna love it."

And I do. It's the first floor of a two-family with lots of windows that open and close just like real windows. It has this big screened-in back porch and a long driveway with a two-car garage.

We decide on a moving day and ask some friends to help. When I ask Buck, he says, "You guys are moving in together?"

"Yeah," I say.

"Oh," he says.

Randy and I play phone tag about the third single and another video and the mythical European tour.

I'm featured in numerous arts section year-end articles about Things That Didn't Happen in '95.

I hear through the grapevine that over a thousand *Cockamamie*s were shipped to retail with a Led Zeppelin CD inside.

I'm thumbing through an old *CMJ*, trying to piece together what's happened/hasn't happened with my record, when I see a radio playlist that has *Cockamamie* coming out on something called Sad Sack/Squint.

Those. Mother. Fuckers.

I ask Randy to call the Gimmee guys and find out where my money is, or my five thousand Squint *Cockamamie*s.

A few days later, Kavallah tells me that she can't seem to track down anyone from Gimmee, that she's been calling them for days but no one's called her back.

It's finally Christmas. In the mail, I get a small red blanket with a "WB" emblem on it, from "Your Friends at Warner Bros. Records." Lola sends me a tall silver candlestick. There are no holiday buckets from any radio stations filled with green and red M&Ms.

I spend a few days down in New York and New Jersey with various members of my family. Tim pulls up in a big black limo with all kinds of exotic presents from Brazil—bright shirts with flowers on them and rocks carved into birds and two bottles of *cachaca*. I want to tell him how badly I miss him, but I don't want to be so pathetic, so childish— and besides, he's already being the life of the party, telling all kinds of stories and getting everyone drunk on caipirinhas, those powerful Brazilian drinks made from *cachaca* and lime juice and tons of sugar. Having my parents' attention on Tim and his big new job feels far more comfortable than when they were showering it all on me and my big record deal. Far more comfortable and a little depressing. A little depressing and kind of embarrassing. One of my cousins tells me she was at a party and "someone was actually playing your record." Another cousin and his girlfriend are standing in a corner mumbling, shaking their heads, looking at me. I hear the word "*Spin.*"

Just before New Year's, Guy and I throw another party. It's my birthday again, but I don't tell anybody.

Everyone comes, but it's not the same. We have lots of liquor and plenty of food, but all I can think about is that I'm sure they're all thinking that Guy and I are living in this nice new place because I'm rich now, even though the truth is that we split the rent, so I'm actually paying less for this nice new place than I was paying for my old crappy place. When they tell silly stories and make silly jokes, they look at me like *I guess you had to be there.* I want to tell funny stories about being on the road, but nothing's coming to mind.

I'm doing some dishes in the kitchen when Buck comes up from behind and puts his arms around me.

"Hey," he says.

"Hey," I say.

"Long time no see."

"Yeah."

"So you're all moved in."

"Pretty much."

"How've you been?"

"Pretty good," I say. "You?"

"Not too bad."

Buck turns me in his arms to face him. "It's nice to see you," he says. We hug. Then I take a step back. "Buck," I say. "I can't."

"What?" says Buck. "You can't hug me?"

"You know what I'm talking about," I say. "I'm living here. I'm living with Guy."

"Hey, Jen," says Laura, who's suddenly at the kitchen door. "The place looks great."

"Thanks," I say.

Buck turns to the sink and washes his hands.

★

The holiday's over and things begin to rev back up. It's decided that "One Year Down" will be the third single, and we begin the mind-numbing search for a video director that always seems to start from scratch.

Randy's phone calls become farther and farther between, and none of them contains any concrete plans about a European tour, or any tour for that matter. Then just as we're gearing up to shoot the third video and release the third single, he quits. He doesn't just quit on me. He quits on everybody. He leaves management and takes a desk job (albeit a very glorified desk job) at Columbia as BigWig's number two guy.

"He can't just *quit*," I tell Neil.

"Jen, Jen, Jen," says Neil. "I know. This sucks. But spilled milk, you know? Let's just move on."

I tell Neil I want Randy to give me back the portion of his commission for which he's obviously not going to be doing any more work.

"Waaaaaaaait a second," says Neil. "First of all, that's not the way these things work, and second of all, Randy's not disappearing off the face of the earth here. He and Kavallah and the rest of the bunch are really committed to making their artists' transitions to their new management go as smooth as possible."

"Kavallah?" I say. "Forget it. I'm done. Randy's quitting? *Fine*. I just want my money."

"Wow," says Neil. "I didn't expect you to react this way."

"Well," I say. "There you go."

When we hang up, I feel sick. I write Neil about five thousand letters explaining my position, which—no matter how I phrase and rephrase it—keeps coming off grabby and sour-grapey and just plain shitty.

But I can't let it go.

We shoot the video for "One Year Down" in L.A. on the dry side of a dam. I let the wardrobe people dress me up in all kinds of outfits, except for the one that includes a bellybutton-revealing shirt.

"Other girls are lining up to get naked and you won't even show your bellybutton," says Head Honcho, who has become my de facto manager. "I don't get it."

I don't tell Head Honcho that I don't get it either.

The night we finish the shoot, Buck and Robby and I get stoned and wander around the fake Disney town that's part of the Disney hotel complex where we're staying (because it's near the dam). As usual, I've eaten nothing since yesterday except for the three beers I've just downed, and between that and the pot and having spent the last sixteen hours jumping around lip-synching in the bottom of a dam, I'm feeling a bit woozy, which is why I lose my balance and fall against Buck.

"Whoa there," he says, and takes me by the arms and steadies me. Then he lets me go and catches up with Robby.

Even though everyone "loves loves loves" the third single and accompanying video, "One Year Down" gets added almost nowhere. The mythical European tour never becomes anything but myth. I get offered the opening slot on a six-week Aimee Mann tour, but, because she's still labelless, Head Honcho thinks it would be "a waste of time and money" and won't give me tour support. When I remind him that, contractually, I have $150,000 worth of guaranteed tour support (of which I know we still have plenty left), Head Honcho tells me that "guaranteed" can be a funny word. And while I have the money to pay for the tour out of my own pocket, the truth is I just can't see spending that much money on something that'll most likely lead to nothing besides the back seat of another van.

There's no bang. No definitive moment. Just a slow petering out.

By the time I'm told that my record cycle is over, all I want to do is sleep.

We receive a record-breaking 107.6 inches of snow over the winter, snowing out the few gigs I'd actually agreed to do.

I'm featured in a *Wall Street Journal* article that opens with the following quote: *"Ain't a man been born can pick a hit for sure"—Ray Charles.* I'm used as a prime example of one of the new overhyped, overpaid artists who hasn't delivered: *Despite the clamor that surrounded her signing, Ms. Trynin's album* Cockamamie *has sold just 35,000 units since its release. Although it was in the top 94 percent of all records released this past year, the results were still regarded as disappointing.*

I keep being recognized. Buying strings. Out at clubs. Even in the grocery store or the post office. I like it when I'm in the mood and hate it when I'm not.

I tag along with Guy who has some business in L.A. While Guy's at his meetings, I wander around alone. I find a cool shirt somewhere and when I hand my credit card to the girl at the counter, she looks at it, then up at me, then back at my card, then back at me. She points down at my card.

"Oh my God," she says, still pointing. "Are you, you're, you're —"

I don't know why this feels good at this particular moment, but it does.

I smile. "Yeah," I say.

"Oh, wow," says the girl. "God, I haven't seen you in for*ever*! I'm Lisa Garner. Remember? Beechtree Elementary?"

Occasionally, I check in on the newly created "WBR/JenniferTrynin .com" Web site where they've set up a message board. Someone writes that I'm really "hot," which makes me feel really good. Until I read the next message, which says, "DO YOU NEED GLASSES? That chick's a dog."

At night, I sit with my guitar in the dark by the window in our new living room. *You're like February, I think you just may be sorry now you ever came, lost in how to make your getaway.* I watch the snow blowing around the streetlight. *Don't lie, don't tell me that we're leaving, you could never go.* I think about lighting fires in the fireplace. *Don't cry, don't put your arms around me, I already know you got nowhere to go.*

★

In the spring, Buck and Robby and I begin recording my next record with Guy. It's the first time I've ever recorded on a schedule, and it feels a little like a job: 11 A.M. till around 1 A.M., five days a week for sixteen weeks, with two weeks off in the middle. On *Cockamamie,* we'd had a million people playing and singing and we'd tried to make it sound like a band. This time, it's just me and Buck and Robby, and it seems as though we're trying to make it sound like anything *but* a band. It's pretty fun, but not nearly as fun as it was to record songs here and there, on the sly, in downtime, over holidays, with whoever was able to show up.

After eight weeks, we've only managed to record the nuts and bolts of about five songs and we're all getting frustrated, especially Guy. Everyone begins pointing fingers. It's Robby's time. It's Buck's feel. It's Jen's singing. Guy "suggests" that instead of taking two weeks off we use that time to rehearse. So we slog our way down to the rehearsal space, grumbling and coughing. We try to laugh like we used to. We try to pat each other on the ass and spritz each other with water. But mostly we just blame one another for our weaknesses, misunderstandings, poor decisions, general wrongthink.

But I still don't see it coming when Buck puts his bass down and says, "I quit."

"You what?" I say.

"No you don't," says Robby.

"Oh yeah I do," says Buck. He puts on his jacket and walks out the door.

"But but but," I'm saying as I follow him down the dingy hallway, up the rickety stairs, and out into the sunlight. "Please," I say.

Buck turns and looks at me. He hugs me. "I'm sorry," he says. "But I can't do this anymore."

And even though I'm relieved as hell to have him gone, I cry anyway. I lie on the couch with a fan blowing at my head, watching TV with the sound off and playing guitar. *Cheap as this may seem, all I've ever wanted to be is free.* I pout. *Is something wrong with me? Trying has cost me everything.* Stew. *I hope that someday we will find that we were fine anyway, just as we were, and all of this will become a blur.* I finish the song in one sitting and call it "Everything." It's not even close to pop and I don't give a shit.

My parting with Buck is pretty straightforward. According to the agreement we'd signed, Buck is to be paid through the end of the month, and keeps his 1-point interest in *Cockamamie* but gets no further points. Pretty simple, except for all the gear he purchased with the equipment and recording funds, most of which is down in our rehearsal space.

Neil, Mr. Boyg, and Guy all tell me to get Buck's gear back—that it's for the bass player who's playing with me, not for some guy who's quit in the middle of recording—but I can't do it. I feel that what's happened is partially my fault, so I figure I should share in the fallout. So I decide that The Right Thing To Do is to split the gear with him, which all in all is worth about $5,000.

I ask Buck to meet me in the parking lot of the rehearsal space to talk, thinking that afterward, I'll help him get his portion of the gear back to his house.

I'm still in my car when Buck pulls up beside me on a bicycle.

"Wow," I say. "Nice wheels."

"Just got it," he says.

"It's King's Foot," I say.

"Hmm," says Buck.

I get out of my car. He gets off his bike and stands there, holding it.

"So," he says.

"So," I say.

"So it's all pretty clear in the contract," he says. "I don't know what there is to talk about."

"The equipment," I say. "We have to decide what to do with all the gear you bought."

"What about it?" says Buck.

"Well, you know, it's just that that stuff's supposed to be for the band."

"Band?" says Buck. "What band?"

"You know what I mean," I say.

"You said way back at the beginning that that stuff was mine."

"What I said was that when we recouped, *then* it'd be yours. But we're not even close to recouping."

"There's nothing about it in my contract," says Buck.

"Well, yeah," I say. "I guess it should've been spelled out, but the fact is that technically—"

"Technically?" says Buck. "*Technically?*" He swings one leg over his bike. "You know what? Fuck you."

"But, Buck, I—"

"No," he says, pushing off and heading for the street. "Fuck you."

Guy tells me to change the locks on the rehearsal space immediately. I tell Guy that Buck's not that kind of person. Guy says, "You watch."

The following day, I go down to the rehearsal space and all Buck's stuff is gone—basses, amps, pedals, mics, cords, everything.

I sit down on my amp and put my head in my hands.

I go to the studio to tell Guy what happened, and much to my surprise, there's Buck's original bass, the one he'd had when he joined the band, leaning against a wall out in the big room.

Guy says I should throw Buck's bass out the window.

I walk into the big room and look at Buck's bass.

Pick it up.

Put it down.

Pick it up again.

Put it down again.

Only one way out of this mess.

I decide to tell Guy about me and Buck. Not just because I'm terrified that Buck's so pissed he's going to show up at our door and tell Guy everything, but also because the only way I can love Guy again is for him to love me again, for real.

Our conversation is a blur, like we're going a million miles an hour in slow motion. But for the first time since all this began, I can feel everything. Guy. And how I love him like all get-out.

Guy makes me promise that I'll never talk to Buck again. Ever.

Ever?

Ever.

Can I talk to him one more time just to tell him what's happened?

No.

Then how's he gonna know?

He's just gonna have to fucking figure it out.

I visit my dad and BB for the weekend at their house out on Long Island. We go to the beach. The sun is high in the sky and I'm wearing a one-piece I just bought and I'm pale as shit. I feel like a dead fish. And that's when I see him, through the glare of the sun off the ocean. Neil. Neil and his wife and his two cute little kids, frolicking in the surf and laughing. I don't know why I get up, go over, say hi. Neil and I walk a little ways together. When I ask him what he thinks really happened, why my record died the way it did, he says, You never know about these things, but that mostly it was probably just bad timing. The changing of the guard at The Company. Danny Goldberg leaving. How the Goo Goo Dolls had that surprise hit over the summer, which took Warners' eye off me. And, of course, the Alanis Morissette thing. "She's on Madonna's label, and Madonna is Warners' cash cow," says Neil. "They gotta look out for her wants. And Morissette's song took off. And for women, you know, especially in rock, it's still just a little . . . unfair, I guess you could say. But in the end, you gotta follow the money, right?"

★

I'm back on the couch with the fan blowing at my head, watching TV with the sound off, playing guitar, but everything's coming out like shit.

I don't have a manager.

I don't have a bass player, or equipment for one if I did.

Then the phone rings. It's Teddy Z.

"I hear you're short a bass player," he says.

"Yeah," I say.

"Well you're in luck," he says, "because I just happen to play the bass."

I smile. A tears-in-my-eyes smile.

The following day, we're back in the studio—Robby, Teddy Z., Guy, and me—when Guy says, "I've been waiting to do this for a long fucking time." He hits the record button on the two-inch machine with the faders down, erasing Buck's bass lines from the basics of the first five tracks.

I get one of the studio interns to return Buck's bass to him. Buck takes the bass and slams the door in his face.

★

We finish the new record. I call it *Gun Shy Trigger Happy*. I decide to change my "professional" name to *Jen* Trynin (not only because that's

what most people call me, but because I think Jen sounds more *rock*).
I cool it with the drinking and smoking and start running and eating
fruit and actually practicing my voice lessons. I cut my hair short, because I've always been afraid to and I want to stop being so afraid all
the time. I try not to take it personally when not one of the eighteen
managers who were all over me before calls me to say so much as "hey."

I run into Aimee and ask her what she thinks about the whole
manager thing.

"They just wanted to fuck you," she says. "They weren't in love."

But finally someone does call, a manager from L.A. who flies out
to meet me, and we hit it off right away. He's cute with nice hands, the
kind I like—square, big knuckled—I feel them on me . . .

NO!

No.

No.

After much tangling, I finally give in to Manager 2 who wants me to
"send a positive message" to the Powers That Be at Warners by doing
my album art with someone from the Warners art department (instead
of with my old *Cockamamie* art pal).

I get assigned to this chick, Lindy, who flies out for our photo-
shoot in NYC at the Chelsea Hotel. After the shoot, we hook up at a
bar with Lindy's boyfriend, Alex Van Halen (brother of Eddie Van
Halen and the drummer in, well, Van Halen), who ends up whipping
out his dick (twice!) before we even order our drinks.

One day, a couple of weeks later, just as we're zeroing in on some
album art concepts, Lindy doesn't show up to work.

She doesn't show up the next day either.

After she never shows up again, I'm finally allowed to do the artwork with my old *Cockamamie* art pal, which is what I'd wanted to do
in the first place.

The song "February" is picked as the first single, but Head Honcho
makes me change the title to "Getaway," because Warner Bros. wants

to release it in the summer and you can't release a song called "February" in the summer.

This strikes me as a bad sign, but I don't make a fuss because I want everyone to know that *this* time, I'm With The Program.

I pick this super-hip and happening director to shoot the video for "Getaway (February)," which has this scene where a bunch of ridiculously gorgeous models pretend to play all my cool electric guitars, which gives me a headache.

Everyone hates the rough cut of the "Getaway (February)" video, because it's *so* super-hip and happening that no one knows what the hell is going on in it. The Whole Video Thing gets put on hold.

I find another bass player to tour (because I couldn't steal Teddy Z. away from Flint Raft). I hire an additional guitar player so that I can focus more on my singing during shows. I also hire a new tour manager and soundman because I want to start "fresh."

I make it crystal clear to everyone and anyone who'll listen that I want to do my own small-club headlining tour unless I can get onto something bigger, supporting a rock band whose music I think is appropriate. For instance, I refuse to go out on the Lilith Fair—this summer's "Celebration of Women in Music" tour—because it features the same kind of women- fronted, singer-songwritery bands from my Sunday-through-Wednesday-night-folk/acoustic-chick-band-wasteland days. And after my No Chicks Opener Debacle, I think that showing up on the Lilith Fair would make me a hypocrite.

"But the Lilith Fair would really increase your audience," says Head Honcho.

"No," I say.

"Why?" he says.

"You know why," I say.

"Well," says Head Honcho. "'Getaway' is already on a Lilith Fair sampler."

I exhale into the phone.

I call Manager 2.

"That was already in the works when I signed on," he says. "And besides, the whole Lilith Fair thing would really increase your audience."

I'm offered a six-week stint opening for Shalah! (who's just about to get off the Lilith Fair).

"No. Fucking. Way," I say.

"Why not?" says Head Honcho.

"First of all, because her music blows," I say.

"It *blows*?" says Head Honcho, and though I can't see him, I know he's rubbing his temples with his fingers.

Shalah! is from the Boston area and we've run into each other over the years the way people who don't like one another can't help but run into each other. I dislike her for many reasons, not the least of which is that she's always gone by her first name with an exclamation point at the end, kind of like she was thinking *Shazam!* She's also the epitome of a Sunday-through-Wednesday-night folk/acoustic-chick-band-wasteland singer-songwriter except that she sings LOUD with one of those opera-style voices complete with trilling vibrato, which she often delivers while loping around the stage, modern-dance style, hitting a tambourine. Otherwise, she plays piano with her legs spread. Her earnest lyrics are chock-full of biblical references concerning topical issues such as The Abuse Of Women In Our World, or how, just maybe, she's actually Jesus Christ "herself." She wears sweaters that go down to her shins, doesn't drink or smoke, and far as I can tell, doesn't laugh. And it's not like I have anything against her being vegan or supporting PETA or not shaving under her arms—it's just that she talks about it all the time.

I can only guess that My Team considers us to be a "good match" because of all the unfortunate things we have in common—namely that we're both on Warner Bros., we employ the same booking agency, and of course, we're both chicks.

Head Honcho tells me to stop fighting the last war.

"Jen," he says, "I wish you could understand that Shalah! is doing you a *favor* by offering to take you out. Her single is really exploding, and you have *no idea* how many strings I had to pull to get you on this tour."

After much over-the-phone finger-pointing, eye-rolling, and mud-slinging, I finally give in.

This time, three weeks before the tour, Robby does *not* break his leg in three places, but he *does* go flying over the handlebars of his bike, severely spraining his arm.

So I replace him. Simple as that.

Cuz this time, nothin's gonna stop me.

★

Because of her testosterone deficiency, Jen Trynin is destined to be compared with Chrissie Hynde, Liz Phair and other mini-malist chick rockers with attitude. But in truth, the stellar pop craftsmanship and tautly atmospheric low-fi guitar-pop arrangements on Trynin's second album, Gun Shy Trigger Happy, *more readily suggest the influence of the Velvet Underground and Alex Chilton . . . This is one gal who needs the current wave of women-in-rock hype like a fish needs a bicycle.*

—Rolling Stone

Her 1994 debut, Cockamamie, *showed admirable grrrlish spunk and a few knockout songs, but promising as that release was, it barely hinted at the giant leap forward this 33-year-old Bostonian takes on her dazzling follow-up.* Gun Shy Trigger Happy *is a musical tour de force—13 meticulously produced cuts that feature Trynin's hypnotic vocals, gritty guitar playing and grown-up lyrics about faltering relationships and lost innocence . . . In this year that is ruled by Lilith, Trynin has matched her better-known peers by delivering one of 1997's strongest and most mature discs.*　　　—People

Trynin's music sparkles with clean hooks and rare intelligence.

—USA Today

The finest rock song slinger to arrive in these late '90s.

— Entertainment Weekly

Strikingly lovely.   —Billboard

Gun Shy Trigger Happy gets great reviews across the board.

Six Boston stations add "Getaway" to their playlists out of the box.

On the day the record is officially released, I do four on-airs and an in-store at Tower Records, which is packed enough to make me happy.

By sheer coincidence, exactly three days before we're scheduled to hook up with Shalah! on her tour, we end up playing on the same bill with her at a radio festival.

The following day, Manager 2 calls me. He says he just got off the phone with Shalah!'s People, who seem "a bit alarmed" by my show. They insist that I play acoustic guitar on the tour.

I call Head Honcho and tell him to tell Shalah's people where they can stick it.

"Jen," says Head Honcho. "Here're the facts. If you don't play acoustic guitar, you're off the tour."

I run five miles. Walk three.

Then I spend the better part of the next thirty-six hours with my band, shortening bridges and rearranging outros so that we can play my songs *sans* all my wah-wah-infused, feedback-producing electric guitar maneuverings.

We go on tour.

While I love my super-cool old Harmony acoustic guitar (in which I installed a pick-up), I feel hobbled without my trusty Les Paul, Super Reverb amp, and ultrasonic pedals galore. All the energy usually expended through my electric guitar maneuverings begins coming out of my mouth—not singing-wise, but talking-wise. I start going a little nutty. My topics are free-range: finding a spider in my bed, why

people fixate on the weather, my mother's glove size (6), not under-
standing what it means to be "flat-footed."

"What the hell are you talking about out there?" asks my new tour
manager.

Sometimes I'm making a modicum of sense, sometimes I'm just
appreciating the beauty of the non sequitur. Sometimes the audience
is "getting it," sometimes they're not. I don't care. I don't really know
what I'm doing but I know I have to do something. I can't just lie down
like a good little doggie and appropriately strum my little acoustic
guitar.

By show 11, I don't know if I'm talking between songs or playing
songs to break up my comedy-infused performance art.

"That thing you said about the bacon grease fuckin' killed me,"
says my new tour manager.

By show 14, we get a standing ovation that won't quit. Shalah!'s
people tell us to get off the stage.

After our set for show 16, we're pounding beers backstage when
my new tour manager comes in laughing.

"Painful," he says.

"What," I say.

"I was hanging out front and Shalah!'s like trying to talk between
songs or something. Like she's trying to joke around. It's brutal."

By show 19, Shalah! develops one of those stealth diseases like
Epstein-Barr or chronic fatigue syndrome.

On the morning of show 20, Shalah! cancels that night's gig, so
we sit around the hotel, drinking and watching pay-per-view.

The next morning she cancels show 21.

On the morning of show 22, she does it again.

On the morning of show 23, she cancels the rest of the tour (about
twenty more shows).

Everybody goes home.

The funny thing is, not long after this, Shalah! manages to drag
herself out of bed to play a few shows in New York. Then she flies
to Bahrain to do a week's worth of USO shows in the Persian Gulf.

Later on, when the cancelled Shalah! shows are rescheduled, no one calls us.

Great reviews for *Gun Shy Trigger Happy* continue to pour in. It's picked by *Entertainment Weekly* as the #2 Record of the Year (Behind U2's *Pop*). I'm presented with a plaque from *Stereo Review* for Record of the Year at soundcheck during a sold-out show in New York. However, it's becoming clear that "Getaway" is not destined to be a hit, about which Head Honcho is very sad (as is everyone, ESPECIALLY ME), but at least, says Head Honcho, we didn't rack up the extra expense of redoing the failed "Getaway" video.

"Yeah, well," I say, "maybe 'Getaway' would've had a better shot if we'd actually *had* a video for my first single."

"Settle down," says Head Honcho.

We're down in D.C. to be taped for some new HBO show called *Reverb* that's going to be airing live performances of "up-and-coming new bands." This is all fine and dandy except for one thing. It seems as though the *Reverb* people actually want to shoot Shalah! for their show, and *somehow*—a "somehow" that I suspect has something to do with Head Honcho—we've been shoved onto the bill as well at the last minute, which makes the whole thing feel like a pity-taping.

However, I'm determined to be a good fucking sport about it.

I'm heading down the long hallway to front of house for soundcheck when I see Shalah! making her way back. She's about to bump right into me when I say, "Hey."

Shalah! looks up. "Oh," she says. "Hello." She keeps walking.

"You guys about done checking?" I say.

"No," she says.

In the end, we have barely enough time to drag our gear up onto the stage and arrange it in front of Shalah!'s band's gear before it's time for us to play. I'm lugging my amp into place when I feel someone towering above me.

"You guys are on at 9:15," says some gigantic, bald, black-clad crew dude with a pen stuck above his ear like it's piercing right through his skull. "Your set's thirty minutes."

I put my amp down in the middle of the stage. "But our set runs like forty-five minutes," I say.

"You got thirty," he says.

By the time we take the stage with our revamped, three-songs-shy set list, I've downed five beers, maybe six. The club's capacity is about five hundred and it's maybe half full. The audience is mostly gathered at the back of the room, leaving one of those awful chasms between us and them. The crowd is feeling strange to me, awkward and distant, like the whole place is filled with our parents' friends' kids who were forced to come to the show.

But before I know it, we've launched into "Better Than Nothing" and everything changes. Everyone begins clamoring toward the stage, coming right up to the edge and banging their fists at my feet in time to the music, singing along, making me feel as if I'm being raised high into the air, like I'm growing ridiculously tall, funhouse-mirror tall, and I feel awake and alive for the first time in a long time. We rip into the next song and then the next and the next, ramping and bumping through every twist and turn, the audience right with us, swooping down and flying up.

Just as we're coming in for a landing, coasting into our last song, I happen to look to my left and glimpse the bald crew dude standing offstage, waving his arms at me. The song ends with my guitar still ringing and the audience clapping. *What?* I mouth to the bald crew dude. He makes a throat-slitting gesture and yells, "YOU'RE DONE!"

My heart is racing and I'm soaking with sweat. Done? We just got going.

"We just got one more," I say to him, halfway into the mic, which makes the audience clap louder. The bald crew dude points at his watch.

"YOU'RE *DONE*!" he yells again.

I turn toward the audience. "Well, we got one more song for ya, but it doesn't look like we have time," I say. People begin to boo and hiss, and then someone cries, "One more song!" Someone else picks it up, and in a second they're chanting, "One more! One more!"

I look back at the bald crew dude just as Shalah! walks up and stands next to him, folding her arms. As much as it kills me to do this, I raise my eyebrows at her like *Please?,* to which she bites her bottom lip and shrugs her shoulders.

So I raise my right hand way up in the air and let it crash down against my strings, sending a wail of guitar noise out into the room as the chanting gives way to a roar of applause. Then, *"YOU'RE DONE!"* comes booming through the monitors this time, and the applause scatters like a flock of birds.

I lean into the mic, intending simply to say, "Thanks a lot, good night," when I realize my mic's gone dead.

I stare out at the audience.

Blink blink.

Then I swing my guitar around my back and step in front of the mic and out to the lip of the stage.

"Seems as though we don't have time to play our last song," I yell—audience: *Boo! Hiss! No way! One more!*—"which really sucks, because it's a pretty good little tune called 'Too Bad You're Such A Loser'"—a few *WOOHOOs*—"which begins kinda loud and then gets really soft and then gets really loud again and goes into this galloping part and then into like this Crosby, Stills and Nash thing and then everything gets really fucking loud again and nutso and faster and then slower and then faster again and then louder and louder until BAM it ends, which is when all you guys would've been clapping and screaming like MORE MORE—" which is when I begin clapping and jumping up and down as the audience begins clapping like hell and jumping all over the place and there's whistling and screaming and *woohoo*ing like no tomorrow and then suddenly the house music comes on BLARINGLY loud and the lights come up and right beside me is the bald crew dude with his hands on his hips, like some kind of rock-club superhero.

"Get your shit off *now,*" he says, spraying a bit of saliva against my face on the word "shit."

"All right already," I say, unplugging my guitar, glancing over my shoulder toward Shalah!, who is, of course, no longer there.

Head Honcho: "I heard you wouldn't get off the stage."

Me: "It's that they wouldn't let me stay *on* the stage."

To say that everything goes downhill from here makes it sound too gradual.

Advances of the second single, "Writing Notes" (which I consider to be my best and most beautiful song ever and everyone *knows* is going to be a HIT HIT HIT), are sent to radio stations without any artwork.

I tell Manager 2 this is a bad sign.

Manager 2 tells me I'm being paranoid, that singles go out without artwork all the time.

I do a four-week, small-club headlining tour during which I begin to realize something very disturbing. I'm bored. And not a simple bored, like that time at that airport with Robby. A much deeper and more finely tuned bored, like in the center of my chest, like to the tips of my toes. I'm always spacing out. During interviews. Onstage. I find myself rushing through soundcheck so I can get outside in time to see the sun set. I feel myself caring more about when I'm going to find time to take my daily run than I do about the actual shows.

When I return home from the tour, I finally figure out that "Writing Notes" was never "officially released" to radio.

Manager 2 tells me not to worry about it, that some "preliminary research" is being done concerning another single.

Some discussion occurs concerning "future touring opportunities."

Manager 2 assures me that arrangements are being made "as we speak" for a three-week tour in Australia and New Zealand.

Until three weeks go by and nothing is confirmed.

During four back-to-back Australian phoners, I piece together (from the interviewers' questions) that while the new album started out strong, interest seems to be waning.

Manager 2 finally fesses up that the Australian tour is off.

We do some three-gig runs on the East Coast, for which we receive no tour support. I act as driver and tour manager. We don't have our own soundman.

I begin wincing whenever I hear my name.

Every time I sit down to try to work on a new song, the mere sound of my pick hitting the strings makes me feel sad. And spooky. Like my hands belong to someone else.

★

We're onstage in a crappy little club on a long, crappy street in Asbury Park. There are maybe eleven people in the audience—meaning there are at least a few people getting drunk at the bar. We're about three-quarters of the way through the set when I see a big black limo pull up outside. For one stupid moment, I remember the way it used to be, way back when, back when big black limos used to pull up outside of clubs where I was playing.

I can't quite see who all is getting out, but a minute later, a short figure comes limping through the side door of the club.

A woman.

An older woman.

In a tan sweater, tan slacks, tan shoes.

With a mask across her mouth, and an oxygen tank.

I'd heard that Lola "hadn't been feeling well," but no one told me she was on her last fucking leg.

For the rest of the set, Lola hunches at the back of the room with her driver next to her like a bodyguard. She sways a bit to the music. I keep thinking I can hear the whine of the oxygen tank.

After the set, Lola and I stand talking out on the crappy street by her limo. I tell her how sorry I am that she's, umm, not feeling well. She says, "This ol' thing?" pointing at the oxygen tank. But, she says, she's worried. Worried about me. Worried about my place at The Company. Then she goes on to confess how things have never been right there, not since Mo-and-Lenny left, not since The New Regime, how she feels I was never given the kind of chance I deserved, how she can no longer vouch for The Company. She says she wouldn't blame me if I "wanted out."

Back on the couch, no pizza, no guitar, TV off, lights out.

Is Lola trying to tell me something?

Maybe *Warners* is just looking for an out.

Let's say Warners drops me. Then what? Am I expected to go trolling around for another deal? What major label is going to want some thirty-something has-been-who-never-was? And I can't imagine any self-respecting indie offering anything but a big fat raspberry to some failed major-label sell-out who got what she deserved.

And even if Warners does want to keep working together—do I really have it in me to write another record?

Let's say I *do* write another record and Warners *does* put it out— I'll be at least thirty-five by then, and who ever heard of a rock star breaking at thirty-five?

And what if I never break? Do I *really* want to spend the rest of my life doing shitty shows in out-of-the-way towns at hole-in-the-wall clubs?

I talk to Guy. About getting out.

"Out like forever?" he says.

"I don't know," I say. "Maybe."

"You sure that's what you want?"

"Yes."

Guy looks at me with tears in his eyes.

"Don't," I say.

"Okay," he says.

I call Neil.

★

A few months later.

It's a hot August afternoon. I'm in the driveway lying in a lounge chair, the plastic sticking to my arms, sweat dripping into my eyes. At my feet is a fan rigged with three extension cords running out from the kitchen, where I can hear Guy clanging around with a baseball game on.

I've never sat in the sun before in my whole life.

I pull a piece of Bazooka from my pocket. Unwrap it. Stick it in my mouth. My fortune: *Something you want is just within your reach.*

I remove my Peter Fonda/*Easy Rider* sunglasses. Swab my eyes with a paper towel ripped from the roll beside me. Put the sunglasses back on.

This is before I begin wearing makeup and high boots and short skirts.

Before I return to school.

Marry Guy.

Buy a house.

Have a child.

Write a book.

Before all this, all I do is lie in the sun with a #2 pencil and a big book of mind puzzles open on my stomach.

Which one of the designs on the right is the mirror image of the design on the left?

The last thing in this ever-loving world I can do right now is create something.

Make seven squares by adding only two lines to the pattern.

I just want to solve things.

If three-dimensional, which of the following patterns could be folded into a hexagon?

It's just something to do.

While the wind is blowing warm.

Sun high up in the sky.

The trees.

Until the phone finally rings, telling me, once and for all, that it's done.

CODA

Aimee stops by just to say hi, to see our house, to meet our daughter. She looks beautiful, as she always does. She's playing in Boston tonight. Big show. Sold out.

We sit in the den drinking coffee as my little girl is quietly crying in my lap.

"I'm still thinking about maybe having kids," says Aimee. "But, like, yipes, you know?"

"Yeah," I say.

Then she says, "Do you ever miss it?"

"I don't know," I say. "Sometimes. I guess."

It's true that my life is much quieter now, without the music, the bars, the boys. But the loudest silence of all is the absence of my old daydream, the one where I used to picture myself in the future, sauntering through the streets of some city, freewheeling, beautiful, unafraid. What I miss most is no longer having this dreamy vision of myself floating somewhere on the horizon. Because the truth is, once my future finally arrived, I was still just me—a little nervous, kind of plain, always preparing for the worst.

———

Now it's evening and I figure Aimee's just about to take the stage. Guy's working late. Our daughter's finally asleep. I'm down in the basement slopping clothes from the washer into the dryer. *When I was a child, I spoke as a child, I understood as a child, I thought as a child; but when I became a man, I put away childish things.* This is what rings in my head now. Every time I stare out a window, or take a night run, or touch my daughter's impossibly soft cheek.

ACKNOWLEDGMENTS

With wholehearted dedication to M&G.

Thanks to Becky Saletan, Becky Saletan, Becky Saletan, Stacia Decker, David Hough, Evan Boorstyn, Kent Wolf, and everyone at Harcourt; Bill Clegg, Elyse Cheney and Stephanie Hanson; Jonathan Horn and Susan Amster; Tim Huggins, Laura Zigman, Tom Perrotta, Brad Watson, David Gessner, Sandy Kaye, and Dennis Lehane; Jay Allison and Jonathan Katz, Thomas Beller, and Julianna Baggott; Cassy Hayman and everyone at A Place To Grow. And, of course, nothing but thanks to all the people who were part of one of the most incredible experiences of my life, especially: Buck, Robby, Burns, and SoundBoy; Neil and Mr. Boyg; Head Honcho, Lola, and Howdy Doody; Randy and Manager 2; Aimee, Teddy Z., Johnny, Ivana, my cousin-of-a-cousin, and everyone who played on *Cockamamie* and toured with me on *GSTH*. And lastly, a sincere and heartfelt thanks to each of my six parents, my brother, and Malcolm S. for their unflagging support and encouragement while I wrote this dang thing.

In memory of Mark Sandman and Mikey Dee.